Youth Crime and Youth Culture in the Inner City

Bill Sanders

Routledge
Taylor & Francis Group

LONDON AND NEW YORK

First published 2005 by Routledge
2 Park Square, Milton Park, Abingdon, Oxon OX14 4RN

Simultaneously published in the USA and Canada by Routledge
270 Madison Ave, New York, NY 10016

Routledge is an imprint of the Taylor & Francis Group

© 2005 Bill Sanders

Typeset in Baskerville by Bookcraft Ltd, Stroud, Gloucestershire
Printed and bound in Great Britain by Antony Rowe Ltd,
Chippenham, Wiltshire

British Library Cataloguing in Publication Data
A catalogue record for this book is available from the British Library

Library of Congress Cataloging in Publication Data
A catalog record for this book has been requested

ISBN 0-415-35503-6

For Mumsie!

Contents

Figures

Tables

Acknowledgements

This book would not have been possible without the help of many individuals to whom I owe my deepest gratitude.

In particular, thanks go out to Tim Newburn, David Downes, Nikolas Rose and Bridget Hutter, my supervisors at the London School of Economics. Thanks are also due to Geoffrey Pearson, Les Back, John Pitts and Janet Foster for comments on earlier drafts and passing me on through various stages of the doctorate.

Much appreciation is owed to the people who worked at Lambeth Youth Justice, several police officers in Lambeth, and dozens of youth and community workers in the borough who were interviewed or contacted during this research. Without their insights and experiences this work would be incomplete. Also, and importantly, thanks are due to the several detached youth workers in Lambeth whose dedication, hard work and perseverance are greatly underpaid and often underacknowledged. I hope this book helps to highlight the profound difficulties faced by those who work in this profession.

To my new wife, Cheryle, whom I met in London: your love and support are without parallel.

Finally, thank yous, big ups and shout outs go to all the young people who were interviewed. I hope this book properly represents your worldviews.

Preface

My upbringing was both outside England and outside the inner city. Six years of living in central Brixton, though, offered me an idea of what daily life must be like for English inner-city inhabitants. The sights, sounds and smells of Brixton, what can be expected from walking down the area's high and back streets, where the 'good' and 'bad' areas are, and some restaurants and cafes worth checking out are well remembered. Due to my length of time in Brixton, to a degree, I became localised, and enjoyed many of the area's small perks. I discovered a couple of places to buy inexpensive CDs, shops selling cheap refillable shaving razors, and some off-licences that are open every day of the year. I enjoyed much of what Brixton had to offer, and could take people on guided tours, showing off the area's many attractions.

Some extraordinary events occurred during my time in Brixton. Nelson Mandela visited, and gave a talk at the Recreation Centre. The vibe he generated amongst the throngs of people who came to welcome him was one of wonder and respect. I caught a glimpse of him as his motorcade departed. Mike Tyson also came to Brixton to check things out, and had to duck into the local police station to avoid getting mobbed by his fans. Activists once 'reclaimed the streets' and turned Brixton High Street into a giant party, complete with banners demanding that Effra Road be dug up as 'a river runs below it'. On the day of Princess Diana's funeral, Brixton seemed relatively empty, and the chorus of the broadcasted funeral procession was audible in the streets. A racist homophobe exploded a nail bomb on Electric Avenue, about 40 metres from where I stood at the time. The shockwave caused by the explosion was not too dissimilar from the tremors caused by minor earthquakes in Southern California. These events will never be forgotten.

In October 2002, I moved out of Brixton to live with my fiancée in Tottenham, North London, an environment not too dissimilar from Brixton, and then finally out of Tottenham a year later to take up a position at Columbia University. I always knew my time in Brixton was temporary. My plan was to get in, do research, and get out, and the plan unfolded accordingly. Throughout the course of this research, the knowledge of eventually leaving Brixton never really left my mind. Brixton was only my temporary home, a chapter in my life that I opened and closed. I put myself in and took myself out of this environment. The majority of people living in Brixton and Lambeth more generally probably do not have these options. In other words, that many people in Lambeth would be able to pick up, move out, and resettle elsewhere is unlikely. My inner-city experiences, being both temporary and relatively controlled, can never form a complete picture of what being *from* the inner city is truly like, to be born, raised and educated there. I only experienced a taste of inner-city life, a glimpse of the realities of Brixton's long-term residents.

Youth Crime and Youth Culture in the Inner City endeavours to illustrate the complex series of normative judgements young people make regarding their offending behaviour. It aims to offer a glimpse into the 'moral universes' of young people with a particular focus on their histories of offending. I wanted to offer some insight into the minds of young people as they committed 'crime', and the overall role of 'crime' in their lives. While these were my research tasks, I enjoyed many fantastic experiences during my time in Brixton, and England more generally. I spent the greater part of my 20s there. I met people from around the world, and bathed in multiculturalism. I made dear friends, several of whom I have seen marry. I also have a godson who lives outside Brighton. What I call my overall 'British Experience' extends well beyond the work presented here. I established connections in England that will hold for the rest of my life.

I truly enjoyed my time in Brixton, and think it to be a vibrant and exciting multicultural environment. Rather than a 'British Experience', I underwent more of a 'Brixton Experience', for this area was where I spent the majority of my time. Many fantastic and wonderful people and aspects about Brixton and Lambeth more generally exist, but these should not belie the borough's dark underbelly. The conditions and histories of crime – including serious offences such as robbery, burglary and crack and heroin sales – within the borough surely add, unnecessarily, to the pressures and tribulations that inner-city residents, already living in an overcrowded borough with a high unemployment rate, must suffer. The many businesses skirting on the lines of legality by trading in 'hot' goods also add to the atmosphere of crime in the area. Lambeth's citizens may not be direct victims of these crimes per se, but living in the wake of these behaviours surely compounds their daily grind, their daily struggle. These things are important to bring up; such activities and behaviours do not occur with such frequency or such visibility everywhere, though they happen in Lambeth, and have been doing so for a very long time. If nothing is said then surely nothing will be done. High rates of serious offences will not go away by themselves, as evidenced by their prominence within Lambeth over decades. I hope this book in some way serves as a catalyst for positive change in the borough.

Bill Sanders
Brooklyn 2004

Introduction

Why study young people and crime? Many forces drive researchers to study social phenomena, some of which may stem from the researcher's history. What might best be described as a personal 'connection' between a sociologist's biography and their topic of study has been suggested as an incentive (Becker 1963; Corrigan 1979; Hobbs 1988; Polsky 1969; see also Geis 2002; Lofland and Lofland 1984), and indeed a personal connection served as an impetus for this research.

My initial interest in criminology partially stemmed from growing up around gangs in San Diego, California. San Diego, like many major US cities, has criminal street gangs (Klein 1995; Spergel 1995). The gangs exist in various communities in San Diego (Sanders 1994), including the residential suburb where I lived in North County. I knew guys in the gang throughout my teen years, and still run into some of them when I occasionally go back to visit. Their faces are not easy to forget; we attended the same schools, were in the same classes and lived around the street from one another. This upbringing also helped shape my interest in *how* to research crime and delinquency. For instance, that only some of the guys I grew up with joined the gang, not all of them, was interesting to note. Qualitative approaches towards the study of crime and delinquency – such as interviews, observations and ethnography – have a great potential for uncovering reasons for such a discrepancy. These methods, generally speaking, allow for subjective interpretations and understandings of social phenomena to emerge, including those in the general field of crime and delinquency (Berger and Luckman 1967; Goffman 1959, 1963, 1967; Groves and Lynch 1990; Weber 1947). Furthermore, these qualitative methods offer the opportunity to bridge the often large gap between a researcher of crime and delinquency and the 'criminals' they research (Nelken 1994), and allows us an opportunity to find out what 'crime' really means to others and how it fits with their daily lives.

My original intentions for this research were 'gang' oriented. I intended to come to London, find an area to study young people, hang out with them, determine how they compared to US-style street gangs, and write about it. *Youth Crime and Youth Culture in the Inner City*, however, turned out to be much more than expected. This book offers an interpretative account of young people, crime and culture in a multi-cultural environment. It examines a reality experienced by young 'white', 'black' and 'mixed-race' people who have offended, as translated through their voices and the voices of those who have worked closely with such individuals. It offers my analysis on several topics related to various categories of behaviour that, by definition, are illegal. This book aims to offer a contemporary picture, both physically and theoretically, of young people with various histories of offending in an inner-city London borough.

This research is much needed; there is a dearth of interpretative studies on young people within urban settings who commit crime. What do we know about young people who offend in London's inner-city areas in the early years of the new millennium? How do young people make sense of their offences? How do they talk about them? How does offending fit in with the rest of their lives? The present study attempts to answer these questions. Also, and importantly, inner cities are often equated with crime (Foster 1990; Graef 1993). Recent British Crime Survey data have shown a disproportionate amount of 'street' crimes, victims of these crimes and fear of crime in inner-city areas (Kershaw *et al.* 2000; Mirrlees-Black *et al.* 1996, 1998; Simmons *et al.* 2002). These considerations may give rise to feelings of lawlessness and helplessness associated with inner cities. But is this really the case? By researching crime in the inner city, this study is addressing a major social concern in an area that typifies where this concern is substantial.

Specific themes examined within the book include sociological, criminological and more general concerns. One of these is motivation – criminology's 'Holy Grail' (Groves and Lynch 1990: 360). Why do young people offend? This question is difficult to answer, and several general theories of crime and delinquency attempt to account for such behaviours. One line of reasoning – strain theory – contends that young people turn to offending as a way to reach their desired goals, and that offending is the result of them being denied legitimate access to what they want in life (Agnew 1992; Merton 1938, 1957). Another major theoretical standpoint suggests that we have various social bonds – investments, commitments, attachments to and beliefs about our society – which, in effect, keep us from offending (Gottfredson and Hirschi 1990; Hirschi 1969). These control theories argue that when these bonds become weakened or are altogether removed, an individual may offend. Others have suggested that crime may be a rational choice (Coleman and Fararo 1992; Cornish and Clarke 1987). Rational-choice theory holds that people carefully calculate their offences by weighing out perceived risk against perceived gain, and only commit them when the former is deemed acceptable in lieu of attaining the latter. An additional theory suggests a seductive nature of crime, where people offend in order to transcend their everyday rational worlds and enter an alternative 'carnivalesque' reality where they indulge in fantastical 'sneaky thrills' (Katz 1988; Presdee 2000).

This book is not aimed at testing or proving any one of these major theories of crime and delinquency. However, it attempts to see how they fit with the interpretations offered by young people about their offences. Likewise, this book cannot exactly answer *why* young people behave illegally, although I move towards explanations for various offences by piecing together existing bits of some contemporary theories. Aside from seeking motivation, additional phenomenological aspects of the young people's offending – such as how they select appropriate victims or targets, the extent to which they plan such acts, and how they feel after committing their offences – are also explored within the book. Information on the young people's motivation, planning, target selection and their attitudes towards various offences are referred to as that pertaining to their 'moral universes' or their worldviews.

Youth Crime and Youth Culture in the Inner City also addresses structural and cultural conditions of the young people's urban environment in attempts to evoke or explain specifics about their offending. In particular, I explore the extent to which structural deficiencies within the borough, such as high population density and high unemployment, may have given rise to additional, illicit and illegal forms of economic activity, such as selling drugs and the trading of 'second-hand' merchandise (Coleman 1988; Foster 1990; Hagan 1994; Sullivan 1989). From here, I attempt to assess the degree to which the presence of such activity, and, invariably, those involved with it, may have been influential on young people's decision to offend (Sutherland 1947; Sutherland *et al.* 1992).

Other perspectives on crime and delinquency that I explore in this research attempt to account for the moral climate towards specific offences. Is there a broad 'culture of offending' (Matza 1964; Sykes and Matza 1961) amongst young people in the inner city where certain offences are 'allowed', or are there smaller 'offending cultures' where such behaviour is 'required' (Cloward and Ohlin 1960; Cohen 1955)? Perhaps young people who offend in the inner city comprise the 'criminal Other' – individuals relatively detached from conventional values and lifestyles (Nelken 1994)? Alternatively, maybe these young people are more like everyone else than previously expected. This book examines the extent to which such perspectives are valuable in capturing explanations of crime and delinquency amongst young people.

Cultural attributes of young people themselves are considered in relation to their offending. This examination is steeped within the tradition of 'cultural criminology' – the explorations and analyses of the intersections of culture and crime (Ferrell and Sanders 1995; Hall and Jefferson 1976; Hebdige 1979; Jefferson 1993; Presdee 2000; Willis 1978). The importance of this lies not only in how we view young people who have offended, what we think they look like and get up to, but also in finding out if anything about their own cultural minutiae is significant in better explaining aspects about their offending. For instance, there exists in the inner city a variety of mediated images of 'crime and deviance', which, in part, offer up portrayals and stereotypes of individuals considered 'criminal' or 'deviant'. These images, in turn, have the potential to become internalised by a vast audience, suggesting who should be considered criminal or deviant in our society (S. Cohen 1972; Sparks 1992; Surette and Otto 2001). Postwar Britain has seen a veritable rogues' gallery of young offenders with the teddy boys, mods and rockers, punks, skinheads, hippies, ravers, and, perhaps more recently, yardies and gangstas. And while the image of the young offender has certainly changed in appearance over the second half of the twentieth century, how much has it changed fundamentally? Are the groups fairly similar to one another, each being a continuation of Britain's 'history of respectable fears' (Pearson 1983)? Or have their structure and functions recently changed, maybe being more similar to US-style gangs? Certainly previous literature has failed to find gangs in Britain (Downes 1966; Foster 1990; Parker 1974; Robins 1992), but some social and economic conditions in the UK had, near the end of the twentieth century, shifted towards those in the USA linked with the emergence of gang behaviour (Downes 1998). 'Yardie' and 'gangsta' are also terms heard in the media, and reported in journalistic accounts (Davidson 1997; Thompson 1995). Concomitantly, popular music is saturated with hip-hop's tattooed, self-proclaimed 'thugs' and 'rude bwois'. Yet to what extent are these accurate portrayals of young people who offend in the inner city? By addressing various aspects of the young people's cultural worlds, how they represent themselves and how they are perceived, an additional aim is to draw attention to how (and if) such aspects are important in comprehending crime and delinquency in their lives.

In order to answer my questions, getting very close to young people who have offended was important. This occurred through various efforts. *Youth Crime and Youth Culture in the Inner City* is not an ethnographic study per se, but it was carried out in the spirit of ethnography: *in situ* and over time. Whyte's (1955) *Street Corner Society*, Liebow's (1967) *Tally's Corner*, Becker's (1963) *Outsiders*, Parker's (1974) *A View From the Boys*, Foster's (1990) *Villains*, Robins' (1992) *Tarnished Vision* and Bourgois' (1995) *In Search of Respect*, to name a few, were all highly influential works. Like these researchers, I sought to analyse crime and deviance 'up close' through direct experience, interaction and communication. Rather than generating data through what are generally considered 'participant observational' methods, this research is primarily based on semi-structured, in-depth interviews with 31 young people with various histories of offending, supported by similar interviews with 67 professionals who have worked with young people who have offended in miscellaneous capacities. This information is complemented by six years of field notes on general information about aspects related to crime and delinquency in an inner-city London borough generated from living, working and playing there. In the first chapter I discuss exactly how I came to London and 'hit the ground running' in terms of attempting to find and interview young people who have offended and those who have worked with them. I also highlight some of the trials and tribulations I encountered in the process of finding paths that would (hopefully) lead me closer to young people who have offended, and discuss some of the strengths and weaknesses of the methods that were eventually employed. In addition, Chapter One offers some background information on the young people and professionals interviewed, and discusses how my information about them will be presented. Furthermore, I address some issues of conducting research on crime and delinquency in a multicultural area.

The 31 young people interviewed each have different histories of offending. Some have committed very serious offences, such as street robbery or burglary, whereas others have a relatively tame record of offending, perhaps an odd fight or theft when younger. For analytical purposes, I divided the 31 young people into two generic groups: those more involved in offending and those less so. These categories are based on the classification and total number of offences the young people said they committed with the exception of fighting, and the amount of times they said they had been arrested, if any. Throughout the book comparisons are made within and between these groups to account for similarities and differences in the young people's perspectives – their moral universes.

Prior to discussing and analysing the offences committed by the young people, examining the area they grew up in is important. The second chapter aims to do this. Within the sociology of crime and delinquency, several theories focus on the environmental context and social and economic status of an offender. These include: 'social disorganisation', 'subcultural', 'strain' and the idea of the 'underclass' (Agnew 1992; Merton 1938; Sampson and Groves 1989; Shaw and McKay 1942; Wilson 1987). However, at no point in this book do I suggest any direct link or correlation between structural aspects of the young people's environment and their involvement in offending. Chapter Two illustrates and explores the young people's urban surroundings, so as better to contextualise this behaviour. The point here is to paint the 'background' scenery, to set the environmental tone. Specifically, I offer some socioeconomic statistical information about the inner-city borough, as well the recorded rates of various offences that have occurred within it. Furthermore, I detail discovered and recorded forms of illicit and illegal economic activity within the borough that comprise part of an 'underground economy', and address how this economy may fit into the lives of ordinary people (Foster 1990; Robins 1992). A further analysis centres on the potential influence this economy may have on the young people's involvement in offending (McGahey 1986; Pitts 1999; Sullivan 1989).

Robberies, burglaries and thefts are the topic of Chapter Three. The themes explored in this and other chapters that directly discuss their offences include traditional criminological concerns, such as motivation, planning, learning, skills and reactions to such offences. Chapter Three attempts to find out what goes through the mind of a young person when: they enter a house illegally; stuff expensive clothing in their jackets and leave without paying for it; or dash by and grab someone's bag or purse. The focuses of these analyses centre on the phenomenological context of these behaviours (Gibbons 1971; Groves and Lynch 1990; Jacobs and Wright 1999; Katz 1988; Shover 1996). In other words, I examine the young people's actions immediately revolving around their illegal acts. Also in this chapter I explore the extent to which adults and the underground economy within the area influenced the young people's decisions to become involved in these acquisitive offences.

Illicit drugs are a great social concern. Drug use is very widespread amongst young people and drug markets have the potential to offer them lucrative returns and real dangers. Chapter Four explores these topics. It first looks at how often young people used drugs and their overall attitudes towards them. Cannabis dominates this discussion, but some young people mentioned experimenting with other drugs, such as cocaine, ecstasy, LSD, speed and aerosol inhalants. From here, I discuss how drug use amongst young people is theoretically conceptualised. Does drug use take place within closed, confined circles amongst society's failures (Cloward and Ohlin 1960; Merton 1957)? Or has the use of some drugs become so widespread as to be considered a 'normal', routine aspect of youthful behaviour (Parker *et al.* 1995, 1998)? Perhaps it lies somewhere in between. In the second half of the chapter I examine the interpretations and attitudes of the few young people I interviewed who said they sold crack, heroin and/or cannabis, and find out exactly how they carried it out and why. Their interpretations of these behaviours are compared against that of drug-selling youths previously researched (Fagan 1996; Padilla 1992; Ruggiero and South 1995).

Chapter Five is about expressive offences, such as vandalism, joyriding and graffiti. I look at the frequency of these behaviours and find out exactly how they were committed and with whom. From here, I analyse the significance that the young people attributed to such acts. Why would they purposely destroy public property? What attracts them to smashing car windows or 'tagging' a street name? What function does joyriding serve? Perhaps, as has been suggested, they commit them for 'fun' or 'just for the hell of it' because they are 'bored' with 'nothing to do' (Corrigan 1979; Presdee 1994, 2000). Or maybe they just enjoy being 'bad' (Katz 1988)? I attempt to tease out explanations for these behaviours and answer other questions related to the young people's expressive offences.

Chapter Six concerns violence. It starts by looking at the nature of young people's fighting. By this I refer to why the young people said they fought, whom they fought, and how these fights were carried out. Next, I look at the young people's attitudes towards and use of weapons, namely guns and knives. How prevalent was the use of firearms and 'choppers' amongst young people in this inner-city borough? Are 'guns on the streets' becoming a 'sign of the times'? I try to answer these questions. In the final part of the chapter I look at the extent to which territory was something that the young people fought over, and their degree of willingness to 'defend it' (Anderson 1999; Shover 1996). From here, I compare the young people's territorial issues to those exhibited by US-style street gangs in order to account for similarities and differences (Decker and Van Winkle 1996; Fagan 1996; Klein 1971, 1995; Sanders 1994; Spergel 1995; Vigil 1988).

In Chapter Seven I shift away from directly addressing the young people's interpretations of their offences. Instead, I look at other aspects of their lives, such as how they present themselves in public, what they get up to on a daily basis, and their interactions with police officers in their neighbourhoods. These three completely different cultural aspects of their lives are grouped together here in order to explore the extent to which they intersect with the young people's offending. The overall aim is to find out if we can learn anything relating to this behaviour by closely examining these cultural indicators (Ferrell and Sanders 1995; Hebdige 1979; Willis 1978). First, I look at the style of the young people, which here refers to their clothing, music and overall demeanour, aiming to detect significance and meaning. Next, because the young people said they spend much of their time with their friends, I investigate what they get up to together. In the final section of this chapter I analyse the experiences those in my sample have had with police in their environment.

The concluding chapter reflects on the discussions in the preceding chapters. In particular, I focus on the limits or rules those in my sample, and perhaps other young people in the inner city from similar backgrounds, followed (or still follow) when they committed (or still commit) their offences. These self-imposed and, no doubt, culturally informed rules seem to outline a culture of offending – their normative judgements regarding their illicit or illegal acts. I explore what these judgements may suggest. Are they mindless thugs bent on chaos and destruction, or are there limits they imposed on themselves when behaving illegally? Is crime a 'free for all', or are there guidelines that young people adhere to which regulate their offending? I attempt to answer these questions. I also examine the extent to which young people see themselves committing offences in their futures. Do they believe that they will be 'doing crime' for the rest of their lives, or do they have more typical employment expectations? Additionally, I ask: What can my data reveal about young people who offend in the inner-city borough more generally? Interviews with many professionals who have been working with young offenders in the area for several years offered comments in parallel with the young people's interpretations of their offences. I draw out these parallels, so as to offer a general impression of young people with histories of offending in the borough. From here, I explore the extent to which some of the more general theories of crime and delinquency can adequately explain or evoke the young people's offending, and then offer my own theoretical views on the young people's offending behaviour. A small supplementary chapter offers some advice on what might be done about certain acquisitive and drug-related offences.

This book is about black, white and 'mixed-race' young people who have offended in an inner-city London borough. It explores how they make sense of behaviour generally defined as 'crime', attempts to understand the fine distinctions they make regarding this behaviour, and examines the relationship between offending and specific cultural aspects of their lives. My interviews and observations are very rich in detail and personal experience, and, as such, are able to offer much insight into the minds and lives of young people from the inner city who offended from a fairly unique perspective: up close and personal. The general idea is to offer a peek into the world of these young people, to examine their 'moral universes' in relation to their law-breaking behaviour, and to understand crime and delinquency in their lives as seen through their eyes.

1 Research in the inner city

In my attempt to study US-style gangs in England, I needed to find an area where they might exist – a densely populated, multicultural, inner-city area, in a large urban city with a high rate of crime and unemployment (see Klein 1995; Spergel 1995). So I packed what I could into two suitcases, grabbed my trusty old Apple computer and headed to London. The capital seemed like a good place to start, and, besides, some friends living in the East End extended an invitation to stay with them until I got settled. Where in London to study? My first impressions of London were that the north and west parts of the city are relatively affluent, and that areas in the east and the south are somewhat 'rough'. I knew that some research on young people and crime had already been conducted in London's East End (for example, Downes 1966; Hobbs 1988; Willmott 1966), and that Foster (1990) did her research somewhere in South London. I figured that south of the Thames was an ideal place to study gangs because research on young people who have offended in this area seemed relatively scant. Where in the south of London? This decision was not difficult as there was one place I repeatedly read about and heard in the news: Brixton. Brixton, however, turned out to be a relatively small area with loosely defined boundaries, typical of many areas in London. London's boroughs, however, have solid boundaries, making the collection of demographic and other data about them more feasible. As such, I decided the study should be in the borough containing Brixton – Lambeth.

Upon further inspection, Lambeth looked like an excellent place to conduct research. Importantly, all of the demographic characteristics I looked for in an attempt to find and study street gangs were in Lambeth. Furthermore, very little research on young people who have offended had been conducted in this borough (although see Burney 1990). No question; I had found my setting. So, in the middle of June 1996 I moved into a room in a two-up, two-down terraced house located directly behind the high street in Brixton – the same room where the majority of this book was written.

My general idea was to do an ethnographic study in Lambeth to determine if criminal and/or juvenile street gangs existed. I wanted to find a group of young people that somewhat resembled a US-style gang, befriend them, observe how they interacted with one another at close proximity, talk to them to see how they made sense of their offences and look at how offending fitted in with the rest of their lives –

Figure 1.1 The author in front of his residence in February 1997. The house to his right would later become occupied by crack cocaine and heroin users and sellers.

just like other researchers (for example Parker 1974; Patrick 1973). However, I knew this would be difficult. I knew no one in Lambeth, had no connections with anyone who could act as a middle person between myself and young people, and did not even know my way around the borough. In order to collect data on young people who have offended I hit the ground running, and attempted several ways to find some willing to speak with me. It proved to be a very difficult task.

In the spirit of ethnography, I not only moved into the area of study, but also took a job in a second-hand clothing store, and did some volunteer work with a local, community-based organisation that worked with young people who have offended, which I refer to as 'The Design'.[1] I figured these practices would not only acquaint me with Lambeth, but also help me meet people and make friends, and,

in a sense, make me more a part of Lambeth. I also reckoned this would help intro-
duce me to young people who have offended, and those who work with them.

After my first year in Lambeth, the research started taking shape, yet not exactly
as planned. I failed to find a willing group of young people to conduct a participant-
observational study with. I made some progress with a group of them on my street,
several of whom had histories of offending, but they consistently flaked out on our
arranged meetings. My hopes of a such a study slowly dwindled. I needed to shift
my plan of attack if I wanted to gather information on gangs (or their absence) in
Lambeth. Indeed, as others have noted, collecting first-hand data on groups such
as 'young offenders' is very difficult (see Lee 1993; Maguire 2000).

Taking stock after roughly twelve months in the field I counted a series of interviews with those who worked with young people who offended in Lambeth, such as
police and probation officers, youth justice workers, detached youth workers, and
those at youth and community centres. These interviews contained a wealth of
information about young people in Lambeth in general. Also, around April 1997, I
befriended one young person, Nathan, through my volunteer work at The Design,
and talked with him extensively about his offending. Initially, my intentions were
not to involve any of the young people met through The Design in my research, but
after several meetings with Nathan, it became clear he was exactly the type of
young person I sought to interview – one with a history of offending. On our
second meeting, I told Nathan of the study and asked if he would mind participating. I received permission from both The Design and Nathan's mother, and
everyone was told of my researcher status and intentions, once, if not several times.
Nathan and I met up about fifteen times, where we took in a movie, ate at a fast-
food restaurant and discussed various aspects about his life, including his offending.
Our relationship officially ended when Nathan was put on remand for robbery.

From looking at my interview and observational data collected during the first
twelve months of the research, from June 1996 to June 1997, it became clear that
US style-street gangs were *not* in Lambeth and that they never really have been.
Absolutely nothing was mentioned by these respondents to suggest that young
people in Lambeth joined gangs or engaged in gang-like behaviour (such as
possessing identifiable colours or insignias, or long-standing territorial disputes).
Informal observations in the borough also failed to record any groupings similar to
US-style gangs, and conversations with neighbours and young people on my street
suggested that US-style gangs did not appear to exist in the borough. The professionals and young people were specifically asked about delinquent groups or collectives of young people who have offended on a consistent basis, in some sort of
combination, not necessarily 'gangs'. No one I interviewed or came across in the
first twelve months really talked about anything like US-style gangs, and the word
'gang' itself was not even mentioned by them, a point noted by other researchers in
England (such as Foster 1990; Patrick 1973). Furthermore, little evidence existed to
suggest young people gathered in 'posses' or as yardies, groupings perhaps somewhat akin to gangs previously reported in the British media (see Ruggiero and
South 1995). Mick, a detached youth worker in Brixton, said 'this posse thing' was
largely based on media 'hype'. He elaborated:

The way the media portrays things. The media is all about hyping things. Any youngsters will go around in groups. I think what [the media] tend to do is go out and say, uh, 'A Black Posse of Young Men'. They don't say a group of young men. They say posse or they say gang. Right and that's the way the media portray that … [Young people he has worked with] are not as bad as the media portray them, this posse thing.

Because a participant-observational study of young people and crime was not looking feasible, and because US-style street gangs did not seem to be in Lambeth, I decided to shift both the focus of this research and how to carry it out. Nonetheless, my central purposes remained intact: to find out what offending means to young people in the borough. Over the course of the first year, I collected a small handful of in-depth interviews with those who worked with young people who offended in Lambeth; established a friendly, ongoing relationship with Nathan, an 'active offender'; and, more importantly, made a series of connections with those who might be able to put me in contact with other young people who offended, or those who work with them in the borough. Roughly the next eighteen months, between June 1997 and October 1998, were spent networking these connections and conducting as many in-depth interviews as I could with young people who have offended in Lambeth and those who have worked with them.

About two and a half years into the research I decided that I had collected enough interviews. In total I conducted 31 semi-structured, in-depth interviews with young people with various histories of offending, and 67 with 'professionals' – police officers, youth justice workers, youth and community workers, and detached youth workers. The young people interviewed were pulled from three distinct pools: a group from a youth and community centre, a group from an educational unit, and several whom I met through Nathan. Both the young people and professionals interviewed were asked similar questions regarding offending. Specifically, I asked the young people if they had done anything they knew was illegal or something they knew that a police officer would stop them for. All were explicitly aware of what I referred to. During the interviews the young people reflected on their offences and the professionals reflected on those committed by the young people they worked with.

The age range of the young people in my sample is 13–23, but the majority were aged between 14 and 16. Also, from the pool of available young people to interview, only three were female. The gender bias of this research stemmed, in part, from the approach. At the youth centres and off-site unit where many of the interviews were conducted, young women were the exception, and were thus unavailable to be interviewed. When interviewed, the professionals' responses concerned young men, not young women. This observation suggests that the professionals' conceptualisation of collectives of young offenders in the borough is largely gender specific. To be sure, that most crime is committed by boys and men is a frequently made observation in many criminological studies (Messerschmidt 1993, 2000; Newburn and Stanko 1994; Sutherland and Cressey 1978).

All but a few of the interviews were tape-recorded and conducted with the aid of an interview schedule. Those with the young people were held either at the educational unit or at the community centre where I met them, or at Nathan's home. Nearly all of the professionals were interviewed where they worked. In-depth and informal interviews were not only the most available methods, but perhaps the most feasible and effective. They allowed access to the young people's worlds, and we can somewhat gauge how they behaved or are going to behave based on what they say. Their interview responses are not to be taken as absolute truths, but rather as 'fallible evidence' of their 'realities' (Maxwell 1996; Wengraf 2001). These interviews were also beneficial because they allowed for more elusive sociological concepts, such as values, beliefs and norms, to be accurately examined (Arksey and Knight 1999; Rubin and Rubin 1995) – concepts addressed throughout this book. These concepts play central roles in theories on crime and delinquency, and addressing the values and norms of the young people in relation to their offending behaviours allows us the opportunity to determine the extent of the accuracy of these theories in explaining or evoking these behaviours. In-depth interviews are very useful at drawing out the circumstance, context and incentive regarding the young people's offending (Hakim 1987; Rubin and Rubin 1995).

Interviews with the professionals proved invaluable. Youth justice workers, youth and community workers, and detached youth workers spend a considerable amount of time working with young people in Lambeth, and they said they probed them on similar questions to those I had put to my sample (for example, Why are you committing these offences? How do you feel about them afterwards?). Import-antly, similarities existed between how the young people I interviewed interpreted their offences and what the professionals said about the young people they worked with on many points, including: why they commit offences; what they spend money earned from their offences on; what kinds of drugs they use; how they get along with police officers. As such, the comments from the professionals often serve to support points and arguments made about my sample of young people.

The discrepancy between the number of professionals and young people inter-viewed may be explained by the difficulties in accessing young people who have offended. Basically, in Lambeth I found it much easier to find willing and accessible professionals to interview in comparison to such young people. I did, however, make several attempts to interview others. For instance, for about six months I corresponded with a police officer and a prison liaison officer about interviewing young people from Lambeth on remand in Feltham, a young offenders' institution. While it looked promising at the start, I was eventually denied access due to 'insuffi-cient staff'. I also tried to interview young people through the help of detached youth workers, youth and community workers and youth justice workers, but these attempts were all in vain. Not only was it difficult to find a way to get the informa-tion I wanted, but when one path became seemingly clear – in-depth interviews – I then found it very difficult to find young people with histories of offending available and/or willing to be interviewed. I felt lucky to have the 31.

Notes on access: bragging, empathy, doing something different

The difficulty in obtaining first-hand information about young people who are 'active' offenders is well documented (Jacobs and Wright 1999; Maguire 2000; Wright and Decker 1994; Wright *et al.* 1992). Indeed, accessing young people with histories of offending in Lambeth was not easy. For young people in the borough, the idea of talking to a complete stranger about all the offences they committed (or were still committing) may have not sat so well with them. Through much effort, I found 31 of them willing to talk to me about their offences.

Why would young people want to talk with me about their offences in the first place? One observation noted during the interviews with those from the community centre or the off-site educational unit was that they appeared to use the interview as an excuse to escape from their engagement at that time. Even though the young people at both locations attended these places voluntarily, they mentioned something along the lines of not wanting to participate in their current activity. In this sense, the interviews lured them away, offering a break from their routine behaviour.

Another useful research tool that I think helped me gain access was my 'foreignness', and how respondents may have perceived their position in relation to mine during the course of the interview. For instance, Hannertz (1969) mentioned his Swedish nationality gave him an advantage over local white people when researching black people and black culture in America. Furthermore, my accent is classless and not regionally bound (seemingly a quality by which people in England somewhat gauge one another), and may have aroused their interest simply due its difference. In other words, they might have simply thought it intriguing to speak with 'the foreign guy' or 'the stranger' (see also Merton 1972). Many of the young people interviewed were very interested in learning about specific things in the USA, and enjoyed talking about what they knew or believed about the country, and asked about my own upbringing, experiences and opinions. Conversations with them held before, after and sometimes during the interviews often strayed into issues of US youth culture, such as music, fashions, issues of the opposite sex, and other interests.

Bravado amongst some of the young people may have been another reason they agreed to be interviewed. For instance, Wright, Decker, Redfern and Smith (1992) commented on their respondents' predilection to brag about their current 'score', and how they enjoyed telling others about their offending. One of them said, 'What's the point of scoring if nobody knows about it?' (p. 154; see also Armstrong 1993; Hobbs 1993; Jacobs and Wright 1999; Shover 1996). Padilla (1992: 17–18) also made a similar point when discussing a group of young people he researched called 'The Diamonds' who sold crack: 'I discovered that, in general, like many other teenagers in US society today, Coco and other members of the Diamonds have had a craving to tell and share their stories with the adult world for a very long time.'

Donning the 'white lab coat' when conducting sociological field research and doing it 'by the book' are not always the best ways to gain access or obtain accurate responses. When conducting qualitative research a researcher must rely on a great deal of social skills in order to establish a proficient relationship with the subject (Ackroyd and Hughes 1992; Arksey and Knight 1999; Armstrong 1993; Hobbs 1993; Shaffir 1991). Such interpersonal skills were most needed in this research – in-depth interviews with young people who have offended. Researchers have, no doubt, benefited from the social skills acquired from their personal experiences when studying social phenomena. For instance, imagine the relative ease with which Ned Polsky, a billiards aficionado, accessed pool-hall regulars when researching *Hustlers, Beats and Others* (1969), or how Howard Becker, a jazz musician, probably had few problems infiltrating the lives of marijuana-smoking jazz musicians when researching *Outsiders* (1963). These researchers were probably afforded access to these lifestyles and offered accurate information about those who live them largely due to the parallels between them and their topics of study.

The interpersonal skills acquired from my upbringing around those in involved in crime, my previous employment working with young people 'at risk' of offending in various mediums, and cultural aspects about my life probably aided my access to the young people, and helped secure their rapport. Like many of the young people interviewed, I, too, have grown up around crime, and have friends and relatives who have been in legal trouble. These issues were also brought up peripherally in some of the interviews. Moreover, many of these young people and I shared similar tastes in fashion and music. A likeness existed in the way we dressed and our favourite types of music. We also shared slang words, particularly the term 'what's up?' While the use of this word is relatively ubiquitous in the USA, its use in London appeared, at least during the course of the research, to be very 'hip'. These qualities, along with my long hair (at the time) and earring, might have suggested to these young people that great differences existed between myself and a stereotypical 'academic' complete with camel-hair patches on the elbows of a tweed jacket. What I suggest overall is that, on various levels, many similarities between the young people interviewed and myself were apparent. To some degree, these parallels in life experience and semblance in culture helped me gain access to these young people, and enabled me to draw out accurate and elaborate information from them (Arksey and Knight 1999).

Different young offenders

So that I could explore patterns, the 31 young people were divided into two generic groups based on the classifications and numbers of offences they said they committed, the number of times they mentioned being arrested, the offence(s) that led to the arrest and whether or not they said they had recently (at the time of the interview) offended (see Table 1.1). The groups are labelled those 'more involved in offending' and those 'less involved in offending'. Throughout the book comparisons are made both between these categories and within them on various themes related to the young people's offences and other aspects of their lives. The groups are used for practical purposes, and serve only to distinguish between different types of young people who have offended. Like Foster (1990: 20), when describing the 'levels of

Table 1.1 Reported arrests and offences by the young people by offending category

	Age	Reported arrests	Offence categories									Total reported offences (not fights, joyriding)
			Vandalism	Joyriding	Fights	Shoplifting/theft	Theft of car	Theft from car	Burglary	Robbery	Drug sales	
More involved												
Sonny	14	1		3	*			10	20–30		c	33
Quentin	17	5	3	*	*	8			8	12	c	41
Travis	18	15	*		*	*	*	*	*	*		*
Marc	15	15			?	5		1	30	7	cr,h,c	43
Tolu	15	never	*	*	?			4	7		h	*
Karl	14	13			*	80			20–30	10		120
Martin	16	3	3		?		2	4	8	3		20
Noel	15	7		60–70	?				40			20
Tom	16	30	10		?			10	15			35
Kenny	15	13	*		*	*			16			*
Norman	15	never	*	*	?	*	25		13			*
Theo	20	10		*	*				10			10
Keenan	15	4–5		5	?	*				2		*
Nathan	16	5	*	*	?			5	2	3		*
Lenny	23	1			*					4		4
Kevin	15	4–5	*	4	5	*						*
Less involved												
David	14	15	10	*	*			3	1			10
Todd	14	never		*								3
Larry	15	2		*	*	1						1
Brian	22	2		*	5	1		5				6

continued on next page

Table 1.1 (cont.) Reported arrests and offences by the young people by offending category

			Offence categories									
	Age	Reported arrests	Vandalism	Joyriding	Fights	Shoplifting/ theft	Theft of car	Theft from car	Burglary	Robbery	Drug sales	Total reported offences (not fights, joyriding)
Darrell	16	2	2–3	2	*				1			4
Jack	15	1	*	*	20	18			2			20
Terry	15	1	*			7				1		*
Betty	16	never			*	1						1
Frank	13	never			1							0
Kellen	15	never	*		~							*
Winnona	15	1						1				1
Eric	16	1			~	1						1
Isaac	17	1			1	1						1
Tracy	15	1			*							0
Tim	16	2	1–2		2							2

Note
c = cannabis, cr = crack cocaine, h = heroin.
* = Mentioned 'too many to count'.
~ = Mentioned 'not that many' or 'only a couple'.

villainy' ascribed to those in her study, the labels of the offending groups here only serve 'as a crude analytical tool within which to consider … attitudes and behaviour'.

Those considered 'more involved in offending' committed serious offences, including burglaries, street robberies and/or selling drugs. About half of these young people mentioned *still* committing some offences at the time of the interview. All of them, except Tolu and Norman, have been previously arrested. Lenny, who committed relatively fewer offences in comparison to others within this group, is placed within this group due to the nature of his fights. He talked about being a 'debt collector', and physically threatened or assaulted those who owed money to his 'bosses'. While Lenny openly talked about the numerous fights he had been in, and his involvement in a couple of robberies, he remained vague about those he worked for and the nature of his debt collecting.

The young people considered 'less involved in offending', for the most part, only said they committed comparatively minor offences, such as shoplifting, theft from cars, joyriding, vandalism and some fighting. Generally speaking, these young people committed fewer offences overall. Three of them – Terry, David and Jack – said they were marginally involved in more serious offences, such as robbery or burglary once or twice. Frank, Winnona, Eric, Isaac and Tim only committed one or two offences, some of which led to their arrests. Four have not been arrested, but, for the most part, those who were, were only arrested once or twice. David's case is slightly unique in this respect, being arrested *ten times in the same place within the same week* for smashing beer bottles on the ground. His arrests, while high in comparison to the others, are not for serious offences. David and Todd are the only two within this group who said they still commit relatively petty offences, such as breaking windows and joyriding.

The data also threw up a couple of peculiarities that need to be explained. One may be explained by the approach. For instance, according to their accounts, more young people had committed burglaries than had shoplifted goods. With the exception of being specifically questioned about their fighting, the young people were not read a list of offences, then asked if they had committed them or not. Rather, I asked them if they committed *any* illegal acts or about behaviour they knew the police could stop them for. Thus, a possibility exists that some of those more involved in offending – such as Noel, Tom and Kenny – may have thought their burglaries eclipsed their shoplifting in terms of severity and, as such, decided not to discuss committing other relatively minor offences, though not necessarily prompted to do so. Also, the number of offences the young people said they committed and times they mentioned being arrested were, for the most part, their estimates and not exact counts. This may help explain the use of well-rounded figures such as Marc's '30' burglaries, Sonny's '20–30' robberies, Noel's '40' burglaries and Tom's '30' arrests. Also, the number of fights the young people were involved in proved difficult to quantify, as many of them either said something along the lines of being in 'too many fights to remember', 'loads of fights' or 'hundreds of fights' or, alternatively, they mentioned being involved in 'a couple of fights', 'not many fights', or that they 'rarely' fought.

Overall, these groups are relatively undeveloped, and only serve to roughly distinguish between different young people with variable histories of offending. Comparisons both between and within them on various topics related to their offending behaviour should prove revealing. These groupings do not claim to be representative of young people who offended in the borough or elsewhere for that matter. However, given recent findings from the British Crime Survey (Simmons *et al.* 2002) that a significant proportion of offences are committed by young men between the ages of 15 and 24, those in my sample more involved in offending, in the main, may somewhat reflect the images of such individuals (see also Flood-Page *et al.* 2000). Alternatively, those less involved may somewhat reflect the images of young people who are only temporarily and/or marginally involved in a couple of relatively less serious forms of offending (Audit Commission 1996; Flood-Page *et al.* 2000).

Some background data on the young people

Table 1.2 lists the housing tenure, household income and education of the young people interviewed, as well as how many adults they lived with. The correlation between the social and economic background of an individual and that individual's propensity or actual involvement in offending has been the cause of much debate (for example, Dunaway *et al.* 2000; Wright *et al.* 1999). Nowhere in the book do I suggest a causal relationship between the young people's involvement in offending and their social and economic background. My data threw up mixed patterns in these respects. The information presented below simply serves to illustrate the social and economic conditions these young people grew up in, and helps to better contextualise their behaviour.

All but four of the young people in my sample lived in public-sector housing, mostly on crowded council estates. However, those less involved in offending tended to live in privately rented houses and public-sector houses; those more involved within council flats. All the young people in my sample, except for the two who had jobs, were in some form of education or vocational training at a local Lambeth institute. However, some distinctions were apparent in their education. About half of those more involved in offending attended or had completed their education at an off-site educational unit. The other young people, in the main, attended or completed mainstream school. Those in my sample also predominately come from single-parent (mother) households. This, however, is not to suggest any causal relationship between an individual being raised by a mother only and that individual's involvement in or disposition towards offending. For instance, recent research by Toby and Farrington (2001: 37) suggested 'it would be a mistake to conclude that disrupted families in general have criminogenic effects', and how boys raised only by their mothers 'are no more criminogenic than intact harmonious families'. Nonetheless, those less involved in offending tended to come from dual-parent households. Seven of the young people's families receive income support, and five of these seven were more involved in offending. The parents who were employed worked at relatively low-income occupations; several of them, such as Nathan's mum, worked in the public sector as social workers. However, the parents of those less involved in offending worked in comparatively more skilled and specialist occupations.

Table 1.2 Who they were raised by, income, housing and education[a] by offending category

	Adults, income	Accommodation	Education
More involved			
Sonny	Mum, bus driver	Council estate	Off-site unit
Quentin	Mum, social worker	Council terraced house	College
Travis	Mum, income support	Council estate	College
Marc	Mum, child minder	Council estate	Off-site unit
Tolu	Mum, housing officer	Council terraced house	8 GCSEs, M
Karl	Mum, income support	Housing association house	Off-site unit
Martin	Mum, income support	Council estate	Off-site unit
Noel	Dad, carpenter, Mum, cleaner	Council maisonette	Off-site unit
Tom	Mum, income support	Council estate	Off-site unit
Kenny	Mum, income support	Council estate	All right, M
Norman	Mum, primary school teacher	Council estate	8 GCSEs, M
Theo	Mum, school dinner lady	Council estate	Comp. Off-site unit
Keenan	Dad, carpenter, Mum, cleaner	Council estate	6 GCSEs, M
Nathan	Mum, social worker	Council terraced house	Off-site unit
Lenny	Both parents are tailors	Privately rented house	Comp. College
Kevin	Dad, engineer, Mum, social worker	Privately rented house	Off-site unit
Less involved			
David	Mum, manager of an arcade	Council estate	Off-site unit
Todd	Both parents run a pub	Privately rented house	5 GCSEs, M
Larry	Mum, social worker	Council terraced house	5 GCSEs, M
Brian	Mum, social worker	Council terraced house	Comp. School
Darrell	Mum, social worker	Housing association maisonette	re-sit GCSE, M
Jack	Grandparents, pension	Council estate	9 GCSEs, M
Terry	Mum, income support	Council flat	11 GCSEs, M
Betty	Both parents, Dad, own business	Privately rented house	11 GCSEs, M
Frank	Mum, social worker	Council flat	Well, M
Kellen	Mum, income support	Council semi-detached house	8 GCSEs, M
Winnona	Residential care facility	Residential care facility	Off-site unit
Eric	Nan, dressmaker	Council semi-detached house	10 GCSEs, M
Isaac	Mum, caterer/promoter	Council terraced house	College
Tracy	Dad, scaffolder, Mum, secretary	Council terraced house	Poor, M
Tim	Dad public administration, Mum, cleaner	Council terraced house	Comp. school

Note

a 'Off-site unit' refers to an off-site educational support unit. '*n*' GCSEs refers to the number of GCSEs the young people said they were studying at a mainstream school. 'Well/all right/poor' refers to what the young people said about their school performance. 'Comp. School/College' refers to those who have completed their education at a mainstream school and received some college training. M = mainstream school.

Overall, the young people interviewed predominantly: came from backgrounds that may generally be considered 'working' or 'lower' class; lived with one parent in public-sector accommodation belonging to either Lambeth Council or Housing Association; and had finished their education or were attending an off-site educational unit. In the main the backgrounds of the young people the professionals said they worked with were similar.

In terms of patterns, those more involved in offending within the sample came from comparatively lower-income, single-parent households, and were attending or had completed their education at an off-site educational unit, whereas those less involved were more likely to be living with either one or two working adults who generated a relatively larger income, and were attending or had completed their education at a mainstream school. While housing tenure remained fairly consistent for all groups, general differences were apparent between those more and less involved in offending in terms of household size, household income and adults in the home. However, no clear causal patterns emerged linking these aspects of these young people's lives to their various levels of offending.

Keeping in mind the complex nature of the relationship between a young person's background – their general socioeconomic status in this case – and their involvement in offending or their propensity to offend is important. My data threw up mixed signals when comparing individual cases. For instance, Lenny – who, according to his accounts, was involved in some serious offences, such as robbery and what seemed to be some level of racketeering – lived with two working parents in a house in a relatively 'nicer' area of Lambeth. Lenny was also the only one in his family who offended. Alternatively, Isaac, who was marginally involved in a couple of minor offences, lived in less affluent area with his mum in a terraced house belonging to Lambeth Council. Isaac also has several relatives involved in different levels of serious offences, some who have smuggled cocaine into Britain from Jamaica. Given the background of these two young men, it might be expected that Isaac, coming from a relatively 'poorer' background, would be more involved in offending and Lenny, coming from a relatively 'affluent' background, less so. This, however, was not the case. The difficulty in making accurate predictions based on the young people's background is further illustrated by looking at Nathan's family. I interviewed Nathan and his three brothers, and found that little could be explained about their offending from looking at their housing income, housing tenure, and who raised them. For instance, all four boys were raised by their mother, who was employed as a social worker, and they have lived in some sort of terraced Victorian homes belonging to Lambeth's Housing Association all their lives. The eldest of the four brothers, Brian, and the youngest one, Larry, only told of their involvement in a couple of relatively minor offences they had committed earlier in their lives. The two middle brothers, Nathan and Quentin, on the other hand, reported a number of more serious, ongoing offences, one of which saw Nathan end up on remand in Feltham. In this case, four brothers growing up in the same house all had different offending histories. These examples suggest the difficulty in teasing out explanations about the young people's offending from addressing their general background. Perhaps, as recent research suggests, other important considerations need to be addressed, such as social psychological aspects of the individuals themselves, when exploring the nexus between someone's socio-economic status and their involvement in 'crime' (Broidy 2001; Dunaway *et al.* 2000; Wright *et al.* 1999).

Interviewing the professionals

The 67 professionals interviewed worked in various contexts with young people who offended in Lambeth. These interviews serve to complement and support the points made about my small sample of young people. The ages of the young people the professionals said they work with are roughly between 14 and 20. The professionals interviewed comprised 13 police officers, 2 probation officers, 21 youth justice workers, 21 youth and community workers, 7 detached youth workers and 3 journalists who report on crime in general in the borough. I attempted to cover the spectrum of those in occupations in the borough where 'work' with 'groups of young people who have offended' might be conducted, and believed these professionals were the best to interview (Becker 1970; Lee 1993; Lofland and Lofland 1984).[2] These professionals either worked in locations across Lambeth or with young people who lived all over the borough.

The police interviewed were primarily Criminal Investigations Department (CID) officers working in robbery, burglary or drugs divisions, or specialists working with young people who have offended in Lambeth. The focus within their interviews was on young people aged between 15 and 20. This 'snowball' sample was generated through my introduction to one officer, which led to others, and so on.

Unfortunately, only two probation officers from the borough were interviewed. Numerous attempts to interview other probation officers failed, and, understandably, many of them mentioned not having the time to offer an interview.

However, I interviewed many of those at Lambeth Youth Justice. Youth justice workers work with young people up to age 17 who have received a community penalty at court. I asked the head of Lambeth Youth Justice for permission to conduct the interviews, and then individual youth justice workers themselves. Interviews were primarily held with youth justice workers who worked most closely with young people, such as those who acted as 'appropriate adults' while the young people were in police custody, wrote pre-sentence court reports or conducted group sessions with the young people that focused on their offences. Only a few of those in more administrative positions were interviewed because of their limited contact with the young people.

I also interviewed adults working at youth and community centres throughout Lambeth. They discussed their work with young people who had offended in the past. Details for all of the youth and community centres were found in public directories. Several contacts were established through my volunteer work at The Design. This volunteer work also served as a reference point for other youth and community workers wishing to confirm my researcher status.

I interviewed several detached youth workers in Lambeth whose contact details were also found in a public directory. Detached youth workers are similar to youth and community workers, yet often conduct their work with young people away from a community centre and more 'on the street'. The detached youth workers occupied a unique position because of their relationship with the young people. All of the detached youth workers interviewed were highly spoken of by several youth and community workers and youth justice workers. These professionals mentioned how the detached youth workers could best answer my questions because they thought they worked most closely with young people 'on the street'. Indeed, the detached youth workers interviewed seemed to be closer to the young people they worked with than the other professionals interviewed. Some detached youth workers even mentioned having consistent contact with the young person's family. As Mick, a detached youth worker in Brixton, said: 'It's like I know them from the community. Like parents, sisters, brothers, uncles and aunts, so it's very much kind of a close-knit community in terms of those are the kinds of youngsters that come to the centre.'

Norma is another detached youth worker from Brixton. She described the work she and her team conduct as 'street work' and defined it in the following way:

> Street work and estate work is essentially the same type of thing. What it is, is working with young people in their environment. So what you find is that a lot of the young people that we work with tend to congregate on various streets normally those on commercial areas such as those of the McDonalds or the Pizza Hut where they tend to hang out. And it mainly tends to be working with small groups or individual on a one to one basis. And that tends to be providing information and advice, befriending, guidance and support rather than the sort of normal recreational facilities that might take place in a youth club such as table tennis and that sort of thing.

Ayo, a detached youth worker from Stockwell, also talked about the nature of his work:

> Some, not all of them [young people], have committed crime or have gone to jail and prison … The whole point of the [street] work is basically to redirect young people who have some, who have failed. Some are probably heading in that direction at this moment and, umm, basically opportunities … I might meet someone who I feel at this moment are a danger to themselves and encourage themselves to go to the centre … It's basically redirecting people.

The ethnic backgrounds of the professionals interviewed varied somewhat,[3] reflecting Lambeth's multicultural status. When asked about their ethnicity, about half of the youth and community workers, half of the youth justice workers and one probation officer identified themselves as being 'black', Afro-Caribbean or West African, having a combination of parents from such backgrounds, or 'mixed race', describing one parent as 'white' and the other as 'black', Afro-Caribbean or West African. The other half of the youth justice workers, youth and community workers and one probation officer described themselves as 'white', British, Irish or

European. *All* of the journalists and detached youth workers interviewed identified themselves as being 'black', Afro-Caribbean or West African. All of the police officers interviewed identified themselves as being 'white', British, Irish or European. Part of this bias stems from the absence of white detached youth workers and black CID officers in Lambeth during this research.

Access to the professionals was much easier to obtain than was access to young people with histories of offending in Lambeth. Most were not difficult to find and were generous with their time. A few, however, were reluctant to speak with me at first – in particular, the detached youth workers and some youth and community workers. Nonetheless, as with the young people, parallels in our lives emerged that may have eased my access to them. For instance, many of the professionals, like myself, have worked with young people considered at risk of offending. I previously worked as a child care worker in Riverside, California at a 'gang suppression unit' with young people also considered at risk of offending. Additionally, I worked as a child care worker in a 'group home' (residential care facility) in Riverside. I found the social and youth work extremely demanding, low paying, highly stressful and all too often not very satisfying in terms of the progress made with the young people. Similar sentiments were expressed by detached youth workers, youth and community workers and youth justice workers in the borough. For instance, Mick, a detached youth worker from Brixton, said: 'I've been in this business like I said to you. It don't pay you nothing. You don't get no rewards out of it.' Mick related this to a couple of things, one of them being the lack of support from the local authority.

> It becomes a very emotional time for me because it becomes very demoralising with the hours you put in to make something still go. Cuz if you don't have a local authority who can see what you're trying to do in terms of trying to preserve and trying to nurture and try and bring some young people through to become responsible adults of tomorrow, that takes a hell of a task to try and convince a local authority to do that.

Young people also frustrated Mick's efforts. He continued:

> And that is the [bad attitude] problem we have ... I'm talking about young-sters from the age of 12 ... They have the best trainers, they have the best garments. They're walking around with Walkmans and you're looking at youngsters and you're saying to yourself, 'Hold on a moment.' And they have an attitude like, 'Fuck you!' Give them all the trips. Take 'em everywhere. And ya say, 'But why are you carrying on like that? It's only a pound a day to come on the trip. Ya pay a pound a day. Ya mother or father pay five pounds for the week. Five pounds for the week! We take ya cinema, we take ya rock climbing, we take ya everywhere.' I got one of the programmes here! They go every-where – sailing the whole lot. And when you get out of the tube at the end of the day they can't even say 'thank you' ... It's real negative. They have this kinda 'fuck you' attitude. And the thing is I see it time and time again ... it really pisses me off right, y'know.

During the interviews with the professionals, I asked them for some general background information on the nature and history of their work with young people in Lambeth, and told them about my research agenda as well as my own work with young people. I found that many of us had things in common. I empathised with their work, being familiar with working with at-risk young people. These experiences we shared allowed these interviews to proceed in an open and casual atmosphere. My previous work experience with young people in the USA also piqued the interest of many professionals, especially youth justice workers, youth and community workers and detached youth workers. Some expressed an interest in how services oriented around young people who have offended operated, gangs in the USA, police–community issues and other topics. Also, some of the youth justice workers mentioned they had previously worked as youth or child care workers. Thus, my history as a child care worker served to advertise my status as a researcher with a history of doing work similar to many of my respondents. The rapport I established with many professionals interviewed *vis-à-vis* our shared work experience allowed for my relatively smooth access to them.

Field notes: the job, the street, the skatepark

Most of the information related to the young people is drawn from the interview material, but my own experiences and observations are in here as well. Throughout the research I lived in a large room (by Brixton standards at least) in a two-up, two-down terraced house turned into four bedsits, located directly behind the Brixton high street. I had moved from within 200 yards of the beach in San Diego to within 100 yards of two railway lines, and was paying over twice as much for it. Between June 1996 and June 1997, I worked at a second-hand retail clothing shop on Coldharbour Lane – a major road in the area. Living and working in Brixton proved helpful in finding my way around Lambeth. Furthermore, communicating with locals and fellow co-workers helped me understand British colloquialisms, some Jamaican patois, and what I considered a British–Jamaican hybrid slang (Back 1996; Robins 1992).[4] Acquiring these skills proved invaluable, as they allowed for more fluid conversations with Londoners and, especially, young people from Lambeth. For the first couple of months, though, I had to ask the locals to repeat themselves, and to do so slowly.

Observations were also recorded in other ways. In early April 1997 two representatives from a voluntary local playground organisation in Brixton asked, on their behalf, if I would be willing to teach basketball to local young people. The opportunity of teaching basketball to local Brixton youths was certainly appealing, not to mention curious. I agreed to take this on, and immediately started a weekly two-hour session on an outdoor court located only a few hundred yards from my home. The organisation made a cloth banner with my name on it, announcing the times and dates drawn in large pen markers. While the rain ruined the banner in a few weeks, I got to know many young people and others. My coaching career continued until the beginning of October 1997 when persistent rain put a stop to it.

I also frequently went to the skatepark on the border between Brixton and Stockwell. Like a stereotypical Southern California 'dude', for me skateboarding is a passion (not to mention a cheap and exciting way to keep in shape and active). More importantly though, the skatepark is a good place to make observations, or meet people who may be beneficial to the research. The Stockwell skatepark is a youth 'hang-out' that attracts many young people on bicycles, skateboards, roller blades and even the odd roller-skater trying their best on the skatepark's transitions and jumps. I befriended several young people there whose knowledge about the area, crime, drugs and other things was tremendously helpful in one way or another in the course of this research.

During my time in Lambeth a conscious decision to 'do research' did not always exist.[5] My intentions were not to record observations every time I left my house or peeked out my window, but on many occasions events somewhat relevant to my research occurred in plain view. For instance, I recorded observations from walking around the borough, waiting for the bus, going to work, shopping and any additional daily business. These may be considered 'unobtrusive measures' of collecting data (Webb *et al.* 1966).

I bring up the skatepark, basketball court and the other observations made around Lambeth in relation to their utility in collecting data on young people in the borough. These observations were not deceitful, and whenever possible I revealed my research identity and intentions. Fellow employees, neighbours, those at the basketball court and the people befriended at the skatepark were informed of my researcher status and the general topic of my study once, if not several times. However, my role as employee at the shop, neighbour on the block, coach at the court, or just your average somebody or 'bod'[6] at the skatepark, seemed to garner more attention than my student status.[7] All they seemed to remember was me being a student doing 'something somewhere'.

Research on crime in a multicultural borough

Ethnicity is an important consideration in any discussion of crime, but more so in a multiracial, polyethnic inner-city borough such as Lambeth. Topics of ethnicity within any academic discipline can evoke strong emotions and reactions, especially when related to themes of crime and delinquency, for several reasons. 'Blacks' and Asians, which would include those generally considered 'mixed race', are significantly over-represented within the criminal justice system in the UK as perpetrators of crime (see Audit Commission 1996; Fitzgerald 1998). British Crime Survey data also suggest these same people are generally at a higher risk of being the victim of an offence than whites (see Kershaw *et al.* 2000; Mirrlees-Black *et al.* 1996, 1998; Simmons *et al.* 2002). Sensitivity over this subject may also arise due to the portrayals of 'blacks' as criminals within the mass media. For instance, Hall *et al.* (1978) examined how the media associated young black men with perpetrators of street robberies or muggings, and the adverse effects of this in terms of whom police officers viewed as suspicious (see also Burney 1990). Russell (2001) discussed the media's large role in stereotyping young black men as criminals, and how these portrayals, in fact, did not reflect the actual number of black men recently arrested for serious street crime. Furthermore, inner-city areas where black people live have been associated with crime in popular movies and hip-hop music – music that originated in the inner city (see Fernando Jr 1994). From films such as *Boyz in da Hood* and *Menace II Society* to 'gangsta rappers' such as Tupac, Biggie Smalls and 50 Cent, the image of the modern-day inner-city gangsta seems to be a black one. But are these images accurate representations of young people in Lambeth?

Lambeth is a multicultural borough with people from a variety of European and other ethnic backgrounds. Lambeth is, however, generally considered a borough where many black people live. Lambeth's black population, which in this context refers to people whose ethnic origins are from Caribbean countries (Jamaica, Trinidad, Barbados), West African countries (Nigeria, Ghana, Sierra Leone) and East African countries (Eritrea, Ethiopia, Somalia), accounted for roughly a quarter of the borough's total population, one of the largest black communities in the city. Also, the total black population of Lambeth was much younger than the white population, a point reflected in the ethnic composition of all schools. In Lambeth, roughly half of all students were of West African, East African or Afro-Caribbean descent, the largest black student population in London.[8] Lambeth's white people, including Irish and all other Europeans, accounted for about 60 per cent of the total population. The remainder of Lambeth's population was primarily comprised of people of Indian, Chinese and Vietnamese descent.[9]

About half of the black people in Lambeth were of Afro-Caribbean descent. Afro-Caribbean people have been living in the borough in large numbers since the 1950s and have firm roots within the community. Lambeth was one of many areas across Britain where immigrants from the Caribbean, particularly Jamaica, initially settled, answering Britain's postwar call for labour (see Glass 1960; Harris and James 1993; Patterson 1965; Pryce 1979). Specific areas within Lambeth – such as Brixton, Stockwell and Streatham – have been home to Afro-Caribbean immigrants and their children since the first postwar wave of immigration. The remaining half of Lambeth's black population consists primarily of people from West African backgrounds, with those of East African descent representing the smallest black population in the borough.

The trend in the UK, where black people, particularly Afro-Caribbean people, are significantly over-represented at various stages of the criminal justice system, (see Audit Commission 1996; Fitzgerald 1998; Kirk 1996) is evident in Lambeth. People within the borough's black communities have been disproportionately represented in local criminal statistics for some time. For instance, between 2000 and 2002, roughly half of all offenders were black, mainly black men. During this time black men were also over-represented in arrests for robbery and violence against the person – both very serious offences.[10] Furthermore, the youth justice workers and the youth and community workers interviewed generally said about half of the young men they worked with were white and the other half black, and the detached youth workers said that nearly all of the young men they worked with were black. As less than a quarter of the total population in Lambeth was black, these over-representations are significant. How can they be explained?

One way to address this question is to look at police–community relations, or rather the relationship between the police and people within black communities (see Fitzgerald 1998). Lambeth, and particularly Brixton, has a history of less than amicable relations between the police and these communities, particularly young black men (see Burney 1990; Scarman 1981; Spencer and Hough 2000), the very same group of people who are over-represented, both literally in statistics and figuratively in media representations, as perpetrators of crime. Black people in Lambeth, as in other areas, have expressed their frustrations with police in terms of being needlessly stopped and searched, the effects of differential policing, prejudiced officers, and deaths of black people in police custody (Burney 1990; Runnymede Trust 1996; Spencer and Hough 2000; see also Keith 1993). On occasion, these frustrations have been vented as violent upheavals. The Brixton riots of April 1981 were some of the most damaging the country had ever seen, not just to the businesses and buildings, but also in terms of relations between police officers and the black communities (see Benyon and Solomos 1987; Scarman 1981). Indeed, Lord Scarman's report sought not only the cause of these riots, but also to discover what the government could do to prevent them from happening again, such as training officers to police multiethnic communities and implementing locally based programs (see Benyon and Solomos 1987; Scarman 1981). Riots on a smaller scale and for similar reasons returned to Brixton in 1985, and again in 1995 – about six months before I arrived.

But how much have relations between the police and young black men improved since the early 1980s? This question is difficult to gauge given the research's approach; this research cannot serve as an accurate barometer of 'race relations' in Lambeth. However, at the turn of the century, even with Lambeth's Community Police Consultative Group and Racial Harassment Committee, relations between the police and parts of the black community in the borough seemed unsettled. For instance, a representative from the Movement for Justice, a community-based campaign concerned with 'building an integrated and independent civil rights movement' and 'combating racism and inequality', while city-wide, said they deal primarily with police brutality cases and deaths in police custody in Lambeth.[11] Spencer and Hough's (2000) research findings also confirmed what previous studies have indicated: relations between police and 'the community' in Lambeth, particularly black people, are not so good. From this we can gather that, since the early 1980s, little seems to have changed in terms of relations between the police and the black communities in the borough.

But what are the ramifications of this ill history? One possible result is that these negative relations may lead to police officers conceptualising black people, particularly young black men, as the 'criminal Other' – someone likely to be up to no good, who has just committed an offence or is about to (see Jefferson 1993). Such conceptualisations can have adverse effects on young black men in terms of being suspected of an offence, which, in turn, can lead to them being over-represented at other stages in the criminal justice system: arrest, incarceration, probation (Benyon and Solomos 1987; Jefferson 1993; Keith 1993). This 'criminal stigma' and experience can, in turn, have devastating consequences for the remainder of that individual's life. And if the MacPherson Report's (1999) conclusions about London's Metropolitan Police being 'institutionally racist' is an accurate gauge, then this process of criminalising young black men has probably happened (and continues to do so) in Lambeth. Young people's experiences with the police in Lambeth are given proper attention in Chapter Seven. As this is an interpretative account of young people and crime, the important question to answer here is whether or not the young people themselves brought up issues related to their ethnicity in relation to their experiences with or interpretations of their offending. How significant did they consider their ethnicity in terms of these behaviours?

The 31 young people interviewed came from a variety of ethnic backgrounds, and somewhat reflected the ethnic diversity of Lambeth. Seven said 'Jamaican', one said 'parents are from Ghana' and another said one parent was 'Jamaican' and the other was 'from Guyana' when asked about their ethnicity. Twelve of the young people described their ethnicity as 'English', 'British', or 'my mum's English, my dad's Irish'. Five described themselves as 'half-white, half-black', or 'part Jamaican, part English', or something similar. One said 'part Chinese, part Guyana, part Jamaican', and Nathan and his three brothers said 'my mum is English, my dad is from Sri Lanka'. All but two of the young people in this research, Norman and Isaac, were born in Britain. Overall, about two-thirds of the young people interviewed were what might be generally considered black or 'mixed race', and the remaining third white.

So did these young people discuss their ethnicity in relation to any aspect about their offending? The main focus of this book is to explore the various interpretations the young people offered about their offences, and to examine how offending fits in with the rest of their lives. *Surprisingly, very little was found to suggest that discrepancies or distinctions existed from their interpretations based on ethnic differences.* In other words, young black and white people alike offered very similar interpretations of issues related to their offending behaviour. Only two young people said they felt the police had stopped or 'harassed' them because of their non-white ethnicity; the others did not, in any way, relate their ethnicity to aspects of their offending, not even their experiences with the police. This is not to deny the impact differential policing has had on young black men in Lambeth (Audit Commission 1996; Fitzgerald 1998), or that blacks are a 'visible minority', subject to the prejudices of a predominately white police force (Benyon and Solomos 1988; Keith 1993). Nor is it to deny the housing and employment discrimination suffered by black people in the UK, particularly Afro-Caribbean people since their mass arrival around the end of World War II (Glass 1960; Harris and James 1993), and the consequent implications of this on future generations of black people within the country, including the young people in my sample (Gilroy 1987; Harris and James 1993; Pryce 1979). And while such social conditions are consequences of living in a 'racist society', what seems to be the overall case in my research is that these young people did not bring up their ethnicity when discussing various topics related to offending. Patterns of offending were very similar for the white and black people in my sample, a point consistent with other research (see Audit Commission 1996). In fact as young people they appeared to have more in common than not.

For one, cultural miscellanea were shared by young black and white people in my sample. For instance, all of them adopted a similar style, employed the same argot and had comparable music preferences. The Jamaican/Afro-Caribbean influence on the ways *all* the young people dressed, how they spoke and the music they listened to was apparent, a point noted by others (such as Back 1996; Brake 1985; Cashmore 1984; Gilroy 1993; Hebdige 1979). For those in my study, their overall style – which includes what they wore, how they talked and, to a lesser extent, their overall demeanour – was heavily influenced by the music they listened to, such as US hip-hop, jungle, drum and bass, Jamaican reggae and UK garage. Furthermore, the way the young people spoke and dressed incorporated influences from Jamaican patois, British slang and US hip-hop argot. Interviews with professionals confirmed this. For instance, Brenda, a youth justice worker, best summed up what type of slang the young people she worked with employed:

> On the streets at the moment, there's one basic language that they all speak. Be it Chinese, Vietnamese, Portuguese, Jamaican they all speak this sort of, ummm … patois. It's parts of patois. On the bus you hear white kids talking about 'Yeah, she was feisty man!' They all have this sort of cloak the way that they speak and understand each other. Well, what I'm saying is that there are aspects of patois that is commonly used and turned into English words like 'feisty'. People say you're feisty as opposed to 'cheeky'. Now that word is almost gone. Kids use the word feisty meaning you've got a lot of mouth or you're pushing your luck. This little girl was using the word 'safe'. 'Woah, you're safe, man', and that stuff that came out of the Jamaican patios, the Jamaican vernacular. They have words that they, that the Rastafarians use, words like 'safe' or 'star'. Rather than using someone's name, they call you 'star'. The kids are picking it up. It's Chinese kids, it's all sorts of kids. And that's acceptable. That's part of the street talk that's acceptable. They pick up particular words I think from the Caribbean community. It's like a blanket language that they all speak.

Some slang words used by the young people were borrowed from US hip-hop culture. For instance, the term 'Five-O', which refers to police officers, was derived from the television show *Hawaii Five-O* – a crime drama set in Hawaii. Another term used by the young people to describe police officers was the 'Fedz' – a term found in hip-hop lyrics referring to US federal law-enforcement agencies. Other slang words used by the young people were borrowed from Jamaican patois, such as 'rude boy', 'batty man', 'breadren', 'lick' and 'screwing'. Others still suggest an English/British origin. One such term was 'init?', a slurred version of the English colloquialism 'Isn't it?' Likewise, some young people interviewed often ended their sentences with other rhetorical questions, such as 'y'get me?', 'y'get what I'm saying?', 'y'know what I mean?', or 'y'know?'. Some argot spoken by the young people was similar to the East London Cockney rhyming slang. For instance, some referred to skunk cannabis as 'punk'.[12]

Moreover, all of the young people in the study mentioned, at least in passing, having both white and black friends. Back (1996: 53, 71), in his research on multiethnic urban communities in England, mentioned 'an interactional level of reality where the salience of "race" is denied', 'a domain where race is temporarily deconstructed', as well as how 'identities are being forged between black and white young people.' Similar points can be made in this study. The young people interviewed did not make distinctions about their friends based on ethnicity. To them, ethnic differences did not seem to be very significant, at least on the surface. In other words, for the young people in my sample, in terms of their experiences with offending and who they interacted with, ethnicity did not seem to be a big deal.

Also, I found little evidence of racism while conducting this research, unlike Hobbs (1988: 11–12) who considered many of his respondents during his work in the East End of London as 'racist'. Based on how the young people and professionals talked and acted during the interviews, nothing emerged to suggest racism, and none expressed any prejudiced opinions. *This is not to say that racism does not exist in Lambeth, for this surely cannot be the case, only that I failed to find it when examining the interpretations of young people from different ethnicities.* This even holds true when discussing the relationship between the young people and police officers in Lambeth. While a few young people and even professionals mentioned being physically abused or harassed by police officers who shouted racially charged derogatory names at them, *many* of the young people interviewed, regardless of their ethnicity, talked about negative or hostile relations with the police, and offered similar interpretations about how they had interacted with them. Again, no clear differences emerged in the responses between the black, white or 'mixed-race' young people interviewed.

White researcher/black people

Is it really significant if the ethnicity of a researcher is distinct from that of those researched? Does my status as a researcher (white, middle-class) studying black young people who come from the lower/working classes bias my research findings? Have the ethnic differences between myself and some of the respondents affected the way I presented my data or made my arguments? To all of these questions, I would say no. The ethnic differences between myself and some of the people in this research have not skewed my findings. Throughout this research I have remained conscious of the sensitivities inherent in discussions of 'race' and 'research on young people and crime', and the presentation of my data has been straightforward.

But why bring this up? A couple of reasons come to mind. For one, I personally came across several individuals expressing concerns about a white researcher studying black people. A few fellow students, a couple of respondents, some academics and some others spoken with in Lambeth seemed to find it peculiar that a white American was studying crime in a black British neighbourhood, and suggested this being slightly inappropriate. They seemed to imply: only black people should study black people; why would *they* tell *you* anything? Some even bluntly said just that. For instance, Mick, a detached youth worker in Brixton, came out and said at our initial meeting something to the extent of, 'Let's be honest, Bill: you're a white guy asking questions about young people and crime in Brixton, and that's suspicious'.

To be sure, not many people I came across mentioned anything about this difference in ethnicity in relation to my research. For the several who did, though, I can understand the concern. Some sociological research conducted by 'whites' presents 'blacks' in a negative light. A classic example of this being *The Bell Curve* (Herrnstein and Murray 1994), which suggested, in part, that black people in the USA were intellectually inferior. Their research has been fiercely criticised, not least for the cultural bias associated with how they measured intelligence (see Fraser 1995, for example). Some research in England on black people by white researchers has come under fire for its xenophobic attitude. For instance, Patterson's (1965) account of Jamaicans in Lambeth as 'dark strangers', however unintentional, over-emphasised an 'otherness' associated with the black people in her research (Harris and James 1993: 1). *The Bell Curve*, *Dark Strangers* and others, have, no doubt, caused a furore in academic circles that has perhaps fuelled a certain fear held by white, middle-class researchers who avoid researching black inner-city environments, so as to reduce the risk of being perceived as racist (Bourgois 1995; Sampson and Wilson 1995). This may be one of the reasons so little qualitative research on young black people, crime and the inner city exists. Perhaps this reflects the 'politics of fieldwork' – 'the general avoidance of reporting any sorts of "bad behaviour" blacks, lower-class, or non-Western men might engage in' (Warren 1988: 39). Certainly, in the UK, the trend has been to steer clear of researching multicultural environments up close and personal.

Why is this? Some have suggested that black areas are best studied by black researchers. For instance, Corrigan (1979: 14) mentioned this when he suggested that research in black British neighbourhoods should be done by 'someone who has experienced these oppressions' (see also Hobbs 1988). How much research has been conducted by those 'experienced' since the work of such sociologists? The answer is: not much. The few qualitative studies since the mid-1970s addressing young black people in the inner city and crime, notably the works of Burney (1990), Graef (1993), Pryce (1979), and Robins (1992), all seem to advocate greater opportunities for young blacks in the inner city to fully participate within society. More research is needed to discuss and refine what opportunities are best suited to their needs and desires. However, if we continue along this methodological solipsism, whereby academics stick to 'like-race' research, we might find, for example, that white, male, middle-class academics from the suburbs of Cambridgeshire can only study other white, male, middle-class academics from the suburbs of Cambridge-shire (Merton 1972). This hinders progress. We should not turn a blind eye to an area where empirical research is much needed: 'crime' in the multicultural inner city.

The rise in multiculturalism since the 1980s, both in the USA and UK, is important to note. In Lambeth and, indeed, throughout London, people from various ethnic backgrounds intermix. Younger generations of researchers, if not people in general, have grown up around people from varying racial, ethnic and cultural backgrounds, more so today than in years past, both in the USA and UK. Such experiences, in turn, assist in analysing people from different ethnic backgrounds without an 'air of difference' or 'otherness'. In the presentation of my data in this research I certainly attempted to do this. Because some of us were of different ethnicities does not mean that my findings should be considered invalid. Surely to say that an ethnic similarity between respondents and researcher acts as a skeleton key towards the most accurate and elaborate responses is not enough, and claiming that such a similarity would eliminate any bias is difficult. For instance, Schuman and Converse (1971) specifically tested the variation between black and white interviewers on black respondents, and found that assumptions about more accurate responses based on an ethnic similarity between researcher and subject were unfounded. Overall, to declare a piece of research invalid or unworthy of academic value based on variations of ethnicity between researcher and researched is simply unacceptable. Literature within the naturalistic tradition would support this (see Back 1996; Finestone 1957; Graef 1993; Klein 1971; Liebow 1967). In brief, to suggest a researcher should only study subjects from similar ethnic backgrounds is tautological, misleading and inaccurate.

Like the young people interviewed, I, too, have grown up in a very multicultural environment, and speaking and interacting with those from different ethnic backgrounds is not novel. During these interviews and other informal 'chats', I focused on bringing up topics we might both be interested in, and, as suggested earlier, it was found that we shared some personal experiences and preferences. I think this common ground may have overriden any potential or perceived difficulties in establishing access with the young people from different ethnic backgrounds. Also, about a third of the young people interviewed were 'mixed race', which, amongst them, predominantly referred to having one white and one black parent. In such cases measuring their difference from a white researcher, like myself, becomes even more difficult.

Some of the suspicions a few of the black professionals may have had being interviewed by me – a white researcher – were assuaged by the common ground we shared. Several of them were precious about the young people they worked with, and were very weary of being exploited by someone else with their own agenda. I got the feeling that some of them had been misquoted or misrepresented by other white researchers or journalists, and indeed several confirmed this, particularly the detached youth workers, all of whom were black. However, after informing them of my previous work with young people and the aims of my research, most became very helpful, answering many questions and offering valuable time. Again, this common ground between us probably helped me gain access and establish rapport.

In many ways those interviewed and myself were both 'like' and 'unlike'. These young people and I experienced similar life events and interests, and the professionals and I both worked with young people who had offended. In these respects, similarities existed between us. Simultaneously, the young people and I were 'unlike' because I grew up in outside working- or lower-class inner-city areas, and the professionals and I were 'unlike' because of our employment in completely different professions. Furthermore, all of them differed from me because of my American status, and dissimilarities existed between many of us because of my white ethnicity. Methodologically speaking, my position as a researcher was similar to that of 'Marginal Man' (Linder 1996; Park 1950). Marginal Man initially referred to ethnic hybrids – individuals who were ethnically 'marginal' because they possessed both a black and a white parent, but Park applied this concept to cultural hybrids. My position as a researcher in this exercise was akin to this cultural concept of Marginal Man, both different from and the same as those researched. I believe this balance helped me gain access with those interviewed, particularly the young people. For instance, the parallel experiences between the young people and me suggested my familiarity with their language, their offending and their lifestyles, which, in turn, may have brought us closer and eased my access. Alternatively, my American accent, upbringing and, in some cases, my ethnicity, as well as my status as a researcher put some space between myself and those interviewed. To them, my status was, perhaps, considered an 'inside outsider' (or is that an 'outside insider'?) – someone close enough to understand and appreciate their situations, yet distant enough to remain inconsequential to their lives (Merton 1972). The professionals may have viewed me in a similar way, but for different reasons.

On a final note, the particular sensitivities involved in this research have not gone unnoticed. Much care has been taken throughout this book to avoid reinforcing or provoking stereotypes and over-dramatisation, not only due to the topic, but also the location. Using the borough's real name and not a pseudonym was not an easy decision. For many years areas in Lambeth, particularly Brixton, have received negative attention in the press. Mick, a detached youth worker in Brixton, commented on this:

> I think Brixton is a nostalgia for the world public, no sorry, the world media, for parts of this country to recognise Brixton is always one of those volatile areas that can kick off. Not saying that Brixton doesn't have a reputation that a disturbance couldn't happen tomorrow morning; it could. And I won't deny that. But one thing, right, I would say to you as well, right, that Brixton has a hell of a lotta business interest or a lot of potential or people that are prepared to pour money into Brixton to make Brixton a better place.

Whether or not to name Lambeth as the area of study or use a pseudonym was something I struggled with for a couple of years. Initially, I decided that those within the borough might not appreciate the extra attention this research would generate, and thus decided to keep it anonymous. However, young people's involvement in crime and delinquency in Lambeth, and indeed the inner cities more generally, is an area of great social concern. I eventually decided to name Lambeth to draw attention to this concern, to make the lives of those who live there more tangible. Wilson (1987) suggested that problems associated with inner-city areas need to be addressed honestly and candidly, so as to highlight potential avenues for positive changes. I only hope this research serves in some way to help bring about these changes.

2   Lambeth

Prior to discussing and analysing the offences committed by the young people in my sample, examining the area where they grew up is important, so as to better contextualise such behaviour. This chapter aims to do this. The first section offers a brief history of the borough, followed by some current socioeconomic statistical data, such as its employment structure, unemployment and crime rates, family and housing composition, population density, percentage of population receiving income support and others. The purpose is to attempt to categorise what 'type' of borough Lambeth is. The second section focuses on additional, illicit forms of economic activity within the borough that comprise part of an 'underground economy'. The final section of the chapter addresses how the underground economy fits into the lives of ordinary people in Lambeth by looking at what some professionals and young people said about it. The point in bringing up the borough's underground economy is not only to determine what exactly these other economic activities are, but also to explore their potential role within the young people's offending.

Some general information on Lambeth

The borough of Lambeth, located south of the Thames near the centre of London, is one of the city's largest boroughs geographically, and, at the turn of the millennium, was the fifth most densely populated.[1] Lambeth is broken up into several smaller areas. There are Waterloo and Vauxhall, which are located on the north end of Lambeth adjacent to the Thames, and Streatham, which is in the south bordering the borough of Croydon. Clapham is in the west of Lambeth and Camberwell is in the east. Other areas in Lambeth include Kennington, Stockwell, Norwood, West Norwood and, of course, Brixton (see Figure 2.1). The young people interviewed lived in areas all over the borough, and were not concentrated in just one. Likewise, the professionals worked with young people from all over Lambeth.

Lambeth has generally been considered an English working-class borough for many years. However, it remains slightly different from other working-class boroughs previously described by researchers studying young people and crime in England (for example, Downes 1966; Mays 1954; Parker 1974; Willis 1977; Willmott 1966). Many transformations in British working-class cultures have

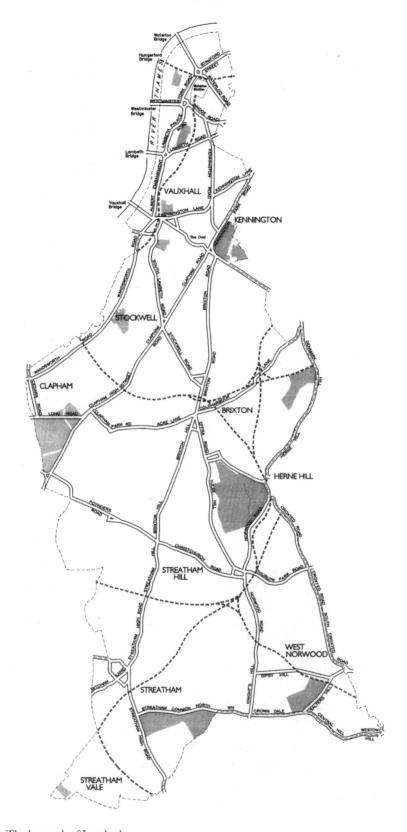

Figure 2.1 The borough of Lambeth.

occurred since these times, such as a rise in multiculturalism, an increase in consumerism and individuality, and a sense of loss of former community controls (Downes 1998). So while Lambeth may be generally considered lower or working class, the conditions of Lambeth's workforce, housing tenure and economic activity are remarkably heterogeneous. Lambeth had diverse and inconsistent socioeconomic conditions between and within areas throughout the borough. The borough was simultaneously home to affluence and shortage, magnificence and simplicity, sanctuary and danger. The overall background of the young people interviewed, however, only somewhat reflected this diversity. The majority lived in public-sector housing, usually on a council estate, and with one parent who worked at comparatively lower-income jobs, if at all. As such, the young people in my sample predominately came from socioeconomic backgrounds that might generally be considered lower class or working class.

Lambeth is an 'inner-city area'. The British Crime Survey (Simmons *et al.* 2002) defines such areas as having a high population density, low owner-occupation and low proportion of professionals – certainly the picture of the borough since just

Figure 2.2 Electric Avenue from Atlantic Road.

before World War II. However, Lambeth has a long and diverse history. This definition of 'inner-city area' would not have applied in the early parts of the twentieth century. Lambeth was once considered relatively upmarket. For instance, Electric Avenue, which today is the location of Brixton's bustling outdoor market, was one of the first streets of Victorian London to have street lighting. Also, the number of entertainment venues in central Lambeth made it somewhat akin to the West End of its day. Indeed, the wide high streets in Streatham and Brixton, which once served as carriageways for the more affluent, act as reminders of the borough's rich past. Several beautiful parks and commons exist, and the Oval cricket grounds have been annually hosting national competitions for some time. In terms of demography, southern parts of the borough were once homes for the wealthy, central Lambeth housed 'artisans and bohemians', and the northern parts of the borough were working-class docklands (Chamberlain 1989; Patterson 1965).

In the 1930s and 1940s Lambeth went through some radical social changes, and the status of the borough rapidly declined. These changes were due, in part, to the social mobility out of the area, transformations in the housing and employment markets, and the extensive bomb damage caused during World War II (Glass 1960; Patterson 1965). Perhaps the most significant adjustment to occur in Lambeth, though, was the steady flow of immigrants arriving from the West Indies. During the postwar call for labour to help rebuild ravaged Britain, many places in Lambeth, now considered Brixton, Streatham, Stockwell, Clapham and Camberwell, were areas where some of the early Caribbean migrants settled. These areas were, in part, deemed ideal to house these newcomers due to the undesirability associated with the area, such as the extensive bomb damage and the abundance of vacant, old and dilapidated Victorian houses found throughout (Glass 1960; Patterson 1965). Living space was at a premium in Lambeth during the immediate postwar period. Many arrivals from the Caribbean were crowded into these run-down houses, charged unreasonably high rents, and/or faced housing discrimination (Glass 1960; Patterson 1965; Pryce 1979).

Black people in Lambeth have been suffering some form of discrimination and racial prejudice since they first arrived. These prejudices were not only manifested as housing restrictions and verbal and physical racist attacks, but also, perhaps more crucially, in terms of employment opportunities. Generally speaking, the Caribbean migrant workers filled jobs that the native British people did not necessarily want, such as semi- and unskilled labouring jobs, or, as Pryce (1979: 269, 270) put it, jobs 'at the bottom of the occupational structure' – 'slave labour' and 'shit work' (see also Glass 1960; Harris and James 1993). Moreover, these jobs filled by the recent newcomers eventually became superfluous, leading to significant levels of unemployment amongst them (Harris and James 1993; Pryce 1979). Pryce (1979: 269) elaborated:

> [West Indian and Asian] immigrant labour … was used to fill the new back-breaking 'de-skilled' jobs deserted by white workers as a result of technical innovation which transferred certain skilled aspects of work from workers to machines and proliferated an abundance of unattractive jobs requiring shift

work, sweated labour and long hours in foundries, factories, hospitals, in construction work and in assembly lines … West Indian (and Asian) workers have been exploited as a 'reserve pool' of labour in the service of British capitalism, because they can be discarded at will in periods of unemployment and their arrival from the Third World can be controlled by legislation. *This explains the economic and social conditions of West Indians in Britain today, rejected in the areas of housing and employment and discriminated against by trade unions and by racist and restrictionist immigration policies* [emphasis added].

Acknowledging that various discriminatory practices have had a knock-on effect on future generations of black people in the borough is important. Pryce (1979: 269) directly related the constraints of contemporary 'West Indian lifestyles' to this 'general process of "immiseration" and racism, which is institutionalised in the British social system because of Britain's imperialist past and the contemporary neo-colonial nature of migration' (see also Gilroy 1993). The histories of white and black young people in Lambeth, and indeed the rest of the country, are thus fundamentally different.

Lambeth at the turn of the millennium is a borough of two sides: 'richer' and 'poorer'. Looking at the poorer side, Lambeth is one of the most deprived local authorities in England.[2] Unemployment, including long-term unemployment, has been and continues to be relatively high.[3] Lambeth also has the second highest rate of those living in public sector housing, with roughly half of the borough's housing run by the public sector[4] Furthermore, Lambeth ranked as the sixth highest borough in London having a concentration of families within the lowest median gross weekly household incomes, which accounted for about a quarter of all families.[5] Black people have been disproportionately represented within these statistics.

Lambeth has a long history of high rates of offences. British Crime Survey data have shown falls in overall reported offences in the last couple of sweeps (Kershaw *et al.* 2000; Mirrlees-Black *et al.* 1996, 1998; Simmons *et al.* 2002). And while crime has also fallen in Lambeth since the late 1990s, overall, crime rates remain relatively high. Over ten years ago, Burney (1990: 7) remarked how '[n]obody nowadays would deny that Lambeth has a serious street crime problem'. In the early years of the twenty-first century, these words still ring true. Lambeth had relative high overall crime rates between 1996 and 2002, and rates for violence, burglary and especially street robbery were (and remain to date) some of the highest in London.[6] In fact, 2001/2002 British Crime Survey data show Lambeth had *the* highest rate of street robberies in the country and the second highest rate of burglaries (Simmons *et al.* 2002). Black people in Lambeth, particularly young black men, have been disproportionately represented in these local crime statistics as perpetrators of recorded offences,[7] and British Crime Survey data have shown that black people have been included in those considered most at risk of being the victim of certain offences (Kershaw *et al.* 2000).

Looking at the data presented thus far about Lambeth only offers us a glimpse at one side of life in the borough. Statistics suggest that Lambeth has pockets of affluence located throughout. For instance, Lambeth ranked high amongst all London boroughs in terms of its 'economic activity'.[8] This suggests that Lambeth's economy is not stagnant, and that a relatively high flow of money is being made and spent within the borough. This high economic activity is generated, in part, by 20 per cent of the workforce in Lambeth employed at jobs that provided the highest median gross weekly household income in the borough, such as those in real estate, renting and business professions.[9] Indeed, a comparatively high rate of people in Lambeth have qualifications at degree level or above.[10] Also, while a high percentage of public-sector housing in Lambeth exists, so too does a comparatively high rate of private-sector housing.[11] Housing in the borough is also relatively expensive. Lambeth ranked within the top half of all London boroughs as having the most expensive housing.[12] These privately rented houses are not located miles away from the crowded council-controlled estates or housing-association property, but they are alongside one another. And while areas of the borough, such as Brixton, Stockwell and Streatham, have a higher concentration of large, sprawling estates when compared to other neighbourhoods in Lambeth, these same areas remain interconnected with some of the most expensive houses in the borough. Indeed, a sheer visible discord exists around residential areas in Lambeth.

The bohemian and artisan elements that once characterised central Lambeth were still alive at the turn of the millennium. According to a July 2003 issue of *Time Out* magazine, there were more artists and writers living in Brixton per square mile than anywhere else in the UK. Several small art galleries are housed in Lambeth, and the borough is bordered by the Tate and the Tate Modern in the north and Camberwell Art School to the east. The Ritzy Cinema in Brixton, one of the oldest in London, shows independent and European-made films alongside mainstream productions. An annual legalise cannabis rally has been held in Lambeth, where an activist march beginning at the Oval has culminated into a massive party in Brockwell Park for the last several years. Lambeth also contains a significant gay population, with several gay bars, a large gay superclub – The Fridge (one of Lambeth's old theatre halls) – and annual gay festivals have been held in Clapham Common and Kennington Park. Venues such as The Academy (formerly The Astoria) have catered to musicians and performers from around the world. Several well-known bands have lived in the area, including Bassment Jaxx and Alabama 3. Other large clubs – which play house, techno, garage, drum and bass, jungle, hip-hop and reggae, and attract thousands of young people every weekend – are peppered throughout the borough. One summer's day during my time in the borough, central Brixton was 'taken over' by May Day activists, who literally 'reclaimed the streets' by holding a massive party and blocking off main roads. Indeed, Lambeth's reputation for art and bohemia has survived into the twenty-first century. This reputation is further evidence of the borough's heterogeneous population.

Lambeth is a borough where people from a variety of different backgrounds intermix throughout. Dated high-rise estates face towards streets that cater to beautifully maintained Victorian houses and newly developed buildings and centres. Superannuated, small terraced houses, which line some of the more major roads within the borough, hide spacious, expensive and privately owned detached houses. The housing surrounding the skatepark is a classic example of this. On one side the skatepark is the large, sprawling and crowded Stockwell Park Estate, and on the other side are refurbished, spacious and (relatively) expensive Victorian terraced houses. The houses on my street are another good example of how affluence literally lives next to poverty. On one side of my house in Brixton was a completely refurbished home, purchased for more than £200,000, while the house on the other side was occupied by heroin-using and -selling 'squatters'. Not just housing, but the condition and longevity of the shops and businesses in the borough are mixed. New restaurants, clubs and bars in the borough, which have been popping up throughout this research, spill out into streets adjacent to large estates, and areas where evidence of hard drug use exists. A Tesco is located next to a Lidl Shop and a Kwik Save near a Sainsburys.[13] Well-known retail chain outlets line the borough's high streets and outshine the many drab second-hand shops and inexpensive general stores along the side streets. So, while Lambeth may generally be considered working or lower class due to the background of the majority of those living there, evidence of money being made and money being spent was apparent throughout.

Lambeth's underground economy

An established, illicit economic system exists in Lambeth, complete with an autonomous, subterranean labour force that provides goods and services for those within the community. Research in England and the USA has described and detailed such economies and referred to them as 'underground', 'informal', 'secondary' or 'irregular' (for example, Bourgois 1995; Foster 1990; Hobbs 1988; Robins 1992; Shover 1996; Sullivan 1989). 'Black market' is also a popular term heard in the movies, or on television or the radio. For purposes here, I borrow the term 'underground economy' in order to describe this illicit economic system in Lambeth. This term, however, is not to imply that this economy is hidden from public view; many of its activities are highly visible. Three areas of this underground economy are explored in this section: the availability of illicit drugs, the trading of stolen merchandise, and miscellaneous observed and recorded economic activities.

The availability of drugs in Lambeth

Selling cannabis, crack and heroin are practices of Lambeth's underground economy. Such practices are, perhaps, more 'usual suspects' of such economies. As Parker *et al.* (1988: 107) have noted in their study, selling heroin was not 'a new and sinister creation set up from outside, but an adaptation of long-established trading mechanisms which were already central to the irregular economy' (see also Bourgois 1995; Ruggiero and South 1995). Certain areas within Lambeth, particularly Brixton and Stockwell, had more notorious reputations than other areas within the borough due to the availability of certain drugs, namely cannabis, crack cocaine and heroin. Theo commented on how many drug sellers he has come across in the Brixton area.

There's bear [many] men on the corners, man [asking] 'Ya want something. Ya want something.' … It's just gone mad. Everyone's trying to make money now … especially in my area [Brixton] there's feds [police] with dogs, just plain clothes going around busting everyone.

The availability of such drugs did not seem uniform across the borough, but rather limited to specific areas where they appeared to be more readily available, something confirmed in interviews with some professionals. For instance, Quincy, a youth justice worker, said, 'Brixton is the place where you buy your half-ounce of weed'. Fred, a drugs squad officer in Lambeth, said, 'Lambeth is synonymous with heroin'. Russell, a NACRO worker from Brixton, said, 'The area down by Five Ways [in Brixton] is known as "Crack City".' Oscar, a youth and community worker in Brixton, said, 'during the 70s' Brixton was the place to go 'if you wanted to get some ganja [cannabis] … now it's crack'.

Indeed, crack has been available in parts of Lambeth, particularly central Brixton, for years, according to interviews with police. For instance, Rod, a drugs squad officer from Brixton, said of the mid- to late 1980s, when crack cocaine entered the streets of Lambeth:

In 1985, a DEA [Drug Enforcement Agency] agent came over from the States after the crack explosion to give a warning. He was essentially right, but just got his time scale wrong. Things don't happen as fast over here as they do in the States. There was no explosion. It just expanded slowly. So it went from his warning. We started to see crack and bigger seizures of crack. And since then crack has been one of our major problems in the last few years drugs wise.

When I first arrived in Brixton in June 1996, I observed people using crack, and have been offered crack on many occasions in Brixton and Stockwell. These experiences stemmed, in part, from working at the clothing shop on Coldharbour Lane – a road where crack dealers were never far away – and skating and hanging around the skatepark, which is adjacent to Stockwell Road, often patrolled by heroin or crack users and sellers. A couple of years later, I heard less about crack, and more about heroin. Heroin transactions were often reported and, indeed, heavily observed in the central Brixton area, such as on Atlantic Road near the train station and in parts of Stockwell, particularly along Stockwell Road between the skatepark and Stockwell underground station. Individuals smoking heroin have been observed several times at Brixton train station, and seeing discarded needles at this location was not strange. Even one of the young people in my sample, Theo, mentioned, 'I see needles, rude boy, bear [a lot of] needles outside the train station'. Also, it seemed to be common knowledge that the young men hanging around outside Brixton train station during the day sold heroin (this was even reported on the news a couple of times). Aside from the squatters next door, two houses on my street sold heroin, where users frequently lurked. Reportedly, one neighbour firebombed one of the houses in 1997, and another neighbour did the same to the other house in 1999. Also, a makeshift heroin den located ten yards from my house once hid heroin users until being set alight by yet *another* neighbour in 2001. At the time of writing, heroin users were still visiting my neighbours – the squatters – day and night, and I sometimes found discarded needles near my front door. Neighbours have also complained about heroin users in their small front yards sharing needles and 'shooting up'.

I wanted to find out more about this apparent shift from selling crack to selling heroin in Lambeth. Norma, a detached youth worker from Brixton, was working with a group of young men who sold heroin, and she also noted this shift. Offering her opinion, Norma suggested that more young drug sellers in Lambeth were shifting from selling crack to selling heroin because, at least in her experience, it appeared to be 'more economical'.

> It's more economical because of someone on heroin – their usage and their need … they'll get more. They [the young heroin sellers Norma worked with] can probably get £20 to £40 a day from a heroin person [who] needs a fix in the morning, a fix in the evening. With a crack person, you may just buy a couple of rocks a day or what have you, but with heroin the demand for it, y'know? … and also cuz of the flood of heroin on the market at the moment y'know? It's more expensive now … it used to be much cheaper than crack, but now it's selling for selling for as much as crack … it can go from 15 to 25 [pounds] for a little sack … it depends on your habit … some people have a £15–25 a day habit, some can go up to £50 a morning

Aside from being dealt on the street, crack, cannabis and heroin were reportedly sold at local establishments or business 'fronts', such as off-licences, newsagents, mini-cab stations, take-away restaurants, barber shops, beauty salons and other businesses within the borough (Bourgois 1995; Fagan 1996; 'Arif's minimart' in Robins 1992: 90; the 'marijuana "store"' in Sullivan 1989: 240). Those personally known[14] include a mini-cab office in Camberwell and an off-licence in Kennington that sold cannabis and hash, as well as a take-away restaurant in Brixton that sold crack while, ironically, posting a sign stating, 'No drug sellers will be tolerated on these premises'. Evidence for these and similar shops selling drugs 'under the counter' was validated in interviews with many of the respondents. For instance, Quincy, a youth justice worker, commented on how common this practice of selling drugs was:

> Basically, in order for shop keepers to make a living in this time, they need another income. And if that income is from a [drug] juggler, that's what you need to do in order to kinda survive. You're not going to get Kentucky [Fried Chicken] to admit that it happens or maybe Take Two [local take-away] … but known drug jugglers are in the shop.

Fred, a drugs squad officer from Lambeth, commented on the number of businesses that also sold drugs:

I could name you some of them. If we wish to go out, I could show you a lot of garages that are owned by criminals that are highly suspected of, if not known to be, associated with drugs and using them as fronts ... I could name fifteen of such places.

Lewis, a drugs squad officer from Streatham, offered a similar opinion:

What tends to happen is a business will be set up by the people running the drugs and that business will appear. I'm not going to mention which ones they are, but there are a number of them that are, are running these businesses purely for the laundering of the money from drugs.
Can you tell me what types of businesses they are, not the names?
There's a number of textile businesses. There's a number of restaurants.

Even locals had stories. I befriended Marion, the owner of a shop near the clothing shop where I worked. We would often sit and chat. One time the conversation turned to drugs in the Brixton area and how certain shops were selling drugs 'under the counter'. He told me a good friend of his who once owned a take-away restaurant in the area was approached by a drugs seller who wanted to use his restaurant as a type of 'base' where he could sell crack. In exchange this individual said he would give the restaurant owner £500 a week – a deal the owner eventually agreed to. Marion continued by saying how this base was extremely beneficial to the crack seller as it offered him a chance to sell his drugs off the street, thus aiding in keeping his illicit dealing activities hidden from the police. As time went on, the restaurant owner received less and less of his weekly stipend followed with an excuse such as 'business wasn't so good this week'. In the end, so the story went, the restaurant owner had to close his business because the crack seller took over the restaurant with his consistent presence and refused to pay the owner any more money. Marion declined when a similar offer was put to him by another crack seller in the area for such reasons. Other professionals interviewed also said they suspected that those constantly hanging around certain shops in Lambeth were selling drugs. For instance, Mary, a youth justice worker, said: 'I assumed that some of the shops you see in Brixton were a bit dodgy, you know? People always sitting in them. I don't know what they are there for.'

Lambeth's drug economy offers young people a lucrative way to earn some easy cash, not necessarily selling drugs, but just delivering them. For instance, a couple of the professionals mentioned how young people they worked with acted as 'runners' for drug sellers (Williams 1989). Barney, a police officer from Clapham, defined a runner in the following way:

A runner is someone who goes out and gives people [drug users] phone numbers down at the [train or underground] station. [The user] rings them up, they meet them at certain venues and they [the drug sellers] supply.

Norma, a detached youth worker from Brixton, described how the young heroin sellers she worked with used runners:

They don't get their hands dirty like that. They're quite slick … they get some younger people to do the runs, to be the runners, but it's their operation. Their operation is they have a mobile phone, the phone will ring and they'll make a meeting. All over … so they'll get the runner, give the runner the bags, make the runner go and do the drops.

Interviews with professionals suggested juveniles as young as twelve were runners for the older guys. Brenda, a youth justice worker, noted the increase in attention given to young people involved in Class A drug distribution:

Prior to this year my colleagues have been working with kids who have been runners for the drug barons or whatever you want to call them. This year I've seen; my eyes have been open. I've been down to the police station where there were three young people who were used in the middle – gophers for drug dealers. And that's on the increase as far as I'm concerned. Every time it's coming up and we're like, 'Again! It just happened last week!' And it's something I think we haven't realised that it's been going on because they've been good at it or whatever, but it's coming to our attention now that something is going on … I think it's going on much more … I think we will see a lot more of this.

Trading in stolen merchandise

In Lambeth other elements of the underground economy were observed, such as second-hand electronic shops that buy and sell stolen goods, or people who do this door to door, as well as garages buying and selling 'knock-off' motor vehicle parts. Such 'businesses' provide young people in Lambeth with a variety of additional opportunities to make money through committing certain offences, such as theft, burglary and robbery. Sullivan (1989: 119) noted how 'The most pervasive social supports for youthful economic crime … were the markets for the illegal goods and services supplied by youth. Such markets play a *crucial* role in channelling exploratory ventures into more systematic economic crime' (emphasis added; see also Cromwell *et al.* 1991, 1996; Parker 1974; Reiss 1986; Shover 1996).

An important characteristic of these shops in Lambeth was their visibility and candour. The aforementioned businesses trading in stolen goods, particularly the second-hand electronic shops, seemed to be widespread in the borough, something certainly confirmed in interviews with many professionals. For instance, Will, a detective constable from Streatham, talked about a pawn shop near the Streatham police station:

Just from previous dealings with any pawn type shop. One [near here] that has stolen gear, one in Norwood that has stolen gear.

Declan, a youth justice worker, also talked about where stolen goods are taken:

Who are they selling [the stolen goods] to?

They would go from door to door or small businesses. They are renowned ... you go to a back-street garage. You go to a shop or a local shop on the corner.

Bill, a detective constable from Streatham, commented on where stolen merchandise is taken:

> *What do they do with that stuff?*
> [laughs] Well, that's what I'd like to know cuz I'd like to know where they sell it because they generally don't keep it. They don't keep it and all the stuff gets sold around to other people on the estate perhaps or y'know?
> *Do you know that?*
> I know that because I've asked that question, because the police always labour under the misapprehension that it's the sort of Fagin-type character that takes in all this stolen gear and then and then I don't know ... I think there's some type of, umm, subterranean market place going on, y'know where things get bought and sold.

[later in the interview]

> *Could you please give me a bit more on how you think they get rid of it?*
> Friends, neighbours, friends of friends.
> *Do you believe that there is a specific place where they get rid of it?*
> No, I mean sometimes there is, sometimes you hear of a mini-cab firm is taking stuff in, sometimes you hear of a shop that's taking stuff in.

I observed many independently owned and managed second-hand electronic stores in the borough. Stop and Swap (a pseudonym) is a chain of second-hand retail shops found around London, three of which are in Lambeth. While Stop and Swap *does* have a policy regarding buying goods, such as bringing in two forms of identification when selling merchandise, some interviews suggest the shop does not strictly adhere to such a policy. For instance, Will, a detective constable in Streatham, offered his opinion about Stop and Swap:

> I have an opinion on a certain business called Stop and Swap. I think behind Stop and Swap is a more organised criminality than people give it credit for. The amount of stolen gear that I've picked up from there is quite high. I mean I can pick up four items of stolen goods there every week ... you see known criminals that frequent there every day, but that's a legitimate business.

Marc, a young person in my sample who was heavily involved in offending, talked about how many televisions and videos he brought into Stop and Swap throughout the course of a week:

> Do you know Stop and Swap? That's where I used to take [stolen goods], y'get me? But I got nicked cuz like we used come in there like two–three times a day

with just bear [a lot of] stuff, y'get me? It just started to get hot. I got nicked for one of them, but the police don't know there was only one burglary done on that day. They just like they went to the shop and asked for the video camera [CCTV], but they don't know like it was just that day I went in there. They think it's just that one day. Like, if they was to look on the video camera like all the weeks like they would see me in their like every day, but they don't know nothing because they just looked on that one day. I'm lucky that they didn't see none of the other ones.

By fortune I met Bobby, who worked at Stop and Swap, and asked him his opinion on the amount of stolen merchandise supposedly circulating through the store. During our conversation Bobby made it very clear that he and his bosses believed that many people who came into the store were not the rightful owners of the goods they brought with them. He mentioned the same people coming in week after week with large amounts to pawn. Also, Bobby discussed how his boss would manipulate the 'crack heads' who came into the shop by only offering them a fraction of the value of their obviously stolen goods, figuring they would take his first offer for fear of it being reduced or withdrawn. He offered me an example about a 'crack head' coming in with 'a box full of [digital] camera [memory] chips' who had 'no idea what they were worth'. Regardless, Bobby basically said that as long as people have enough identification 'points' – utility bills, driver's licence, birth certificates – Stop and Swap could legally buy goods from them.

Other legitimate businesses were also suspect. Several respondents, including the young people, suggested that mobile phone shops in the borough bought stolen mobile phones and then resold them through a process where certain microchips within the phone could be replaced, which enabled the phones to be reprogrammed and then resold. Albert, a detective sergeant from Streatham, commented on this process:

> The recycling of mobile phones, things like that, just change the identity of them. So, I take a stolen phone into a [mobile phone] shop, which also has a legitimate access to whatever. They reprogramme them, the stolen handset, then they connect you up as a genuine customer. So that's another general tariff. They get money off the company for air time, they get the phone for nothing.

Some mini-cab agencies in Lambeth, reportedly, also had their stake within the borough's underground economy. Some were known to sell cannabis, and in addition some police officers believed that mini-cab drivers played a role in burglaries and robberies. For instance, Darren, a division intelligence officer from Brixton, mentioned:

> There are a lot of illegal mini-cabs about … We certainly have information that these cab drivers helped villains to do burglaries. They would go get a video recorder and throw it in the back of the mini-cab, and the mini-cab would transport it for them. Then the mini-cab driver would say, 'Well, I

didn't know it was a burglary. I thought I was just moving some property' …
In Brixton there are certain cab offices that are regularly used by villains as
transport units. Then you gotta look that some of these mini-cab drivers are
villains themselves with previous convictions for all types of crimes, because
they don't have to be registered any more … but the government is trying to
change this.

Lambeth's underground economy does not solely consist of established shops.
Rather, like those who sell illegal drugs or prop up makeshift cardboard tables and
sell pirated CDs, batteries and other goods, individuals who spontaneously
approach others with goods to sell are a part of the borough's underground
economy. Unlike established shops in the borough, these individuals are not
consistently supplied with goods to sell. Rather, they sell such merchandise around
the neighbourhood when supplied (Cromwell *et al.* 1991, 1996; Shover 1996;
Sullivan 1989), something confirmed in interviews. For instance, Theo talked
about where he once sold stolen goods:

> *Where did you sell them [stolen goods] off to?*
> We just find people, like older people, younger people. Like, who's looking for
> the sets [stereo]. There's always someone looking for a system, if y'know what
> I'm saying.
> *Did you go off and ask people around you?*
> We just go: 'Yeah man is looking for this. Yeah, y'know a man's looking for a
> set?' You get me? You like, 'Yeah. How much? What kind of set?' They go,
> 'Yes! A set with the business isn't it?' Sold it off and got our money.

Steven, a detached youth worker from Stockwell, also commented on how stolen
property is sold this way:

> Around here, y'know I guess, y'know it's probably pretty easy. Cuz even
> though when, y'know someone's stealing stuff, there's always someone who
> would like buy it around here. Cuz them always say, y'know, 'I want this,
> y'know? Everything come to me. I got this, y'know? Do you want to buy it?'
> and everything. Even last week someone came in here [the youth and commu-
> nity centre], y'know with a bike, y'know asked if I wanted to buy it. Said,
> 'Y'know, I got three at home', y'know? So and people buy it off you off the
> street.

Miscellaneous activities

The young people interviewed were not directly involved in, or connected with, all
aspects of Lambeth's underground economy. Nonetheless, these other elements
are worth discussing. For instance, both male and female prostitutes in Stockwell
and Brixton have propositioned me. According to some of the police in Streatham,
the area has had a reputation for prostitution for several decades. Furthermore, I

know *many* people committing housing benefit and social security fraud. It seemed that several neighbours and other locals were all taking advantage of this, and some of the interviews established how common in Lambeth this practice was. For instance, Mick, a detached youth worker from Brixton, mentioned:

> That's one of the biggest licks [thefts] that they are still doing. Like what I said right, when it comes to the social security system at the unemployment centre they are licking it left right and centre. Seriously.

Additional noted components of Lambeth's underground economy include those that set up cardboard boxes as makeshift platforms along the borough's high streets. They sell a number of items including pirated CDs, DVDs and videos; designer perfume; batteries; mobile phone cards; incense; posters; and a host of other products at prices normally lower than the same product in retail stores. Other ways to make money on the street were observed. For instance, the 'travel card hustlers' outside the Brixton underground station who sell previously used travel cards back to others, or those whom Matthews and Pitts (2001: 12) called 'squeegee merchants' who 'work' at high-street intersections with their bucket, window squeegee and towels asking for spare change from commuters stopped at red lights in exchange for washing their windscreens. The activities and practices that could be considered part of Lambeth's underground economy were numerous and diverse, and many others not directly observed or revealed probably exist.

The underground economy and daily life in Lambeth

It is important to look at how this underground economy fits into the daily lives of ordinary people who benefit from it or at least lie in its shadow. Lambeth's underground economy did not materialise overnight. While the length of its existence is uncertain, other researchers have suggested that such economies are 'an established fact of working-class life' in England (Robins 1992: 89; see also Foster 1990; Hobbs 1988), and the likelihood the young people interviewed grew up with this underground economy is high.

The legal and illegal ways to make money in Lambeth appeared to exist side by side. This close proximity of legal and illegal worlds is similar to Cloward and Ohlin's (1960: 161–71) discussion of an 'integrated' community, where legitimate, conventional opportunities to earn money exist alongside illegitimate, criminal economic opportunities to do the same (see also Coleman 1988; Hagan 1994; Spergel 1964; Sullivan 1989; Whyte 1955). In looking at the criminal and conventional 'opportunities' within different areas, Cloward and Ohlin emphasised that involvement in specific offences, much like legitimate work, is differentially available to young people based on the presence, or not, of such opportunities (Downes 1966; Parker 1974; Shover 1996; Sullivan 1989). In this sense the bounty of pawnshops, second-hand shops, garages, as well as the illicit drug economy in Lambeth offers young people and others various additional opportunities to make money through offending.

But how were such illegal practices able to exist in the borough, and what measures can be taken to shut them down? More specifically, why was it that many of those interviewed, including police officers, knew of various establishments – such as second-hand shops that buy and sell stolen electronic goods, garages that buy and sell stolen car parts and the like – yet were helpless to do much about it? While some police officers interviewed said some of the businesses bartering in second-hand merchandise were operating illegally, apparently, prosecuting them is difficult, and they mentioned that little could be done about it. For instance, Barney, a divisional intelligence officer from Clapham, said he knew of a couple of such establishments, but commented on how

> there's never been a successful conviction against them … all they've got to say is, 'I didn't know it was stolen', and they've got a perfect defence.

Will, a detective constable from Streatham, offered similar comments:

> It's very difficult for us to prove. We are very cynical about it. If someone is selling stolen gear we think that management has something to do with it … It's very difficult to prove … I wouldn't say the guy [shop worker] knows that it's stolen, it's just that he probably doesn't care.

The sheer number of locations in Lambeth where stolen goods were bought and sold helped deter monopolisation. For instance, the overall number of shops known throughout the borough surely invited competition, whereby some shops might have offered better prices for their goods than others. Furthermore, the proliferation of second-hand shops ensured that somewhere willing to buy stolen items is never far away. In comparison, if only one or two such shops existed in the borough, there might be a higher risk that they might become full of merchandise to the point where the shopkeepers could not accept any more goods. The vast mumber of such businesses that barter in stolen merchandise also suggests they cater to a wide audience of people in Lambeth.

But where do these 'businesses' get all of the brand-name merchandise they sell at prices much lower than the same product found amongst the borough's high-street stores? Perhaps, as Hebdige (1979) noted, such items are the result of the 'miraculous regularity' with which goods fall 'off the back of passing lorries' (cited in Foster 1990: 33; see also Robins 1992). In Lambeth numerous second-hand shops and pawnshops remained open for business throughout the research. The way that stolen goods were reportedly dispersed in the community suggests that such practices are common-place. When people set up their 'cardboard stalls' along the borough's high streets and sell batteries, designer perfume, CDs, videos, posters and other things, interested consumers approached them, something personally witnessed on numerous occasions. Even I bought several pirated CDs from these guys. The point is, overall, the practices that make up Lambeth's underground economy persisted through time, and there seemed to be a reasonable section of the community within the borough buying items from people in the streets with conviction and consistency.

Lambeth's underground economy may be portrayed, both implicitly and explicitly, as acceptable to young people. Explicitly, the simple existence of the underground economy offers them additional ways to make money. In other words, young people in Lambeth, through their daily activity and residential proximity to such economic practices, may easily see or hear of such 'businesses', and thus realise that money can be made by selling stolen gear. This represents an overt way that internal, structural conditions of Lambeth may be influential. An implicit way exists as well in which certain illicit practices of Lambeth's underground economy may have been 'allowed' to continue. More specifically, there seemed to be a lack of community censure within the borough towards the appropriation of goods most likely procured in an illegal manner. A great deal of apathy towards such economic practices exists; many adults I came across during the course of this research did not seem to care about buying stolen merchandise. This, in turn, may have an effect on the value system of young people in terms of their offending, and may serve to normalise it, at least partially. In other words, if few adults express concern over young people bringing in expensive and valuable goods to sell, then why would young people not feel free to make money this way?

The potential impact of the economic practices of Lambeth's underground economy may be understood by considering ideas of 'social' and 'cultural' capital (Coleman 1988; Cromwell *et al.* 1996; Hagan 1994; Shover 1996). For instance, Hagan (1994: 69) referred to social capital as 'aspects of structured groupings that increase their capacities for action oriented to the achievement of group and individual goals', and cultural capital as 'adaptations' to the existing forms of money-making opportunities in an area. Hagan (1994: 70) continued by suggesting that forms of social and cultural capital may be 'divergent and oppositional' in areas suffering from 'disadvantaging social and economic processes'. If the 'divergent and oppositional' practices are those against the law, and the 'disadvantaging social and economic processes' Lambeth's relatively high unemployment rate, relatively high deprivation rate and relatively low median household income, then it becomes clearer that Lambeth's underground economy increases capacities for action through various forms of cultural adaptation. Hagan (1994: 70) continued by suggesting the processes of social and cultural capital within an area may be 'the only or best life choices available, and these adaptations can become powerful influences on later life outcomes'. Thus, if the underground economic practices of Lambeth's underground economy are 'the best life choices' for some in the borough, then the likelihood of them being frequently utilised and highly valued is strong.

While the practices of Lambeth's underground economy are illegal, they play no less of a significant role in the lives of those who consume from and provide for it. As Foster (1990: 34) noted, 'People learn from an early age to exploit their environment using legitimate or illegitimate methods'. If such illicit practices are as common as they appeared to be, then a possibility exists that they may not be considered as illegitimate as might be the case in other communities, and young people may find that the division of illegal and legal worlds in their lives is not salient. For instance, places such as Stop and Swap, mobile-phone shops, the business fronts that sell certain illicit drugs 'under the counter' and other second-hand businesses in the borough are legitimate, conventional businesses that act as outlets for illegitimate, illegal business. In such cases conventional and criminal enterprise may become completely merged, and distinctions possibly blurred between legal and illegal actions. Differences between legal and illegal ways of making money are, no doubt, of little importance to those who benefit from such practices. Furthermore, these opportunities are more or less 'allowed' by a section of the community. Many practices of Lambeth's underground economy did not appear to evoke strong moral outrage by those who consumed from it (Cromwell *et al.* 1996; Foster 1990; Hobbs 1988; Mays 1954; Parker 1974; Shover 1996; Wright and Decker 1994). This point was certainly confirmed by interviews with professionals. For instance, Kwame, a youth and community worker from Brixton, mentioned:

> It's an opportunity ... someone says, 'Hey, ya wanna buy a TV?' Then, why not? Yeah ... you can have all these nice things, so, y'know it would be silly not to.

Steven, a detached youth worker from Stockwell, commented on how people in Lambeth were not bothered where the stolen goods came from:

> Y'know, so people buy it off you, off the street even though people know it's stolen, but like no one really cares about it, y'know? As long as they didn't see you steal it, y'know?

Lawrence, a NACRO worker, expressed similar sentiments:

> I've been brought up in the inner London environment, so you would know. You'd be fool to say that you didn't know. You know, you do meet people. Even the people that you've been brought up with ... that's a common thing now. People accept goods – videos, TVs, y'know? No one considers that a crime as such. Everybody does it. The most honest of people buy TVs and videos off, umm, the back of a lorry.

A couple of the young people interviewed also made comments that support this point. For instance, Marc noticed how 'There's a lot of people that just buys stolen good, you get me? Hook ups.' Isaac made a similar point: 'Well, they know that it's stolen, but they don't care as well. A big store like, umm Stop and Swap, but they wouldn't admit it. Anyway, but they know that it's stolen.'

Comparing these comments highlights the supply–demand exchange of stolen goods in Lambeth, but a hidden irony exists here. For instance, consuming from the underground economy (for example buying stolen goods) brought forth neutral expressions from some professionals (with the exception of the police). Several professionals, particularly the youth and community workers, expressed how they were happy to buy stolen goods, and that it 'wasn't a big deal' because 'everybody does it'. However, *providing for* this economy (for example stealing the goods in the first place) was something they worked to prevent. Nobody wants to have their things stolen, but people seem willing to buy others' stolen goods. In this sense that some professionals found the trading of stolen goods acceptable is somewhat ironic. Young people who commit acquisitive offences assist in providing for Lambeth's underground economy, yet the nature of the professionals' jobs is to help lead local young people away from offending.

Moreover, the young people interviewed did not say their thieving, robbing and burgling was something carried out in other, more affluent areas. Rather, they expressed how they committed such offences in their own backyard (Pitts 1999; Sutherland and Cressey 1978). In this sense, some of these young people steal things from one neighbour, only to sell them to another. So while someone in Lambeth will benefit from buying a second-hand television at a 'really good price', someone else in the borough will have no television to watch any more. And within inner-city environments, according to recent British Crime Survey data, those most 'at risk' include 'the poorest of the poor' – those who live on council estates either earning under £5,000 a year or simply unemployed (Kershaw *et al.* 2000; Mirrlees-Black *et al.* 1996, 1998; Simmons *et al.* 2002). To this degree, these young people who burgle their neighbours are similar to inverted images of Robin Hood: they steal from 'the poor' and sell their swag on to the 'not-so-poor.'

The mere allowance of many illicit practices of Lambeth's underground economy, and in many cases their *approval*, may significantly affect young people's decisions to commit certain offences. Adult influences have a powerful effect on young people in terms of what offences are 'allowed' in the borough, as well as how young people and others may feel about specific offences (Gottfredson and Hirschi 1990; Hirschi 1969; Sutherland 1947; Sutherland *et al.* 1992). If adults approve of the illicit bartering systems of second-hand electronic shops and garages in Lambeth, then young people, in turn, are likely to find that supplying such goods is not censured. Not to sound deterministic, as the presence of Lambeth's underground economy does not necessarily mean everyone within the borough participates in it, nor finds its economic activity acceptable. Furthermore, allowing acquisitive offences such as robbery and burglary to take place is not necessarily a conscious decision. However, by failing to censure the distribution of such goods and services and actually participating in their purchase, sections of the community are inevitably, and implicitly, aiding in the young people's participation in criminal practices that ensure such goods and services will continue to be available. This failure to censure the illegal exchange of goods may be influential in young people's involvement in acquisitive offences, and how they feel about committing them. This may particularly be the case if young people growing up in Lambeth notice that 'everyone's doing it', realise that 'nobody cares' and thus act accordingly (Matza 1964; Sykes and Matza 1957).

Conclusions

In this chapter I examined structural and cultural conditions in the London borough of Lambeth. Lambeth has a long and rich history, being a multicultural borough containing people from various walks of life. The borough is not easy to pigeonhole, not necessarily a 'rich' or 'poor' area. Rather, Lambeth, while historically considered a working- or lower-class borough, was found to be peppered with affluence. These affluent pockets were not located miles away from the large, sprawling estates or old, rundown housing, but rather right next to them. In Lambeth signs of urban degeneration and urban regeneration interweave throughout. However, the background of the young people interviewed only somewhat reflected the borough's socioeconomic variety; the status of the majority was lower or working class. Also, the young people interviewed lived all across the borough, not just in one specific area.

The conglomeration of an illicit drugs market, the trade in stolen merchandise, and a host of other illegal money-making practices comprise an established 'underground economy' in Lambeth. This economy is very beneficial to all kinds of people in Lambeth, being a networking of available sociocultural resources that, in part, grew out of the cracks and fissures of the borough's structural conditions. This economy is prized, as it enables many denizens of Lambeth to enjoy goods and services at a reduced rate, as well as those that are simply unavailable in the regulated 'conventional' economy. Lambeth's underground economy, while illicit in nature, is highly valued by many. Its longevity within the community is enough evidence of this. In addition, though 'underground', in many respects this economy is highly visible. Even as a new arrival to the borough, I located aspects of this economy with little difficulty.

Lambeth's underground economy provides many criminal opportunities. These opportunities are available to young people, and easy ways to make money through the trade in stolen goods, particularly electronic goods, exist in the borough. As long as people are willing to buy 'hot' televisions, videos, hi-fi systems, car stereos, and so on, young people and others will be feeding such merchandise to the many second-hand electronic shops throughout Lambeth where these transactions go down. The illicit drugs market in Lambeth, particularly the selling of crack, heroin and cannabis, also opens doors for young people – some reportedly as young as twelve – into a lucrative market and a chance of making big money. All of these opportunities are, no doubt, very tempting to impressionable young people in Lambeth, who may find or believe that other legitimate ways to 'make it' are either unattainable or unavailable.

3   Robbery, burglary, theft

In the years 1996–2002 Lambeth had relatively high rates of what might be called 'acquisitive' offences, such as theft of or from motor vehicles, shoplifting, burglary and street robbery.[1] This chapter explores what these offences mean to those in my sample. The analysis is organised around four interrelated themes: motivation, planning, the young people's knowledge of 'associates', and how they felt after committing offences. The first section analyses what the young people said motivated them to commit acquisitive offences. The second section looks at how much time they spent planning such offences. The third addresses the young people's knowledge of associates, which here refers to adults and 'businesses' they knew were involved in some degree of illicit activity, such as those who buy and sell stolen merchandise. The final section of the chapter explores how the young people said they felt after committing acquisitive offences. Here the aim is to determine the extent to which they expressed remorse or concern, if any, over such behaviour.

This chapter does not give rise to large theoretical claims, but rather focuses on the various shades of interpretation offered by different young people, and explores how acquisitive offences fit in with the rest of their lives. It addresses 'foreground' considerations or 'the immediate phenomenological context in which decisions to offend are activated' (Jacobs and Wright 1999: 150; see also Gibbons 1971; Groves and Lynch 1990; Hagan and McCarthy 1992; Katz 1988; Shover 1996). Additional aims of the chapter are to expose and address the similarities and differences amongst the young people based on the four identified themes, and offer analytical discussions on their interpretations of their acquisitive offences.

Motivation

Exploring what motivates someone to commit a crime is a traditional criminological concern. However, pinpointing motivation is a daunting task. For instance, Jacobs and Wright (1999: 149) described motivation as 'criminology's dirty little secret – manifest yet murky, presupposed but elusive, everywhere and nowhere'. Here I aim to find out more about this 'dirty little secret'.

In this section I illustrate that those more involved in offending offered relatively instrumental reasons for their acquisitive offences. Most of them said they had committed (with some still committing) robberies and burglaries with the sole intention of getting money. By contrast, those less involved in offending primarily said they only shoplifted petty items, such as food or magazines to use themselves, if any acquisitive offences at all. Several of these young people were only marginally involved in an acquisitive offence due the actions of others, and others said they failed to realise they had committed an offence that occurred 'a long time ago' in their lives. In terms of motivation, significant differences emerged between those who committed a greater number of more serious offences when compared to those who committed fewer, petty offences.

Table 3.1 lists six different incentives offered by the young people as to why they committed (or still commit) acquisitive offences: money; goods; 'leisure' (for example, searching for 'excitement' or because they were 'bored'); 'revenge', meaning the offence is a retaliation against a previous injustice; 'peer pressure'; and 'circumstance', which refers to young people who were only around others who committed the offence, or those who said they did not realise they were actually committing an offence. I take each in turn.

Getting money

Those more involved in offending mainly discussed committing serious acquisitive offences, such as burglary and robbery, in order to make money. When directly asked to explain this behaviour, a typical response was 'I needed the money'. These young people either talked about actually taking money from their victims during a street robbery or, more likely, sold the goods they stole in robberies or burglaries to others. In a couple of cases they actually *found* money when they burgled houses. Karl, for instance, when asked how he found money replied, 'I don't know. I just seem to find it.' Marc also said he found money during burglaries when looking in 'drawers, init?'

> *You just look in drawers?*
> Yeah. One time I found £150 in a man's shoe. I just moved it out of the way, just picked it out of the way and I see money drop out.

Most of those more involved in offending, however, said they received money through burglaries and street robberies *only* after the pilfered items were either sold to one of the many second-hand shops throughout Lambeth, or to others they knew. For instance, Marc sold stolen electronic goods to Stop and Swap – a retail chain outlet that trades in second-hand merchandise; Karl sold stolen bicycles on to others he knew in his area; Travis sold stolen laptop computers to his 'man' – someone who worked at a second-hand electronics shop. Indeed, the young men in this group who committed such offences discussed knowing someone or some-where willing to buy filched goods. For instance, Martin talked about what he did with his stolen goods:

> *What are you taking in the burglaries?*
> Videos, stereos, anything that's worth money.

Table 3.1 Reported motivation and type of offence[a] by offending category

	Age	Money	Goods	'Leisure'[b]	Revenge	Peer Pressure	'Circumstance'[c]
More involved							
Sonny	14	R	R	R			
Quentin	17	R,B,Sh	R,B,Sh				
Travis	18	R,B,TFC,Sh	Sh				
Marc	15	R,B,TFC	Sh				
Tolu	15	R,B			B		
Karl	14	R,B,Sh	Sh				
Martin	16	B,R,TOC		B			
Noel	15	B					
Tom	16			B,TFC			
Kenny	15	B					
Norman	15	B, TOC	Sh				
Theo	20					B	
Keenan	15	R	Sh				
Nathan	16	B,R	B,R				
Lenny	23	R					
Kevin	15	Sh					
Less involved							
David	14		B[d]				
Todd	14						TFC
Larry	15		Sh				
Brian	22		Sh				TFC
Darrell	16				B		
Jack	15	B	Sh				
Terry	15		Sh			R	
Betty	16						S
Frank	13						
Kellen	15						
Winnona	15						B
Eric	16						Th
Isaac	17		Th				
Tracy	15						
Tim	16						

Notes

a   R = street robbery, B = burglary, TOC = theft of car, TFC = theft from car, Sh = shoplifting.

b   'Leisure' refers to those who said they committed the offence 'for excitement', 'for fun' or 'because I was bored'.

c   'Circumstance' refers to those who said they were either with others who committed an offence and did not actually participate in the offence, or those who said they did not realise they were committing an offence.

d   This is an attempted burglary.

What are you doing with them?
Well, we was taking them to anybody that wants a video, or to our [cannabis] dealers, or to a pawn shop, or something like that.

[later in the interview]

What do you do with the cars that you steal?
Well, I know a friend that he just wants all the parts of a car, and he'll give you the money for parts of the car.

Kevin has shoplifted more times than he can remember, and mentioned how he shoplifted easily concealed items, such as toiletries, audio and video tapes, CDs, Playstation games and tools in order to pawn them off to those living around him. Kevin elaborated:

I shoplifted in every single shop in West Norwood ... just like anything I can get my hands on in a shop. I do it if I knew I could sell it.

By contrast, only one young person less involved in offending, Jack, mentioned being motivated by money when he shoplifted and burgled houses. Jack's friends have committed 'about 20 to 30' burglaries, of which he took part in two in order to 'get a little money'.

Looking at what these young people said motivated them to commit acquisitive offences tells us much about how they interpreted such acts. They predominately discussed how money motivated them to rob, burgle and/or thieve. Moreover, they displayed a willingness to take significant risks committing these offences, many of which carry severe legal penalties, in order to satisfy this desire or need for money. But why take such risks? During the interviews, these young people mentioned not receiving money through any other means. None of them had legitimate jobs, and all of them talked about not receiving any money from those they lived with. Travis, for instance, mentioned how his mum:

was going brass pockets [had no money]. Boy, she was a bit broke, init? ... I was just thinking money. I needed the money.

Kenny also said that:

Now and again, if it is really tight with money and I needed money, I go out and rob a house or something.

What do these young people spend this ill-gotten money on? Why did they take such risks? Interview material suggests their money was not spent in order to sustain themselves in terms of buying food, clothing and shelter. Jacobs and Wright (1999: 163), in their study of street robbers, noted that few robberies were committed 'to buy the proverbial loaf of bread to feed their children' (see also

Burney 1990; Shover 1996; Walsh 1986). All of the young people in this study appeared to be provided for by the adults they lived with; all were clothed, housed and fed. The money they earned from acquisitive offences went towards interests other than self-preservation.

Rather than buying food or paying rent, these young people talked about spending the money from offending on designer clothing and trainers, potent 'skunk' cannabis, mobile phones, take-away food, 'raving' at nightclubs and other possessions or forms of entertainment (Jacobs and Wright 1999; Parker 1974; Shover 1996; Walsh 1986; Wright and Decker 1994). Moreover, these young people were not frugal with their illegally earned money, but rather spent it as soon as they acquired it. As Shover (1996: 104) noted, 'The way money is acquired is a powerful determinant of how it is spent'. For instance, Martin talked about how quickly he spent the money made from selling stolen goods:

> Just buy my drugs and sit in my room and smoke my weed and buy some beers. That's it. Pubbing, clubbing and that's it. Money done.

The point that young people spend their money earned from acquisitive offences on self-indulgence was confirmed in interviews with professionals. For instance, Patty, a probation officer, noted that:

> [They are] doing it [robbery, burglary, theft] to get the money, to buy the clothes, to buy the music, to go raving. They spend the cash over the weekend on clothes and raving.

Likewise, Nancy, a youth justice worker, offered a similar opinion:

> I tend to look at [young people committing robbery, burglary and/or theft being] about getting money, living a lifestyle that they can't really afford. And the whole thing about clothes, music, y'know? You need to wear the latest trousers. So they were doing [the robberies] to have some hard cash in their pockets. And the mobiles: they've all got them.

Barry, another youth justice worker, made similar observations:

> We felt the main motivation of the [robbery, burglary, and/or theft] wasn't drugs; it was much more clothes. Clothes are far more of a motivation factor than drugs or something else. Yeah, designer clothes. Designer clothes were huge, especially for them. It dominated their lifestyle: going out and looking good.

Indeed, as Barry noted, clothing was high on the list in terms of what these young people said they bought with their money from offending. Not just any clothing, however, but relatively expensive, *designer* clothing, particularly sportswear, such as Nike, Adidas and Reebok, but also more upmarket, high-street names, such as

Moschino, Versace and Armani. For instance, Travis said he possessed nothing to show for all of the burglaries and robberies he had committed save for 'a bunch of nice clothes'; during the interview Karl showed off his new Armani denim jacket, which he bought after selling other clothing he shoplifted; Norman bought some Nike sportswear with what he earned from burglaries and selling stolen motor-vehicle parts. Indeed, obtaining designer clothing seemed a high priority to these young people.

But why were these young people taking gambles by committing serious offences, such as burglary and robbery, in order to acquire designer clothing and other things? Status has much to do with such behaviours, according to local probation and youth justice staff. Young people better their chances at being viewed by their peers as someone who is hip, respected and cool by having the 'right' clothing and participating in the 'right' activities. In short, they achieve higher social standing in the eyes of their friends, in part, through fashion – a valued commodity amongst young people in inner-city areas (Anderson 1990; Campbell 1993; Jacobs and Wright 1999; Katz 1988; Shover 1996). Interviews with other professionals also support this. For instance, Queenie, a youth justice worker, said, 'To be respected on the street, to have some street cred, you gotta look good'. Nancy, another youth justice worker, commented on how some of the young people she has worked with feel they 'need to wear the latest trousers'. Lawrence, a NACRO worker, also suggested the popularity of designer label clothing in Lambeth:

> We're living in the age where young people have to wear that. If they haven't got that then they're looked down upon, so, y'know it goes part and parcel with being part of the youth culture … It's a common thing. It's not surprising: 80–90 per cent of the youths today would wear the [designer] label clothes.

Declan, a youth justice worker, concurred:

> To wear reasonable clothes, you know, like in society, you're not cool, you're not hip, et cetera unless you have Nike, Reebok, Adidas and the trainers and the rest of it.

The designer clothing, trainers, exotic cannabis, nightclubbing and the other activities the young people in my sample enjoy are expensive and in sharp contrast with the overall physical aesthetics and relative socioeconomics of much of Lambeth. Moreover, nearly all of these young people came from low-wage, single-income families, living in public-sector housing, most of which was on crowded council estates. As such, it is doubtful whether their parents or the adults they lived with could afford to keep up with the goods and activities these young people desired. More to the point, these young people committed acquisitive offences in order to obtain designer clothing, cannabis and trainers, and participate in approved youthful activities to the levels *they* desired, a point validated in interviews with professionals. For instance, Steven, a detached youth worker from Stockwell, said:

You have to ask yourself where they get the money to buy the stuff that they are buying, y'know? Like the Moschino, y'know? They're not cheap, y'know? And I know your parents might buy you the odd one or two, but like your parents aren't gonna buy you a whole rail full, y'know?

Kwame, a youth and community worker from Brixton, offered similar comments:

I presume that they are catered for at home to some extent ... but the thing is at that age, your parents can't afford it. These are working-class parents. They'll feed you, and clothe you, but they can't afford £200 jackets.

Status was important to those in my sample, and perhaps remains so for other young people in Lambeth with similar backgrounds, for several reasons. Through presenting themselves as fashionable and 'cool' (for example wearing designer clothing, going out raving) these young people somewhat distanced themselves from their current socioeconomic position (Campbell 1993; Finestone 1957). A possible result of this more affluent appearance is elevated social status amongst their peers. Other research has shown that money earned from acquisitive offences often goes towards the purchase of materialistic, superficial goods, which appear to have no significance other than to present the individual in a manner that heightens their reputation in the eyes of their peers and earn them 'respect on the streets' (Anderson 1990, 1999; Burney 1990; Fagan 1996; Jacobs and Wright 1999; Schneider 1999; Sullivan 1989). For instance, Jacobs and Wright (1999: 156) talked about participation in 'street culture', and how street robbers placed a great deal of importance on the 'fetishised consumption of personal, nonessential, status-enhancing items' that 'knighted them members of a mythic street aristocracy'. For the young people in my sample, a certain sense of worth, a key element of their 'presentation of self in everyday life' (Goffman 1959) was achieved through the adoption of various cultural insignias, such as clothing, trainers, cannabis and raving. For many, theft was one means of acquiring these coveted goods.

In attempting to find out *why* these young people committed acquisitive offences, looking at gender issues is beneficial. Masculine qualities permeate the young people's street culture. Again, 'young people' in this book primarily refers to young men. While it might not necessarily be a conscious decision amongst the young men in my sample, by committing acquisitive offences and participating in this street culture they espoused masculinity. Messerschmidt (1993: 40) discusses how 'most men and women develop sex-specific stereotype behaviours based on "femi-nine" and "masculine" behavioural styles' and that the 'masculine character struc-ture ... requires self-confidence, independence, boldness, responsibility, competitiveness, a drive for dominance, and aggression/violence'. Society rewards those who adhere to their sex-roles and punishes those who deviate from them (Connell 1987; Messerschmidt 1993). Robberies, burglaries and thefts were acts in themselves that allowed the young men to embrace some of these masculine ideals, in a sense, to 'do masculinity' (Messerschmidt 1993, 2000). A hierarchy of 'tough-ness', 'bravado' and 'hardness' is associated with these offences where, amongst young men, the biggest 'badass' is the one most prepared to rob someone or burgle someplace (Katz 1988). In turn the 'badass' drips masculinity. In inner-city street culture young men may 'earn their stripes' and 'prove their manhood' by committing these offences, although I don't wish to sound deterministic, as the great majority of young men in Lambeth do not behave this way. Nonetheless, acquisitive offending provided an arena for young men in the borough to embrace masculine ideals. A couple of the professionals linked young men's participation within this street culture to the absence of male adults in their lives. For instance, Brenda, a youth justice worker, said:

> So there was this thing about single-parent families and offending. And there was definitely a link there, especially with women trying to look after boys. People will be up in arms saying that women can look after boys. They have been doing it all their lives. That's true. But when it comes to adolescence, I feel boys look to the streets for role models. It's this thing about women not being able to teach men how to piss. I think that's quite true. They can do the normal things like eating and drinking and how to dress. But being a man, taking the identity of a man, that's where a lot of boys in our community come into conflict. That isn't there. I think they look on the street for it. We have kids. We've seen dad absent from the home and mum's trying her best. She's got other kids and he's out in the street, breaking every boundary she's put down. And lo and behold, he's hanging out in the street. I think a lot of young kids they find that identity, they fulfil their need out on the streets because all the other boys are like them. They make their own culture, their own identity.

Oscar, a youth and community worker in Brixton, mentioned something similar:

> I certainly think for young people, for young men I mean, if they don't actually have an adult around, somebody who can be a mentor, be it an uncle or father or a member of the family, they choose that in terms of the street, in terms of modelling their behaviour. And it's also about being part of a group where in some sense, in their own sense, some kind of love and support and acknowledgement where they can do things and someone will say 'well done', be it playing football, chatting up women, or getting in trouble with the police. I mean at the end of the day they would be getting some acknowledgement.

Street culture is largely based on materialism and invites 'competition' – another masculine quality. In street culture the one with the most 'wins'. Aside from the acts themselves, the spoils of their acquisitive offences also permitted these young men to champion masculine ideals. These offences enabled the young men to 'get money' from which they purchased the latest clothing, fresh trainers, bags of cannabis, and allowed them to participate in all the youthful activities they desired. This, in turn, allowed for greater independence, greater autonomy and allowed them to take on greater responsibility for their own futures. By possessing these materialistic possessions young men have proven they have 'made it', that, through their own efforts, they rose up and embodied masculine qualities. Also, and importantly, having all this money and goods brought about by acquisitive offences has the potential to attract young women, something of paramount importance to young men in the borough. As Ayo, a detached youth worker in Stockwell, mentioned:

> People analyse what you wear. Everyone has good trainers. Everyone has this, they have that, y'knowhatImean? You want to compete with them ... You have to wear something for certain woman to look at you. They're foolish girls. They're like, 'Yeah, [by looking fashionable] that boy's saying something.'

Sandra, a youth and community worker in Brixton, also related acquisitive offences amongst the young men she has worked with to impressing girls.

> [Robbery, burglary, theft] is a lot about girls. And when you hear the girls talk it's about 'Yeah, man. He's got the latest gear and boy' ... There's a lot of talk about girls. A lot of talk about sex. There's a lot of talk about those kind of things and those are really key important things to them.

Dave, another youth and community worker from Brixton, related money from acquisitive offences to 'getting the ladies'.

> So once they get their money or whatever they know they can get the ladies. It goes hand in hand. They get the clothes. They get the money. They know they can get the ladies.

In films, on television, on the radio and in music videos the successful 'street hustler', the one who earned money through illegitimate street crimes, is often the one with a beautiful woman. Being able to get the girl is a significant masculine trait. Having the money, the flashy clothes, the beautiful girls, exotic weed: within inner-city street culture, the image of the ultimate male; within inner-city street argot, what it means to be 'the man'.

On a final note, several of those more involved in offending – such as Sonny, Travis, Karl, Noel and Norman, who mentioned *still* committing acquisitive offences for money to spend on looking good, expensive skunk and raving – are in danger of being caught up in a cycle of acquisitive offending (Jacobs and Wright 1999; Shover 1996). The cycle is this: they want to buy clothing, fast food, trainers, skunk cannabis and entertainment, so they go and commit acquisitive offences in order to come up with the money to do so, but because these activities and items are ongoing and need constant replenishing, they, in turn, commit more acquisitive offences. In this sense these young people may get caught up in a web of their own creation. In a manner similar to what Jacobs and Wright (1999: 166) said about street robbers in their study, these youngsters 'effectively become ensnared in their own self-indulgent habits – habits that feed on themselves and constantly call for more of the same.'

Other utilitarian motives

Table 3.1 shows that many young people said they committed their acquisitive offences for practical reasons, primarily in order to keep what they stole, something observed in other research (such as Wright and Decker 1994). For those in my sample, this was mostly true when they shoplifted. For instance, Travis laughed when he told me how he was arrested after stealing a can of Pringles (potato crisps) from Woolworths; Quentin stole Ferrero Rocher chocolates from a Woolworths store; Keenan 'like[d] the look' of a silver watch and 'some Warner Brothers' socks and a tie' he shoplifted from stores. These examples suggest that only shoplifted goods were kept, being small and relatively inexpensive, destined for instantaneous use. However, a few of those more involved in offending were partly motivated to commit more serious offences, such as robbery, in order to keep expensive, mainly electronic items, for themselves. For instance, Quentin, Marc, Sonny and Nathan all discussed robbing other boys for their jewellery or electronic goods, such as Walkmans and mobile phones. Marc said he stole mobile phones in order to use them himself. He said: 'I used to shod [sell] some of them, or I just run them up until they cut off.' Sonny mentioned how he took 'mobile phones, watches, headphones, tapes, jewellery – depends on what they got on them', and how he either sold or kept the items. These incentives are instrumental, and committing such offences stems from these young people's desire for more immediate forms of gratification. Obtaining the goods, not selling them, was their goal.

Several of those less involved in offending also said they shoplifted in order to keep the goods for themselves. For instance, Terry talked about 'nicking little things' from 'like Sainsburys and little shops'; Larry said he shoplifted a shirt once because he 'liked it'; Brian shoplifted a magazine and was arrested for this; Jack said he shoplifted 'when I'm hungry and I ain't got no money or nothing'. For these young people, shoplifting is an acquisitive offence they once were willing to commit in order to obtain small items for immediate personal consumption. One of them, David, said he tried to burgle a house of a boy he had previously visited, in order to steal his Playstation games. David broke a window on the side of the house, failed to notice the metal security bars behind the curtains and ran away – it was the only time he tried to burgle a home.

The reasons offered by many of those less involved in offending who committed an acquisitive offence differed greatly from the motivations offered by those more involved in offending. Only two of those less involved said they committed acquisitive offences for money. Furthermore, the acquisitive offences they committed were, overall, of a less serious nature when compared to the ones committed by those more involved in offending. For those less involved in offending, acquisitive offences played a much less significant role within their lives when compared to those more involved. This may partially be explained by their social and economic background. For instance, more of those less involved came from families earning higher incomes, were enrolled in full-time education, and discussed wanting proper jobs in the future when compared to the other group. These young people did not express such a pressing need for cash, and committing acquisitive offences could have seriously jeopardised their future plans. These young people were not willing to take the same risks as many of those more involved in offending.

In pursuit of leisure

Three of the young people – Sonny, Martin and Tom – mentioned committing some offences 'for fun', 'for excitement', because 'there was nothing to do' or because they were 'bored' (Campbell 1993; Corrigan 1979; Downes 1966; Presdee 1994; Sanders 1981). However, the offences these authors primarily discussed were of a less serious nature (for example vandalism or joyriding) when compared to the ones a few young people in my sample discussed committing for fun, such as robbery and burglary. Take Sonny, for instance, who said one reason why he committed street robberies was because, 'I just get, like, a buzz out of it'. Martin, as well, mentioned 'fun and amusement' when asked why he committed some of his burglaries (Katz 1988; Presdee 2000). These motivations are more 'expressive' than instrumental, and committing such offences only served to provide these young people with some 'action' that 'tested their mettle' (Goffman 1967). However, both Sonny and Martin also said they committed burglaries and robberies for money or goods – more instrumental reasons. To this degree, they committed such offences in order to get money, and, perhaps, had a 'good time' doing it. On the other hand, Tom said he committed a spate of burglaries or 'drums'[2] and stole a number of car stereos over a couple of months only because 'there was nothing to do' and 'for fun'.

> *Why did you do the burglaries?*
> Basically, there was nothing to do.
> *What about stealing the car stereos?*
> I didn't know what I was doing. I used to watch Crimewatch on TV and just watched what they were doing and copied them[3] ... I just did them for fun.

Tom offered no other reasons for his acquisitive offences. For Tom, committing burglaries and stealing car stereos helped pass the time and temporarily cured his boredom. He offered no instrumental purpose for his offences, which makes him distinct from the others more involved in offending. But why did he find burglaries and breaking into cars fun? Tom said these offences took place over a short period of time, about a year or so prior to the interview, and led to his arrest. Since this incident, he has desisted from offending altogether. As Tom mentioned, he 'didn't know what [he] was doing' and he saw others committing offences on the television and 'copied them'. Tom apparently failed to realise the severity of such offences during this time, and only viewed them as a way to generate excitement. However, after being arrested several times he changed his tune, and now does things other than offending 'for fun'.

Revenge

Only a couple of young people were motivated to commit acquisitive offences out of 'revenge' or as a way to 'get even' (Cromwell *et al.* 1991; Shover 1996). For instance, Tolu mentioned he committed one of his burglaries because 'someone tried to get mine', meaning that his home was burgled. This burglary made him 'very upset', and, as Tolu mentioned, was a reason why he burgled a house – anyone's house. From Tolu's interpretation of such acts, almost as a parody of the ancient 'eye for an eye' dictum, being a victim of an offence was a justifiable reason for being a perpetrator of the same offence. However, Tolu said revenge motivated him only once, and other burglaries and robberies were committed with the intention of making money.

The other young person who mentioned revenge as an incentive was Darrell, who burgled the house of a boy he 'didn't like' in retaliation to previous perceived injustices. Darrell elaborated:

> Because they was just starting trouble and they left their keys in the door and then someone took them ... we went back in later and took quite a bit of stuff ... in the end, we got caught for that.

Darrell used the burglary as a way to strike back at another boy who was 'starting trouble' with him and his mates. However, this burglary was the only time Darrell committed an acquisitive offence. He interpreted this behaviour as a one-off – something that happened once, which resulted in him being apprehended, and something Darrell will never commit again.

Peer pressure

Offending and the concept of 'peer pressure', or the influence that an individual's acquaintances may have on that individual's decision to offend, received much attention in criminology (Gottfredson and Hirschi 1990; Graham and Bowling 1995; Hirschi 1969; Sutherland 1947; Sutherland *et al.* 1992). While this may be the case, only two young people mentioned feeling pressure from their friends as a reason for their offences. For instance, Terry was marginally involved in an attempted street robbery, and said he felt 'pressure' to participate. He elaborated:

> I'd fallen out with this group of boys a couple of times, so there was this pressure to prove that I was still one of them.

Likewise, Theo also mentioned pressures he felt when asked about his burglaries:

> *Why were you doing the burglaries?*
> Peer pressure, definitely. It wasn't my decision actually. One of my boys was like, 'Yeah, yeah we're going to go on a drum' [burglary]. I would be like following along and like get me, use my strength to open one of the doors, or whatever. It's open, and in the end and we was in there and we was out.

Theo believed he committed the burglaries out of his desire to 'hang out' with 'the little stealing boys', as he called them. However, Theo said he committed these burglaries a couple of years ago, and his interpretations of this behaviour may have shifted within this time. Thus, 'peer pressure' could be a *post hoc* rationalisation, reflecting back on actions that took place years before, as opposed to being the sole reason for such acts. Terry, on the other hand, seemed much more shaken up by his involvement in a street robbery, and his feeling of being 'pressured' into the offence appeared genuine. Not only did Terry and his friends fail to follow through with the robbery, but that robbery was the only time Terry was involved in such behaviour.

A general impression, often advertised in the mass media, is that peer pressure is a significant explanation for why young people offend. We read in the newspaper or hear on the television that Johnny is really a 'good boy' and is only in trouble with the law because he 'hung out' with the 'wrong' crowd, and that these 'bad boys' had 'pressured' him into committing a certain offence. Concomitantly, if Johnny stayed away from the 'bad boys' he would not get in trouble any more. And while peer pressure and the influence of delinquent peers are important criminological concerns, within my small sample of young people 'peer pressure' as a reason for offending was the exception, not the norm. Furthermore, for Theo and Terry, peer pressure seemed only to play a very minor role in their offending. Both of these young people committed several other offences, but only offered 'peer pressure' as a reason for one each: Terry's robbery and Theo's burglaries. For the remainder of their offences, they did not say that 'peer pressure' was a reason.

Circumstance and chance

In this context 'circumstance' and 'chance' refer to those who had no intention of committing an offence, but found themselves in such a situation. They talked about being around others committing an offence, or simply failed to realise their involvement in one. This 'reasoning' was only offered by a couple of those less involved in offending who had committed an acquisitive offence. Such reasons are very dissimilar to those more involved in offending, who were all active participants in their acquisitive offences, and self-aware of their actions and their potential consequences.

Brian and Todd both discussed their brief and partial involvement in stealing car stereos, or 'sets'.[4] Neither of them mentioned being 'motivated' to commit such offences, and only said that on a couple of occasions they simply stood by as others broke into cars. These two did not receive any of the profits earned from selling the car stereos, nor did they discuss any desire to do so. Rather, they explained how they just happened to be around when their friends were committing the acts. Brian and Todd also discussed how such events had not occurred recently, and that the next time their friends go out and steal car stereos they will likely stay home.

A similar story was offered by Betty, who offered no motivation for the acquisitive offences she became caught up in. Betty was only 'hanging around' a friend who stole some make-up from a store. According to Betty, this happened only once. Two others, Winnona and Eric, thieved by chance. They both talked about unintentionally committing an offence, which led to their arrest. Eric mentioned being arrested once for 'theft by finding'. He said he found 'one of those bus hammers' on a bus in Brixton, put it in his pocket and forgot about it. Later, when he was stopped by police officers for 'looking suspicious', they found the hammer and then arrested him. Winnona said she never intended to burgle the house, which she said was a 'squat' and not a 'normal house', and mentioned how she only went in to see her friends. However, because one of her friends took some money she found 'just lying on the side' they were both arrested for burglary. Such instances were one-offs, never to be repeated again, and these young people were not willing to commit acquisitive offences towards any end.

Overall motivation patterns

Significant differences emerged between those more and less involved in offending in terms of what motivated them to commit acquisitive offences. Those more involved primarily mentioned being willing to take huge risks by committing serious offences, such as robbery or burglary, all in the name of acquiring money in order to afford to 'look good', smoke cannabis, eat at take-aways, and go raving through the night – all, perhaps, obvious activities young people enjoy. Having money and what it can buy enhanced the status of these young men, and bettered their chances of attracting young women. Several of them mentioned still committing such offences for these reasons. These young people were in jeopardy of becoming caught up in a cycle of offending. Given the absence of alternative avenues, they might find themselves in a position where they *must* offend in order to maintain the desired image.

The other young people, for the most part, differed greatly on this point. With the exception of Jack, those less involved in offending only shoplifted small goods to keep for themselves, something that occurred infrequently, and most, at the time of the interview, discontinued committing these offences. For many in my sample less involved in offending, motivation and acquisitive offences were not really issues; roughly half committed one such offence, and they (apparently) were either not aware of it, had not intended to get involved in such offending, or did it 'a long time ago'. The overall lack of acquisitive offending amongst these young people points to their dissimilarity from those more involved in offending, and, perhaps, their resemblance to young people who generally do not behave this way.

So what causes these young people to commit acquisitive offences? According to my data, the great majority of such offending was committed, perhaps not surprisingly, in order to get money or goods. But what do their reasons tell us theoretically? There seems to be a number of issues present. In attempting to draft an explanation for such behaviour, it is important to take issues of gender into account. An overwhelming amount of acquisitive offences are committed by males, not just in Lambeth, but more generally. There is a degree of status competition going on amongst these young men, not just in terms of 'getting the girl' but also looking the part and being 'the man'. As such, to an extent, these young men who commit offences are 'doing masculinity' (Messerschmidt 1993, 2000). Ethnicity, like gender, is also of crucial significance. Fundamental differences exist in the histories of white and black people in the UK, and young black men are disproportionately represented in offender statistics. A similar situation exists in the USA. As such, attempts at addressing *why* acquisitive offending occurs may be unique for young black men (Sampson and Wilson 1995; Wilson 1987). Below, a comprehensive theory about the young people's acquisitive offences is not offered. Rather, I review their reasons for this behaviour in light of some of the major theories of crime and delinquency.

The reasons offered by those in my sample who committed many acquisitive offences suggest they used these offences as a means to an end. Through robberies, burglaries and thefts they were able to obtain commodities and activities highly valued by young people throughout the borough. This being the case, strain theories (Agnew 1992; Merton 1938, 1957) seem somewhat able to capture these explanations. Generally speaking, strain theories advocate that people, particularly those in the lower or working classes, commit certain offences when their aspirations outweigh actual expectations, when they cannot or do not 'get what they want'. This 'presence of negative stimuli' may result in an offence. Similar to Merton's (1938) 'innovators' the young people used acquisitive offences (unconventional means) to obtain money and goods (conventional goals). Robberies, burglaries and thefts enabled these young people to overcome their lack of cash, seemingly a 'strain' in their lives, and fully participate in all the youthful activities and have all the 'gear' they see around them. And based on evidence from the young people, obtaining these goods and 'going out' was very important, these being the accolades of their street culture. Norman flashed the gold around his neck against his new Nike tracksuit, Karl sported a fresh Armani denim jacket, Martin had his 'pubs and clubs', and Travis owned 'a bunch of nice clothes': none of these things would have been possible without them committing acquisitive offences. The professionals concurred. In Lambeth young people who commit robberies, burglaries and thefts do so 'to buy the clothes, to go raving' so they can 'live a lifestyle they can't really afford' because such things 'dominated their lifestyle: going out and looking good', and if 'they haven't got that then they're looked down upon'. Matt, a youth justice worker, talked about why the young people he worked with committed acquisitive offences:

> The reasons why they're doing it is because they want to lead a certain lifestyle where they want to wear certain clothes. And the clothes that they want to wear are very expensive ... They want recognition that's in their own way. And the reasons they want that recognition is because they want to meet the girls. They want to rave, they want to have the champagne and everything and all that I think. It's a bit of money to have them sort of things, so it means going out there committing offences.

Many shortcomings of strain theories exist, not least their relative ignorance of gender and ethnic considerations, or their lack of attention to the differential experiences of strain or pressure that young people may perceive, or how they may cope with them (see, for example, Broidy 2001; Downes and Rock 1988). However, the young people's explanations of using acquisitive offences as a means to an end somewhat fits with the strain model.

When looking at the motivations offered by those who said they committed their offences for reasons other than money or goods, it is beneficial to look outside strain theory. For instance, for those who said they committed a couple of offences 'for fun', the theoretical conceptualisation that seems most adequate is the 'crime as an act of transgression' approach (Katz 1988; Presdee 2000). These authors seem to be suggesting that such offending is an end in itself, and that young people who commit offences for such reasons seek vicarious activity, becoming seduced by the fact that these activities are morally devious. Essentially, this theory advocates that people commit offences in order to change the way they feel, to alter their emotions. Sonny, Martin and Tom seem to have committed a couple of their acquisitive offences due to 'the emotional power of the thrill' (Katz 1988: 77); they all said some the acts gave them a 'buzz'. In line with Katz's approach, these young people did mention how 'exciting' these acts were. Tom, in particular, said he only committed his acquistive offences because 'there was nothing to do'. However, Sonny and Martin also said they committed similar offences for money and goods. As such, the 'crime as an act of transgression' theory does not seem to entirely capture these behaviours. While the theory is refreshing in how its focus is beyond the socioeconomic status of the person who has offended, according to these young people their motives for the majority of their acquisitive offences were clearly economic. Katz acknowledges the financial incentive of acquisitive offences, but emphasises more the supposed transcendent quality of the act as the ultimate reason explaining such behaviours. Rather than competing, perhaps both economic and emotional objectives act together to form an impetus for acquisitive offending. This question, however, remains for future research.

When looking at other theoretical explanations of crime, interestingly enough, only two young people mentioned 'peer pressure' as an incentive for their acquisitive offending, despite the classic 'Billy made me do it' approach towards explaining delinquency (Sutherland 1947; Sutherland *et al.* 1992). And while peer relations are, no doubt, important when addressing young people's *opportunities* to commit acquisitive offences (Flood-Page *et al.* 2000; Graham and Bowling 1995), the influence or pressure of others as an incentive to do so receives little support from my data. Also, peer influence may best capture some of the explanations offered by those whose reasons for acquisitive offences fell within 'circumstance'. For instance, according to their accounts, Todd, Brian, Winnona and Betty would not have been involved in an acquisitive offence had it not been for the actions of their friends.

Overall, then, when attempting to find out *why* these young people committed acquisitive offences, aspects of several theories somewhat fit, not one in its entirety. For the young people who committed several relatively serious acquisitive offences, strain theories, which address economic inequality, seem to best capture their explanations. These young people used the money or goods they acquired through such offences to participate in general youthful activities. A couple of them, however, offered other motives for such offences, such as 'just for fun'. The theory that best captures these explanations, what might be called 'crime as an act of transgression', looks beyond the social class of the actors and suggests a seductive quality of offending, and how such behaviour offers an escape from mundane rationality. Cultural deviance theories – such as those which address the influence of community factors, including friends and family, when accounting for motivation – received little support from my interview data. Only a few young people expressed that they offended because of their friends, but a couple of those less involved in offending genuinely seemed to have become caught up in their one acquisitive offence due to the actions of others. In short, then, parts from several criminological theories somewhat capture the motivations behind the young people's acquisitive offences.

Planning offences and selecting targets

How much do young people think about their offences before they commit them? Do they have a picture of the type of person or place they will commit an offence against? These questions are important to address when attempting to outline and comprehend the mind-set of a young person about to commit, or in the process of committing, an offence. Gibbons (1971: 271), for instance, suggested how 'criminality may be a response to nothing more temporal than provocation and attractions bound up in the immediate circumstances' (see also Jacobs and Wright 1999; Katz 1988; Shover 1996). In this section I examine these attractions and stimuli bound up in the offences committed by the young people in my sample by examining how long (and if) they said they planned them and how they selected targets. These analyses, in turn, aim to tell us more about the phenomenological context of their offences.

All the young people primarily discussed how their acquisitive offences were spontaneous, opportunistic decisions. Only a few of those more involved in offending said they pre-planned their offences. This suggests there may be something about the target or victim of the offence that was highly significant within their decision to commit an offence.

First, none of the street robberies was planned. Rather, decisions to commit a street robbery were discussed as being opportunistic, and they said they targeted their victim immediately prior to the offence (Jacobs and Wright 1999; Shover 1996). No one in my sample said they stalked those they were about to rob, but rather just happened across them. For instance, Tolu robbed 'some man' who approached him and his friends in a recreation park at six in the morning; Karl saw a wallet sticking out of a lady's purse and snatched it; Sonny robbed people of their visible valuables saying, 'it depends on what they got on them'; Keenan robbed two boys smaller than him because he 'saw the opportunity, so I took it'; Lenny instigated robberies after noticing 'what he's [the victim] got on – jewellery or whatever'. These examples suggest that the immediate resolve to rob someone on the street was highly influenced by an assessment of the circumstance of the potential 'victim'. Those walking around with visible valuables – jewellery, electronic goods, designer clothing – were potential targets. It also appears that these young people generally selected victims physically smaller and weaker than them. Overall, while the young people who robbed others clearly spent very little time planning such offences, broad categories of people who they would and would not rob emerged.

In a similar vein to their street robberies, burglaries, shoplifting and other thefts were, predominantly, discussed as opportunistic events that were not pre-planned at all, but owed much to circumstance (Cromwell *et al.* 1991; Shover 1996). Interview material suggests the young people's decision on exactly where or what to burgle, shoplift or thieve was spontaneous, and they thought little about such acts prior to committing them. For instance, Quentin stole a bag he thought contained a laptop computer from an overhead compartment on a train, yet 'it was full of golf balls'; Martin stumbled across an 'empty house' at 2:30 in the morning when he was 'pissed and stoned' and attempted to burgle it; Brian and Larry shoplifted, respectively, a magazine and a shirt when they noticed them in shops; Darrell found the keys to the front door of a house belonging to a boy he 'didn't like', and then burgled the house.

All of these examples suggest the central role that circumstance and opportunity played within the minds of these young people, not only in their decision to commit an acquisitive offence, but also where or against whom to commit them. Importantly, their decision to rob, burgle or thieve hinged on the presence of visible valuables. In other words, if something valuable can be seen, then it can be stolen. For instance, Travis's example of why he broke into a car illustrates this point. He discussed that his decision on which car to break into was heavily dependent on the presence of visible valuables. Below is a paraphrased version of one time Travis broke into a car:[5]

> Travis came across a car with its doors unlocked and windows slightly open filled with various bags and other items. He dipped his hand through one of the car's open windows and pulled out a bag containing a laptop computer, which he later pawned for £133.

Martin discussed how he broke into a car in order to steal the stereo only after he saw it. His account below indicates how opportunity played a significant role towards initiating not only an acquisitive offence (taking from a motor vehicle), but also an attempted expressive offence (joyriding).

> *So, the taking of a motor vehicle, what were you and Danny [Martin's friend] doing?*
> We were just trying to just get the stereo and go out and get draw [cannabis] and just sit in his room and smoke it. But as we got in the car, he lifted up the [sun visor]. As he slipped that down the keys fell down. So I looked at him and he looks at me and we both jumped and we took the stereo. We hid it in the bushes. We were just going to take the stereo, but we found the keys. So we get in the car and we were just driving around and out of the blue: police car.

[He said they ran, but were caught by the police.]

> *How did you get into the car?*
> We just got a stone and pinged the window.
> *Why did you do that?*
> It was just the opportunity.

Likewise, Kevin discussed how he stole a wallet from a jacket in a locker room only after he noticed it:

> I found it in the locker and I couldn't see anyone in the changing rooms, so I shouted, 'Has anyone lost a jacket?' And there was one person in there, and he said he didn't. He just looked at me, so I thought, 'Fair enough', then I took it.

Some exceptions to this generally spontaneous picture of offending exist. A few of those more involved in offending mentioned planning out certain offences, suggesting they spent more time thinking about such offences and invested more of themselves in the offence to help ensure its success. Wright and Decker (1994) previously observed that some burglars spent more time thinking about their burglary in terms of location and what was good to steal. Likewise, Travis plotted some of his burglaries to the point of stealing specific computers – the 'Sun Ultra' – from particular office blocks. Noel's burglaries were the most thought-out, systematic and profitable acquisitive offences in the entire sample. In fact, Noel said that none of his burglaries were spontaneous acts – all were planned. Other examples of young people who planned their offences include the several times that Quentin went to a cloakroom and rifled through the jackets belonging to participants of a laser-tag game, when he knew the jackets would be left there unattended; when Karl stole specific mountain bicycles from a Toys R Us store that he knew were sold there on a couple of occasions; the way Norman said he might notice a moped during the day, and 'just wait till night time to go and get it'; and Martin has 'a friend' who buys stolen car parts, and after asking him 'what he wants', Martin and his mates go and find it. Kevin planned shoplifting, and said he shoplifted 'with foresight', meaning he stole things he believed others would eventually want, or 'took orders', in that he asked others around his area if he could get them 'anything'. Kevin elaborated:

> I was doing all sorts. Anything that anyone ever asked for. Like, say someone wanted a pack of razors. On my way out if I saw a pack of razors, I just pick them up. Videos, blank video cassettes, Playstation games, blank tapes.

Overall then, and in accordance with other research, the trend amongst my sample was that they did not think about their acquisitive offences too much prior to committing them (Cromwell *et al.* 1991; Jacobs and Wright 1999; Katz 1988; Shover 1996; Wright and Decker 1994). However, some notable, significant exceptions appeared. Offences where a previous plan of attack was drawn up were more likely to be successful endeavours when compared to offences decided on the 'spur of the moment'. Again, though, amongst these young people, planning an offence was the exception, not the norm. Most of their offences were discussed as haphazard events, where the young person became lucky and stumbled upon a residence with portable valuables, a car with a laptop or an expensive stereo, or an individual with lots of money and jewellery. In a minority of cases the offences were discussed by the young people as being committed in a methodical, systematic way where they knew exactly what was going to be stolen and where to steal it from.

Associates and skills

Within criminology, the idea that adults and peers exude a degree of influence upon a young person's decision to commit an acquisitive offence has received much attention (Gottfredson and Hirschi 1990; Hirschi 1969; Sutherland *et al.* 1992; see also Graham and Bowling 1995). In the last chapter I suggested opportunities to commit offences appeared to be ubiquitous in Lambeth; its underground economy, in part, relies on them to supply it with its life-blood – stolen merchandise. In this section I focus on what those in my sample knew about illegal activity in Lambeth, such as specific businesses, places or adults that buy and sell stolen merchandise, sell drugs, trade in stolen car parts, or commit other offences. Within this section such individuals are referred to as the young people's 'associates'. These data are summarised in Table 3.2. Also explored in this section is the extent to which the young people employed skills or strategies during their offences that may have been passed down or 'transferred' from their associates.

Associates

Of the 31 young people, 27 mentioned at least one associate, usually an adult involved in some sort of illegal behaviour. Knowledge of someone or some part of Lambeth's underground, illegal economy was widespread, but not universal amongst my sample. Generally speaking, those less involved in offending said they knew of fewer associates, while, alternatively, those more involved mentioned more associates. Theo, for instance, knew of numerous shops in Lambeth that conducted illegal business. As he mentioned:

> You wouldn't even know these places. There's probably more, you get me? On the shops, everything, man. Phone shops, the works … There's bear [many] places, man. I don't even know where to start.

While these associates were, no doubt, somewhat influential in the young people's decision to commit an acquisitive offence, from my data pinpointing the nature of any of these relationships in terms of how close the young people were with their associates, how long they had known them and the (potential) intensity of their influence is difficult. Nonetheless, a couple of examples emerged from those more involved in offending that suggest a direct peer influence on their acquisitive offences. For instance, Norman and Martin both said that an older 'friend' introduced them to someone who buys stolen car parts and showed them where to bring the pilfered motor-vehicle parts; Noel mentioned how his older brother, whom Noel calls 'a professional' at burglary, showed him how to target office buildings in order to burgle computers and where to sell the computers. Also, Travis introduced Quentin to his 'man' – an individual who buys stolen electronic goods, such as laptop and desktop computers. Travis, in turn, was introduced to his 'man' by another friend, Drumma. These introductions were significant because they enabled these young people to earn money by selling stolen goods. Indeed, the

Table 3.2 Reported number of 'associates' known by young people, by offending category

	Age	Shops buying or selling stolen goods	Adults involved in offending	Buying or selling stolen car parts
More involved				
Sonny	14		Too many to count	
Quentin	17	8		
Travis	18	1	Too many to count	
Marc	15		Too many to count	
Tolu	15		4	
Karl	14		Too many to count	2
Martin	16	2	2	
Noel	15	1	3	9
Tom	16			
Kenny	15	1		
Norman	15	1	1	1
Theo	20	Too many to count	Too many to count	1
Keenan	15	2		2
Nathan	16		1	3
Lenny	23	1	Too many to count	
Kevin	15		6	2
Less involved				
David	14	2	1	1
Todd	14		1	
Larry	15		6	
Brian	22	2		
Darrell	16	1	1	
Jack	15	1	1	
Terry	15			
Betty	16		2	
Frank	13			
Kellen	15	2	2	
Winnona	15			1
Eric	16		1	
Isaac	17		Too many to count	1
Tracy	15		1	
Tim	16			

availability of a 'fence', or someone willing to buy pilfered items, is essential in prof-iting from stolen goods (Cromwell *et al.* 1991; Wright and Decker 1994). As Crom-well *et al.* (1991: 92) mentioned, 'marketing-oriented complexes of criminal activity undergrid most forms of vice and theft'.

While receiving money for stolen goods may be consistent and fluid with intim-ate knowledge of a specific person or place bartering in specific goods, this relation-ship was not a prerequisite for profiting from acquisitive offences. Rather, those more involved in offending said that their booty from such offences would be bought by 'someone somewhere' within their vicinity (Cromwell *et al.* 1991, 1996; Shover 1996; Sullivan 1989; Wright and Decker 1994). Karl, for instance, talked about selling stolen goods to those 'that live around me, and people I see', and

Marc mentioned how 'There's a lot of people that just buys stolen goods, y'get me? Hook ups!' Indeed, as suggested in the last chapter, this appeared to be a relatively common practice within Lambeth. In my first year living in Brixton I came across *numerous* second-hand businesses that traded in second-hand (perhaps stolen) goods, as well as those peddling such goods door-to-door. It is thus no wonder that young people who have grown up in Lambeth know of many such places and observed such practices. Overall, the distribution of stolen goods and the apparent relative acceptability of this in Lambeth was influential in the young people's decision to commit acquisitive offences, particularly those who committed such offences in the pursuit of money. Without these outlets the opportunity to make money this way for these young people would be seriously hindered. As Cromwell *et al.* (1991: 71) noted, 'The burglar's ability to market stolen property determines the success or failure of the criminal activities. Without someone to receive and dispose of stolen property, theft becomes a meaningless, profitless act.'

By contrast those less involved, overall, said they mentioned fewer associates than those more involved. Furthermore, none mentioned they used these associates towards any illegal end. These young people said they only *knew* of such people and places, but had nothing to do with them.

Skills

I asked the young people about specific skills or strategies they employed within the course of their acquisitive offending, and queried whether these skills were transferred or passed down from others 'in the know'. The aim was to see if they directly 'learned' any specific offending techniques (Cloward and Ohlin 1960; Sutherland 1947). However, almost none of them said they had learnt any special way to commit their offences. These young people were not delinquent apprentices 'trained' by their criminal 'master' in a Faginesque manner. Rather, in terms of learning how to commit their offences, nearly all of them said something to the effect that they learned by themselves, which was evident in the rudimentary manner in which their acquisitive offences were carried out. For instance, Travis and Theo broke windows or bent doors in order to get into cars or houses; Quentin snatched a bag from an overhead compartment on a train; Martin 'busted the lock off the door' or 'mashed' the window in order to gain entry; David and Jack smashed windows in order to break into houses; Norman, Kevin, Terry, Brian, Larry, Keenan and Karl shoplifted by hiding the items in their clothing. Karl's discussion of how he stole clothes from a department store illustrates the elementary execution of such an offence.

> *How do you steal the stuff?*
> Go to the shop. I like that tracksuit bottom. I like that top and will take it in the [changing room], but put a top over it. So I pick up two, like two shirts, and they only think I pick up one, and two tracksuit bottoms cuz I know they're going to fit me, and leave both of them in [the changing room]. Pretend I tried it on, come back out and say I want to try on this T-shirt. And I pick up two T-

shirts, put them in the cloakroom, pretend I tried them on, and I put on the T-shirt and the tracksuit bottom [and walk out of the store].

Overall, the young people did not spend much time learning specialised methods of committing acquisitive offences (such as using tools, picking locks, over-riding security systems). Rather, their offences were carried out in an ordinary, blatant and mundane fashion (Cromwell *et al.* 1991; Walsh 1986; Wright and Decker 1994). These methods of offending were crude but effective, as many of these young people discussed successful offending.

Only one young person within my sample committed burglaries using a specific tool. Marc mentioned a way of breaking into houses more sophisticated than smashing a window or breaking down a door. He talked about gaining entry into houses through the use of what he called a 'floid' – a 5" by 7" piece of celluloid plastic, a specialised tool, which, as Marc noted, 'A lot of people don't know about'. Marc discussed his ability to slide a floid between the door and the lock, if the lock has an angled bolt which latches it shut. According to Marc, gaining entry with the use of a floid is 'as easy as opening the door'. The fact one of Marc's 'breadren' showed him how to use a floid suggests special skills were transferred, and that Marc's relationship with one of his associates was useful in his 'career' as a burglar (Wright and Decker 1994).

Emotions and reactions

Thus far, this chapter has explored motivation, planning, associates and skills related to the young people's acquisitive offending. In this final section I examine how they felt after committing the offences. This tells us a little bit about their values regarding this behaviour, which, in turn, shows how they make sense of it. Values, according to Sykes and Matza (1957: 666), 'appear as *qualified* guides for action, limited in their applicability in terms of time, place, persons, and social circumstances' (original emphasis). By looking at the values of those in my sample, much can be learned about their actions and behaviours, as well as their 'moral universes'. Analysing what motivated different young people to commit their offences offers us a glimpse of their values and their willingness to engage in specific offences. Here, the aim is to explore these values in more depth, by finding out how they felt about their offences afterwards and see how (and if) their offences preyed on their minds afterwards.

Making sense of the offence

Some clear distinctions emerged between the different categories of young people when looking at how they felt after their acquisitive offences. Those more involved in offending primarily failed to express remorse for their acquisitive offences. Travis said, 'Don't care, init? No remorse', Tolu said 'I don't feel bad', Karl said 'I don't feel no way' and Marc said 'No' when asked if he felt bad after any of his offences. Both Noel and Martin said they felt 'nothing' after burgling homes.

Nathan, too, did not express any concern over any of his offences. Rather, he mentioned, 'There is nothing you can do but face up to the crime'. From speaking with these young people, I was persuaded that their lack of remorse over the offences and lack of empathy with their victims seemed genuine. I received the impression they really did not care at all.

So why was this? In attempting to draft an answer, keeping in mind that the young people who committed these offences are primarily young men is important. Perhaps those who said they 'didn't care' or felt 'no remorse' over their acquisitive offences may have put up an emotional façade. Being penitent, fearful and apologetic is not consistent with a 'macho' disposition, something young men more generally, particularly in the inner city, may attempt to maintain (Burney 1990; Katz 1988; Messerschmidt 1993, 2000; Miller 1958; Shover 1996). On the other hand, statements such as 'I don't care' or 'I felt nothing' suggest a tough exterior image. It might be the case that the young men in my study wish to reflect this image. Burney (1990: 52), in her study in Brixton, suggested that 'macho behaviour' was part of a youthful 'style' desired by those who committed street crimes, such as burglary and street robbery. If this applies to those in my sample, then young people such as Noel, Travis, Martin and the others may have been much more concerned about their acquisitive offences than they let on, and only said they 'didn't care' in order to maintain a 'hard' masculine or macho demeanour.

While these young people may have been fronting a 'tough' disposition by saying they didn't care, many also qualified this reasoning by offering an explanation. Some of these explanations were similar to Sykes and Matza's (1957) 'techniques of neutralisation'. Sykes and Matza suggested their techniques were informed by Sutherland's (1947) theory of differential association, particularly his tenet regarding 'definitions favourable to violation of the law'. Through such techniques, the authors basically argued that the values of those who offend are primarily congruent to conventional ones, as opposed to being distinct. Thus, while the acts are illegal, by applying such techniques the individual does not consider themselves to be 'deviant' or 'bad'. These techniques may be *post hoc* excuses for illegal activity, what Downes and Rock (1988: 173) referred to as 'more or less honourable motives for dishonourable acts'. Sykes and Matza, however, theorised that these techniques serve as a buffer between the young people's illicit actions and their self-image, where conflict between the young person's values that allow for delinquency and the values of those within their broader social environment who censure it become 'neutralized, turned back, or deflected in advance' (1957: 667). Thus, these rationalisations could be ad hoc and formed by young people prior to committing their offences. Sykes and Matza continued:

> Social controls that serve to check or inhibit deviant motivational patterns are rendered inoperative, and the individual is freed to engage in delinquency without serious damage to his self image. In this sense, the delinquent both has his cake and eats it too, for he remains committed to the dominant normative system and yet so qualifies its imperatives that violations are 'acceptable' if not 'right'.
>
> (1957: 667)

One technique some in my sample offered was to deny that the victim of their offence actually suffered any injury. In such cases the young person said they had not caused any significant harm when committing the offence, suggesting that how they felt afterwards was related to how they perceived the individual whom they commited the offence against. Kenny, for instance, discussed how he felt after he burgled houses:

> If someone's loaded with money, yeah usually then I really don't feel nothing, cuz otherwise because then I wouldn't do it in the first place. So I just don't feel nothing, just no way. They got good jobs, a big house, two cars and a telly in every room.

This 'rationalisation' was confirmed in interviews with some professionals. For instance, Barbara, a youth justice worker, mentioned this when she talked about a young man who robbed off-licences and newsagents:

> He didn't feel bad about the victims. The victims would usually be like the workers in that particular store … so he didn't see them particularly as victims because it wasn't their money.

Danielle, another youth justice worker, offered similar comments on some young men who robbed building societies:

> When they're doing the building societies or the shops or whatever, it's very hard for them to realise who the victim is, y'know? If it's a street robbery, its like that's the victim on the street, y'know? With the building societies, they don't really associate too much with the victim.

An additional technique offered by some young people was their 'appeal to higher loyalties' when committing offences by keeping other, deeper values in check. This explanation is related to the young person's own moral code, and was as if they said 'at least I don't do *these* things'. For instance, Norman did not express any remorse over his burglaries or stealing motor-vehicle parts, for, as he mentioned, 'I'm not like knocking off old ladies or nothing'. Norman makes an excuse for his offences by saying he commits offences he believes are less serious, unlike robbing elderly women. Likewise, Karl, Tolu and Sonny said they felt indifferent after committing robberies and burglaries because they failed to harm anyone physically. Karl said, 'Sometimes I feel kinda bad if I hurt them' after mugging people on the street and Tolu said, 'I don't feel bad … because the person isn't in danger' after he robbed a couple of bus tills. Sonny also made a distinction between robbing someone and robbing and attacking someone:

> *Do you ever feel bad after you rob someone?*
> I don't know. It depends on what I've done. If I was just taking [money or jewellery] off them, I wouldn't feel so bad, but like if I would fight them, or

beat them up, or something, and I just saw them there lying with like blood and something like that then I would feel a bit bad.

Thus, while these young people robbed others, they obliged a 'higher loyalty', which in this case is a stand against causing the person harm through physical blows. If someone had been injured in the course of the robberies or burglaries they committed then, perhaps, these three young people would have expressed a degree of remorse or regret over their actions.

A further 'excuse' offered by Tolu was the 'denial of responsibility' whereby 'the delinquent … sees himself as helplessly propelled into new situations' (Sykes and Matza 1957: 667). This explanation is related to the young person's own experiences as a victim of such offences, where the sentiment expressed seems to be, 'I commit such offences because someone has committed them against me'. Tolu offered this reason when he discussed how he felt after one of his burglaries. He said, 'I only did that because someone tried to get mine'. A couple of youth justice workers mentioned how some young people they worked with in the past have volunteered similar excuses. For instance, Tex, when talking about a group of young people on an estate, said:

> The attitude was if your bike was stolen on the estates are you going steal someone else's? So what comes around goes around.

Tommy made similar points about some young people he worked with:

> Basically, it was like y'know, 'Everyone does it y'know?' … It wasn't seen as a big thing. They didn't wreck people's houses. They didn't smash anything up. They just took the stuff. They kinda made excuses for what they had done.

Another technique – the 'denial of victim' – was offered by Nathan. This rationalisation is related to how the young person views the potential victim. Here they seem to be asking: is this a 'normal' person or someone who 'deserves' what they have coming? For instance, Nathan, when asked how he felt after burgling a house said, 'but they were only hippies, weren't they'. In this sense Nathan did not express remorse for the burglary because he viewed the 'hippies' as appropriate targets. For Nathan, 'hippies' were outside his view of 'normal' people. Nathan thus 'denied' a victim existed, and did not feel the person was 'injured', but 'punished' (Sykes and Matza 1957: 668). Similarly, Ethan, a youth and community worker from Brixton, mentioned how some young people he worked with felt 'no remorse' when they robbed a drug seller because such behaviour was 'not a big thing'. Ethan said:

> As far as they're concerned, it's like, y'know, it's not really a big thing to rob a drug dealer, y'know?

These excuses and 'rationalisations' expressed by these young people are similar to an 'honour amongst thieves' ethos or a 'code of offending' that they adhere to. It suggests that within their value systems, there exist very fine distinctions about the types of offences they were (or still are) willing to commit, as well as who they were prepared to commit them against. For instance, Kenny mentioned how he 'just don't feel nothing' when he burgled from residences he considered more affluent than his, but said stealing from 'the people who can't afford it [because] they're in the same position as you' is 'liberties'. Karl, Sonny and Tolu mentioned they felt fine about committing robberies or burglaries because no one was physically harmed. To Nathan, robbing a 'hippy' was not a matter of great concern because he failed to consider the 'hippy' a 'normal' person. There appears to be a set of moral 'rules' or guidelines some of those more involved in offending followed regarding acquisitive offences, being only prepared to commit specific offences against certain types of people. Through abiding by the rules, these young people maintain a positive masculine self-image. This suggests that even in the world of breaking the 'rules', a degree of order is still maintained, an additional, subterranean code followed by those who live in this world.

However, the possibility exists that this macho image may only be skin deep, and expressions of not caring may belie true feelings of fear and concern. Interviews with some professionals suggest this. For instance, Lewis, a CID officer from Clapham, commented on how young people he has worked with have acted tough when questioned about a crime, yet started crying when the officers left the room. He elaborated:

> Often they would cry when you saw them in the detention room you'd walk past. As you walked by on past the window and there'd be [someone] sobbing on his own just because he's there on his own … when they were on their own there was this thing that they were not to be seen, if we walk past and they were crying, that would be the first thing stop him crying. That would be the first thing that would stop them crying, them being seen by us.

Fiona, a NACRO worker from Brixton, mentioned something similar:

> *After they get caught how do they feel?*
> They don't feel bad, but they're not boastful on a one-to-one basis. But that's what I know as a worker … I've seen them in the police station crying their eyes out.

Sandra, a youth and community worker from Brixton, also discussed 'macho' emotions:

> One thing I've been trying to do is to try to get to real emotions rather than this kind of circus stuff because I think, and I'm speculating here, that when [offending] happens in a group, it's seen as quite macho rather than [feeling] any pangs of guilt … I suppose in a sense sometimes when they are talking to me, you almost get a sense that they feel a bit bad about the victim, but that's more on an individual basis [talking to them] outside of the group.

So did the young people who committed acquisitive offences really 'not care'? This question was difficult to assess from interview material. Nonetheless, a significant pattern amongst their accounts was that those still committing certain offences were the ones who expressed little remorse over such behaviour and offered 'excuses' or 'rationalisations'. These young people were still in 'the jungle' and remained loosely governed by a specific set of significant distinctions or 'rules' as to whom they will and will not commit certain offences against, as well as the offences they were willing to commit. Such rules are active and within their worldviews they have legitimacy. These young people still abided by 'the code'.

A couple of those less involved in offending – Jack, Betty, Eric and David – also did not express any remorse for their acquisitive offences. For instance, Betty said she 'didn't feel anything' when her friends stole some make-up; Eric said 'I didn't really care' after being cautioned for 'finding' the bus hammer. Likewise, Isaac and Winnona were not at all remorseful over their offences. Similar to those more involved in offending who said they didn't care, perhaps the responses by these young people also served to present a macho demeanour. However, unlike those more involved in offending, these young people no longer committed any acquisitive offences, and the ones they committed were, for the most part, of a relatively less serious nature. So while these young people may have presented a masculine image by suggesting they didn't care, they also may have not expressed remorse over these offences because these relatively petty events were committed once or twice a 'long time ago' in their lives. The basis of their rationale for not caring appears to be very distinct from those who committed a series of relatively serious offences.

By contrast, those who felt remorse after their offences were primarily the ones who were *not* committing acquisitive offences at the time of the interview. This includes young people both more and less involved in offending. As these young people said they once committed acquisitive offences, their reactions could be nothing more than *post hoc* explanations for these behaviours. Nonetheless, these events occurred in their past, and the remorse they expressed seemed genuine. Their responses suggest these young people felt regret over their past actions, wishing they could 'take them back'. For instance, Quentin said he felt 'sincere remorse' over his previous acquisitive offences. Lenny reflected back on his robberies and said, 'At the end of the day, it was cold.' Theo, after burgling houses said, 'I felt bad. I was like shit … It wasn't really me, in my heart, y'get me?' Keenan, after robbing a couple of boys, said he 'felt like I should never done it. It was stupid.' Terry, on his involvement in a robbery, said, 'I really regret what I done … It just seemed pointless to me.' Darrell 'felt small' after he burgled a house.

Overall, responses from these young people suggest that something within their value-systems switched. Was this switch related to the suffering of the victims? Was it related to young people's 'moral code'? Was it related to their experiences of arrest? The data threw up mixed signals in this respect. Lenny was never arrested, and only later regretted his actions as he became older. Similarly, Theo, Nathan and Darrell discussed their remorse long after their involvement in offending. Saying whether these young people's feelings of remorse were related to their arrests or the end of their offending is difficult. On the other hand, Keenan, Tom, and Terry were all recently arrested for their offences. For these young people, feelings of remorse roughly coincided with their arrests and desistance from such behaviour altogether. As such, their experiences of arrest perhaps contributed to their desistance. However, on the whole accurately pinpointing where the feelings of remorse expressed amongst these young people stemmed from is difficult.

Conclusions

In this chapter I attempted to show that, in terms of the types of acquisitive offences the young people were willing to commit and what they said motivated them to commit such offences, significant differences between those more and less involved in offending emerged. In the main those more involved primarily committed serious acquisitive offences, such as robbery and burglary, with the intention of exchanging the stolen items for cash, or, to a lesser degree, to keep the items. The money these young people earned from such offences went towards status-enhancing items and activities they enjoy, such as 'looking good', eating out, smoking cannabis, and raving – all very important commodities in their world. And while those less involved in offending also highly valued the same commodities, for the most part these young people were not willing to use acquisitive offences as a medium to earn the money to make these things happen. Rather, nearly all of these young people were only willing to commit, peripherally be part of, or unknowingly get caught up in a couple of relatively less serious offences, such as the theft of petty items from shops, which were, in most cases, not sold on, but kept for immediate personal use. Overall, in terms of explaining these behaviours, several theories of 'crime and delinquency' were helpful, but none quite entirely captured them.

In continuing to explore the phenomenological context of the young people's acquisitive offences, I examined their selection of targets and 'plan of action'. Most of them, however, mentioned no plan at all. Rather, opportunity played a big role in their likelihood of committing a robbery (for example, the presence of visible valuables) or shoplifting (such as seeing something then 'just wanting' it), and the overall success of their burglaries – whether or not there were items of value in the residences they burgled – was more often than not down to luck. Only in a couple of cases were offences such as burglaries and thefts planned to the extent of knowing the location of specific goods and a keen buyer. Those who did plan their offences to some degree were likely to profit from them, perhaps more so than if the offence was a 'spur of the moment' idea, a significant distinction.

Next, I looked at the influence that adults in Lambeth involved in some sort of illicit or illegal activity may have on the young people. While almost all of those interviewed knew of somewhere or someone doing something illegal in the borough, only a few examples were offered by some of those more involved in offending to suggest evidence of direct peer involvement or influence in this behaviour. And while these 'hook-ups' possibly allowed for smoother transactions between buyer and seller of stolen goods, such connections were not necessarily required in order to make money from acquisitive offences. The sheer number of shops and people that buy stolen goods in Lambeth suggests that, if *anyone* wanted to pawn off household, particularly electronic, goods, they eventually would just by asking around. To this extent, such individuals and businesses are important to address when looking at the opportunity young people in the borough have to offend. I also explored the extent to which the young people employed any specific skills or methods when offending, perhaps those that may have been taught. However, the way that most of them went about committing their offences was self-taught, very crude, but, more often than not, effective.

Finally, I examined the values of the young people by exploring how they felt after committing these offences. Those who continued to commit serious offences seemed to care about them less, which could easily be considered a typical macho statement delivered by a 'hard' young man showing off. Nonetheless, the responses appeared true, for very fine differences were articulated in the type and target of offence these young people were willing to commit. They might not have cared about their burglaries and robberies, but they differentiated between people they would and would not rob or burgle. These specific normative judgements suggest a certain code existed regulating their offending, as well as their self-image. Most of the others who desisted from offending altogether either felt remorse over the serious offences they had previously committed, or didn't care about the relatively minor ones that took place some time in their past. While these responses could be nothing more than *post hoc* rationalisations, they appeared genuine.

4 Drug use and drug selling

Lambeth has had relatively high rates of both drug possession and drug trafficking in London for several years.[1] Mick, a detached youth worker in Brixton, said, 'Drugs is definitely a part of young people's lives today'. Why do young people use drugs? What do young people do when 'high'? This chapter explores how drugs are part of the young people's lives by exploring their use of illicit drugs, and their attitudes towards and experiences of selling such drugs. The first section examines the young people's frequency of use, their behaviours when using drugs, and their attitudes towards different types of drugs. The second half of the chapter addresses how, where and why four of them sold crack, heroin and/or cannabis.

Cannabis and other drugs

Nearly all of the young people in my sample said they had tried cannabis at least once. Many of them who committed more serious offences used cannabis on a daily or frequent basis, and, if not for the money they made from their acquisitive offences, maintaining this level of use would be difficult. And while cannabis use was not uncommon amongst my sample, the same cannot be said of other drugs. *Only 6* of the 31 young people said they had tried other drugs, such as cocaine, ecstasy, LSD, amphetamines or aerosol inhalants, and several of them expressed negative views of 'hard' Class A drugs, particularly heroin and crack, as well as those who used these drugs. Overall, the young people appeared to have a set of differentiated values regarding the use of various drugs.

Skinning up, blazing down, getting a buzz

Cannabis was the most widely self-reported drug used, a point in line with other research (for example Aldridge *et al.* 1999; Flood-Page *et al.* 2000; Graham and Bowling 1995; Parker *et al.* 1988, 1995). In fact *only 5* of the 31 young people in my sample had not tried cannabis, which they referred to as 'draw', 'gear', 'puff', 'herbs' or 'greens'. 'Skinning up' means to produce a marijuana spliff, 'blazing down' means to smoke it and 'getting a buzz' were the ideals expressed by the young people as to why they smoke weed.

In terms of experiences with cannabis, significant differences emerged between those who committed a relatively larger amount of serious offences when compared to the others in my sample. Generally speaking, cannabis use was more frequent, and more central in the lives amongst the former. Table 4.1 shows that about half of those more involved in offending said they used cannabis daily, and all of them said they had tried cannabis at least once. In contrast, only three of those less involved in offending said they used cannabis daily, and over half had either tried it once or twice or not at all. Those most heavily involved in offending used cannabis on a daily basis. This is not to imply any causal relationship between the frequency of cannabis use and offending, as research has shown the direction of this relationship to be far from clear (for example Parker *et al.* 1995; Ray and Ksir 1999; Ruggiero and South 1995; South and Teeman 1999).

The young people can be distinguished in terms of not only the frequency of their cannabis use, but also their ability to pay for it. Many of those more involved in offending used cannabis on a daily basis. Some of them – such as Quentin, Sonny and Marc – *sold* cannabis, which allowed them to smoke it without having to pay for it. But what about the others? As mentioned in the last chapter, these young people did not have jobs and received little, if any, weekly pocket-money from those they live with. Keenan, for instance, said he sometimes got £5 from his mum and that this went towards cannabis. However, even those who received some pocket-money reported that they received too little to cover the cost of an eighth of an ounce (3.5g) of 'bush' cannabis at £15, let alone an eighth of the 'skunk' cannabis most said they preferred at £30 an eighth.[2] These young people would not be able to buy cannabis if not for the money made from acquisitive offences. This is not to suggest that they directly said that they committed acquisitive offences in order to buy cannabis, rather that cannabis was one of the self-indulgent things they purchased. As Martin said about the money he received when he did burglaries:

[I] just buy my drugs and sit in my room and smoke my weed.

Those less involved in offending did not use cannabis as frequently as the others. A couple said they used cannabis on a daily basis, and a couple more mentioned occasional use. However, the majority of these young people had either never tried cannabis or had used it once or twice. Also, no clear connection exists between their cannabis consumption and acquisitive offences. These young people procured their cannabis without having to offend. David and Brian, for instance, both had jobs and bought their cannabis from friends. Larry said his friends always had cannabis and always gave him some. Larry and David also said they occasionally smoked hash (cannabis resin), what they referred to as 'solid', priced the same as bush cannabis. Others, such as Darrell, Jack and Terry, like Larry, said they occasionally smoked skunk, bush or solid – they did not seem to mind which – when one of their friends had it. In relation to their cannabis use, as with many other aspects of their lives, these young people were very different from those more involved in offending.

So why did the young people use cannabis? There appear to be a couple of reasons. For those who only used it once or twice, the reasons seem experimental. In

Table 4.1 Reported frequency of cannabis use by offending category

	Age	Frequency of use
More involved		
Sonny	14	Daily
Quentin	17	Daily
Travis	18	Daily
Marc	15	Daily
Tolu	15	Daily
Karl	14	Three times
Martin	16	Daily
Noel	15	'A couple of joints a week'
Tom	16	'Once in a while, not that often'
Kenny	15	'Whenever someone's got it'
Norman	15	Daily
Theo	20	Daily
Keenan	15	Daily
Nathan	16	Daily
Lenny	23	Stopped 'years' ago
Kevin	15	Stopped daily use three months ago
Less involved		
David	14	Daily
Todd	14	Never tried any drug
Larry	15	Daily
Brian	22	Daily
Darrell	16	'Every other week'
Jack	15	'Once every two weeks'
Terry	15	'If it was there'
Betty	16	Never
Frank	13	Never tried any drug
Kellen	15	'Smoked a bit of weed' when 13
Winnona	15	Once
Eric	16	'Twice a week'
Isaac	17	Never tried any drug
Tracy	15	Twice
Tim	16	Three or four times

other words these young people, such as Karl, Winnona, Kellen and Tracy, had smoked cannabis only on a couple of occasions in order to experience its effects. The ubiquitous references to weed found within inner-city youth culture might make trying the drug even more seductive. Other reasons for cannabis use amongst the young people were its sociability, and the fact that they liked its effects. Cannabis gave these young people a 'buzz', as many of them called it. Also, smoking weed was a very social activity, and these young people talked about 'hanging out' with their friends passing joints around. Finally, smoking cannabis seemed to be a very 'hip' thing for young people in Lambeth to do. As such, those in my sample may have also smoked cannabis in order to promote a 'hip' and 'cool' image (see Anderson 1990). 'Everyone's at it' was the general impression received from several professionals. Ayo, for instance, a detached youth worker from Stockwell, said:

> Weed. Yeah, a lot of people, like, what I've noticed, yeah, is that in London, yeah, people are really into skunk … it's just the 'in' thing now.

Due to the popularity of cannabis amongst those in my sample, and apparently amongst young people in Lambeth more generally, bringing up how this drug may lead to a process of criminalisation is important. By this I refer to how a young person stopped and searched by police officers after being 'pulled on a suss' and found with cannabis, may be arrested, prosecuted, and effectively become labelled as 'criminal' (Becker 1963). Those in possession of cannabis seriously risked this process. Also, a strong association with cannabis and inner-city black youth culture exists. From hip-hop to dancehall, where the great majority of the artists are black, enjoying cannabis is a recurring lyrical theme. Given this, police in the borough may perceive more young blacks in the borough, like the musicians they listen to, are frequently using cannabis, and, consequently, may decide to stop and search them. This might help explain (apparent) differential policing practices in Lambeth. Indeed, a significantly larger proportion of black people in Lambeth get caught for possession of drugs in comparison to white people.[3] Importantly, this may suggest that more young black men in comparison to young white men may be subject to this process of criminalisation and, therefore, labelled 'criminal'. This process, in turn, may help explain the over-representation of young black men in 'crime' statistics, both locally and nationwide (Fitzgerald 1998).

Other drugs

By contrast with their cannabis use, the young people had limited experience with other drugs, such as LSD, ecstasy, amphetamines, cocaine and aerosol inhalants. Only six said they had tried other drugs. Furthermore, their use of other drugs was either experimental or occasional, and none of them said they ever used other drugs regularly. Overall, the young people's reported use of other drugs differed greatly from that of cannabis, very much in line with other research. Glassner and Loughlin (1990: 82), for example, noted that cannabis use in their sample was 'widespread and on going', but that 'the use of other drugs more limited and experimental', and the Youth Life-styles Surveys suggested that the prevalence of cannabis use is much higher than the use of other drugs (Flood-Page *et al.* 2000; Graham and Bowling 1995).

Drug use outside of cannabis was fairly limited amongst those who committed many serious offences in my sample, a point in contrast with other research, which showed that more persistent and serious young offenders had a higher prevalence of using 'harder' drugs, such as ecstasy, amphetamine, cocaine, LSD and others (for example Audit Commission 1996; Flood-Page *et al.* 2000; Hagell and Newburn 1994; Newburn 1998). The most serious offenders in my sample had only *limited* use and experience of these drugs. For instance, Travis and Kenny said they occasionally used cocaine and had tried other drugs. Kenny said he tried LSD once, and talked about using cocaine on 'special occasions … maybe once a month'. Travis said he used ecstasy on some weekends about a year ago when he went raving at nightclubs – perhaps, a 'normal' setting for ecstasy use (Parker *et al.*

1998; Redhead 1993; Thornton 1995). Aside from smoking cannabis daily, Travis talked about the occasional use of cocaine:

> I hardly touch anything. Once in a blue moon I'll buy a little wrap of charlie [cocaine] … that's rarely, four times a year or something.

A couple of those less involved in offending had also tried other drugs in the past. For instance, Darrell mentioned using speed about six months ago, but did not discuss using it recently. Another time Darrell said he 'smoked charlie [cocaine] before in a joint'. He continued:

> I just done it that one time to try it. It was quite nice, but I wouldn't do it all the time. It's not worth it.

David said he tried LSD once, which 'made me see things I didn't want to'. He used it once, did not find the occurrence pleasant and mentioned never wanting to use it again. David and Darrell's experiences with other drugs were distinct from those of Kenny and Travis, who said that using cocaine from time to time was acceptable. Betty and Tracy had used speed and inhaled the gases released from an aerosol hairspray can 'a long time ago'. The girls took hairspray aerosol cans and wrapped them in towels, then inhaled the gases released with the spray. This only happened a couple of times, though, and neither of them mentioned wanting to use these or other drugs in the future. For these young people, illicit drug use in general held little priority within their lives. Similar to David's experience with LSD, and the time Darrell tried cocaine, Betty and Tracy's use of inhalants was experimental.

In parallel with this relative absence of other drugs in these young people's lives, only a couple of professionals mentioned working with young people who used drugs outside of cannabis. Lawrence, a NACRO worker, worked with a group of young men who used ecstasy on the occasional weekend when out raving at night-clubs. Lawrence said their use of ecstasy was limited to such occasions and that 'it's not really their sort of thing'. Mick, a detached youth worker from Brixton, commented on how some of the young people he worked with used crack as 'a party drug … a social thing for them'. Both Mick and Lawrence discussed the use of such Class A drugs by the young people they worked with as something occasional, rather than as something they feared the young people were addicted to or had a problem with. These two examples remain exceptional, as, overall, few professionals discussed young people using drugs other than cannabis.

In terms of *why* the young people used drugs other than cannabis, two themes seem to surface: experimentation and socialising. Young people such as Betty and Tracy, who inhaled from aerosol containers, and Kenny, who tried LSD, seemed to have used these drugs in order to 'see what they're like'. This occurred once, they did not find it pleasant, and did not use them again. The experiences reported by others such as Darrell and Travis, alongside evidence from the professionals, suggest that the use of certain stimulating drugs, such as cocaine (either power or 'crack') and ecstasy, accompanies nights out 'raving'. These young people used these drugs not only because they enjoy them, but also because they allowed them to stay up until late at night and dance – the essential ingredients of raving (Redhead 1993).

Not only were there clear distinctions in patterns of usage but, perhaps predictably, young people's attitudes to different drugs were also sharply differentiated. In general Class A drugs such as crack and heroin were perceived very negatively by many of those more involved in offending in my sample. For instance, Jack said:

> I would never try cocaine. No way. Nope. Don't go to Class A drugs.

Nathan, who smoked cannabis on a daily basis, said if he used crack, heroin or any other Class A drug that all of his friends would 'kick my ass', and continued by saying the same would go for any of his other friends if they used such drugs. Travis talked about crack and heroin and said:

> It ain't really my thing that kinda shit there. I just seen too many people fucked up on them sort of drugs.

Quentin equates crack with more serious offending and offered the following reasons for his disapproval:

> Boy, see this is the thing that amongst my consciousness about not taking it [crack]. A couple of them [Quentin's friends] started taking coke [crack] and that and then started licking it, like flying [robbing] building societies, getting nicked and going to jail like. It's like a route, ya get what I'm saying? And I say, boy, I'm not going to touch that. I see what it does. I don't want to know nothing about it.

Travis, Quentin, Nathan and several others all viewed the use of drugs such as heroin and crack as eventually leading to serious negative consequences because of bad experiences with those who use such drugs. For them, crack and heroin were drugs that 'ain't [their] thing' which they 'don't want to know nothing about'. Theo also distanced himself from crack and heroin users. He derogatorily referred to those who use crack or heroin as 'cats':

> No matter how much you beat and kick a cat, as long as you keep feeding them they will keep coming back for more and more.

Theo, like Nathan, Travis and Quentin, had had negative experiences with crack and heroin users, and did not care for them. The same can be said for Brian. He also referred to heroin and crack users as 'cats' because he, like Theo, said that they acted like them. Brian elaborated:

> They're always like clinging on to you. They will cling on for what you've got. Even if it's a 10p or even if it's a half a cigarette you're smoking, a cigarette and he'll go 'Yeah, yeah can I have that?' and you say 'Fuck it! Here you are!',

and then he'll walk off. You just thinking to yourself, 'What a cat!', yaknowhatimsaying?

While cannabis was largely accepted among my sample, the use of heroin and crack was viewed as deviant, something to be avoided, undesirable, having negative consequences, and generally negatively stigmatised, a distinction noted by other researchers (such as Anderson 1990; Bourgois 1995; Jacobs 1999). For instance, Jacobs (1999: 555–6) noted how to 'be labelled a crackhead is to be considered "the lowest of the low" in the hierarchy of the street'. Professionals interviewed also observed a significant distinction drawn by young people in Lambeth between cannabis use and the use of other drugs, particularly heroin and crack. For instance, Brenda, a youth justice worker, talked about how the young people in Lambeth she works with dislike crack.

> I think cannabis ... it's cool. It seems cool. The kids will tell you right openly. 'Oh, you know I get high.' I think it's anti-social to admit that they use crack or coke ... [they] don't want to be seen using a drug like crack. 'Oh, I don't touch that, man. I don't touch that shit!' But then they'd sell it. But they swear they don't touch it ... I'd say that cannabis is an all around socially acceptable drug amongst the kids. Y'know it's cool. They're just using it, not selling it ... it's cool to admit you smoke weed, and it's not cool to say that you take crack.

Lewis, a CID officer from Clapham, commented on how a group of young people who sold cannabis would not 'want to be seen around' the flats used by individuals selling heroin:

> In fact, they actually disassociated themselves with the heroin addresses. They didn't want to be seen around them.

My findings suggest very significant differences exist in the attitudes the young people in my sample exhibited towards the use of various drugs. Cannabis was not regarded as a big deal, but use of other 'harder' drugs, particularly crack and heroin, was seriously stigmatised and avoided. They wanted nothing to do with those who used such drugs, and a few occasionally used other drugs, such as cocaine or ecstasy, *only* in festive settings. On the other hand, many of these young people used cannabis daily, and many professionals had a lot to say about young people in Lambeth using it. Indeed, cannabis use was not difficult to spot in Brixton, and during my time there some significant changes occurred relating to how cannabis is perceived throughout London, if not the entire UK.

The normalisation of cannabis

The prevalence of cannabis use amongst my sample did not seem untypical of young people of that age and background within Lambeth. Many of the professionals interviewed commented on the frequency of cannabis use amongst the young people they worked with. For instance, Wendy, a NACRO worker, said, '99 per cent of them smoke puff'; Arthur, a police sergeant in Clapham, said, 'It would be unusual nowadays within Lambeth at that age [13–14] not to have tried it'; Eli, a probation officer, said, 'I mean *everybody* is taking cannabis'. I also had many encounters with cannabis during my time in Lambeth. These ranged from the occasional smell of cannabis wafting in the air in the borough to being offered cannabis numerous times on Coldharbour Lane and Atlantic Avenue (and in front of my home in Brixton).

The extensive use of cannabis in my sample and within the borough suggests the drug was not uncommon, but rather open and 'normalised' (Parker *et al.* 1995, 1998). Illicit drug use was once suggested to take place within a 'retreatist' subculture full of society's 'failures' (Cloward and Ohlin 1960: 178–96). More recently, however, the idea has been entertained that '[d]rug subcultures have become assimilated into and now partly define mainstream youth culture' and are found in traditional youth interests such as magazines, music and fashion (Parker *et al.* 1995: 24–5). Rather than looking at drug use as a 'soluble social problem' Parker and others (1995: 24) argued that the use of certain drugs may be a 'functional and powerful social process'.The authors further suggested that 'Adolescents of the 1990s are growing up in and with this new level of drug availability ... [which is] a *normal* part of the leisure-pleasure landscape' (Parker *et al.* 1995: 25, original emphasis). While they initially argued that normalisation applied to many illegal drugs, they later revised this book and maintained that it primarily applied to cannabis. According to Parker and others (1998: 151–4), the normalisation of cannabis use was suggested, in part, by its availability, how many people are trying it, its social acceptability, and how cannabis is advertised in mainstream youth cultures. Normalisation does not imply that cannabis use is a 'normal' activity for young people to engage in, rather how this 'deviant activity and associated attitudes' have moved 'from the margins *towards* the centre of youth culture' (Parker *et al.* 1998: 152, original emphasis). Based on self-reported use within my sample, and the general experience of cannabis use by young people within Lambeth, Parker *et al.*'s 'normalisation' thesis appears persuasive.

Cannabis was obtainable in Lambeth. More than half of my sample said they knew of people or legitimate businesses, such as off-licences, newsagents or take-away restaurants, that sold cannabis 'under the counter'. Other research has noted places selling cannabis in similar ways (for example Bourgois 1995; Robins 1992; Sullivan 1989). A little over half of all the young people knew of at least one shop within Lambeth selling cannabis this way. More of those heavily involved in offending mentioned knowing a couple of such shops, and Quentin knew more than he could count. Even I discovered a mini-cab agency and take-away restaurant in Brixton that sold cannabis.

Another illustration of the normalised character of cannabis use was the open and social way young people consumed it. Cannabis use amongst them was a very social activity, and its context was more akin to, say, colleagues sharing a cigarette during a work break or having a drink at the pub. Several of them, including Travis, Quentin, Brian and Theo, smoked cannabis during the interview. Marc even smoked a joint one time when I walked with him to his off-site unit. According to the young people, cannabis use accompanied routine social activities, such as playing sports, being on 'the computer' (home entertainment consoles such as the Sony Playstation, Sega Dreamcast or Nintendo 64), or 'just hanging around'. This point has been expressed by others. For instance, Glassner and Loughlin (1990) noted how the youths in their study used cannabis and then got on with customary youthful behaviour. Ruggiero and South (1995: 127) also commented on how 'The "Taking care of business" perspective on the active life of the drug user is an important counter to stereotypes of the dazed, dozing and incapable junkie'.

Further support for the normalisation thesis was the social acceptability of cannabis use as expressed by many of the young people. None of them had anything negative to say about cannabis. Even some police officers did not condemn or regard cannabis use as a social problem. For instance, Chris, a detective inspector from Brixton, had the following to say about cannabis use:

> We virtually ignore it. Nine times out of ten when we do bring people in for cannabis they get a caution. It's either that, or it's thrown away in the streets. There are some people who get spaced out on it. You could stop five people on the streets and two would have cannabis.

Albert, a detective sergeant from Streatham, said the following about young people using cannabis:

> You'll find that even if you go out on the street and chat to them as a policeman and they will say, 'Yeah, I smoke a bit of puff', but they will accept it. It's not a problem for people to talk about personal use of cannabis.

About three years after the interview with these police officers, the head of Lambeth police initiated a borough-wide pilot scheme specifically related to recreational cannabis use.[4] The six-month scheme commenced in July 2001 and gave police officers the option of confiscating small amounts of cannabis and issuing a reprimand on the spot – a more lenient penalty than being arrested and cautioned.[5] This policy was favourably received by both the police and community members in Lambeth.[6] This scheme was the first of its kind in the capital (and, indeed, in England), and appears to have received support. This further suggests cannabis use was normalised in the borough. Furthermore, the pilot scheme on cannabis in Lambeth fits in nicely with the central propositions of the normalisation concept: the destigmatisation of cannabis use as a 'deviant', socially marginal activity (see also South 1999).

Unlike reports of heroin users who look at their addiction as 'problematic' (Parker *et al.* 1988: 41), the use of cannabis was not viewed by the professionals or the young people who used it on a daily or occasional basis as a something they needed to be concerned about. For instance, Tex, a youth justice worker, said that cannabis use amongst young people 'wasn't a big deal'. Kwame, a youth and community worker from Brixton, said, 'A spliff? Da da da. It's no big. It's like a cigarette to people'. Steven, a detached youth worker from Stockwell, did not interpret cannabis use as a 'big thing'. He elaborated:

I don't see that as a big thing to tell you the truth. You know, it's just part of growing up. If anyone was to say, 'I never smoked a hit of a joint', living in this society, I think you're a liar. It's part of kids' culture, y'know?

Finally, in this regard, cultural references to cannabis were ubiquitous in the lives of these young people. The use and acceptance of cannabis amongst the young people was mirrored in the lyrics of the music they listened to. Hip-hop rappers, such as Dr Dre, Eminem, Jay-Z and the Wu-Tang Clan, popular with many of those interviewed, frequently rap about cannabis, and Cypress Hill practically make a living singing about smoking weed.[7] Cannabis use can also be heard in other music the young people said they listened to, such as garage, jungle, reggae and even popular music. For instance, the song 'Because I Got High' by Afroman was in the top ten 'pop' music chart list for weeks in 2001 in the UK. This 'cultural accommodation of the illicit' (Parker *et al.* 1998: 156) further suggests that cannabis use was normalised amongst my sample, and to a greater or lesser degree within Lambeth.

Serving up: young people who sold drugs

Using cannabis was clearly in a completely different category to selling cannabis or any other illicit drug. While almost all of the young people had used some drug (mainly cannabis) at one point in their lives, only four – Marc, Tolu, Sonny and Quentin – mentioned selling cannabis, crack cocaine and/or heroin. A striking difference emerged between the quantity of those who used and those who sold. For those in my sample, selling drugs was uncommon, yet using them, cannabis anyway, was not. While the use of cannabis was acceptable to many, supplying it or any other drug was another story. This suggests that very precise distinctions existed within the value-systems of these young people regarding the use and sales of cannabis, crack and heroin.

While the small number of those who sold any illicit drug within my sample may be related to ethical considerations, that they may possess a firm stance against not selling drugs because they believe such behaviour is 'wrong', it may also simply be explained by the lack of opportunity to do so in the first place. Selling drugs requires a 'connection' – someone to supply the drugs. In this respect selling drugs is unlike other offences, such as burglary or shoplifting, offences practically anyone could commit. In other words these offences do not require the participation of a second or third party; selling drugs, however, does. Not only would someone need a supplier, but also a string of 'clients' – those willing to buy the drugs. Many of the young people knew someone or somewhere that sold drugs. This, however, does necessarily imply such closeness with these connections to include the opportunity to sell drugs. So while their lack of involvement in selling drugs may stem from their beliefs that such behaviour is morally unsound, it may simply be due to the absence of opportunity.

Also, and importantly, selling particular drugs – namely crack, heroin and cannabis – was an activity that seemed to occur amongst a greater proportion of young black men in Lambeth (Ruggiero and South 1995). Local crime statistics show that, for instance, between 2000 and 2002, the overwhelming majority of people accused of 'drug trafficking' were black. During this time, roughly twice as many black people as white were accused of selling drugs.[8] Whether this reflected differential policing is open to debate. Nonetheless, it could be the case that young black men in the borough, like Marc, Tolu and Sonny, were afforded greater opportunities to sell drugs such as crack, cannabis and heroin 'on the street' over young white men (Ruggiero and South 1995).

Marc and Tolu said that they sold heroin and/or crack, and Marc, Sonny and Quentin said they sold cannabis. In the first section I focus on Marc and Tolu's views of selling drugs, which is presented as their 'job', with parallels with the principles of conventional employment. In the second section I examine the incentives for and ways that Sonny and Quentin sold cannabis, patterns very different from Marc and Tolu's activities.

Selling crack and heroin

Several researchers noted how young people who sell drugs view this as a principal form of 'employment' or 'enterprise' (for example Anderson 1990; Bourgois 1995; Hagedorn 1988; Moore 1991; Padilla 1992; Robins 1992; Ruggiero and South 1995; Taylor 1989; Williams 1989). Padilla (1992) said that 'the Diamonds' – a group of young people who sold crack – used the language of work to describe selling drugs. Tolu and Marc did the same. Tolu, for instance, talked about how selling heroin was his 'job' and said that he 'worked' for 'the boss'. Marc called selling crack or heroin a 'business' and that when he sells drugs he is 'working'. Norma, a detached youth worker from Brixton, also talked about selling heroin as the young men's 'job', and those who purchase heroin as 'customers'. Furthermore, Marc and Tolu said they 'work' at selling crack or heroin five days a week, much like someone else at a 'conventional' occupation. Such principles essentially 'mirror the demands of legal enterprise' (Ruggiero and South 1995: 126).

The crack and heroin drug economies in Lambeth are massive enterprises, with people working at various levels of distribution (such as street-level dealers and those who supply them; see Ruggiero and South 1995). A hierarchy of command exists, much like a 'normal' business. Within this business Marc and Tolu play small roles. For instance, if selling crack or heroin were a fast-food business, Marc and Tolu would be taking orders at the till in one of the franchises. Anderson (1990: 244) previously made a similar comparison when he said that 'the drug economy is in many ways a parallel, or a parody of the service industry (with an element of glamour thrown in)'. Indeed, the metaphor of 'serving' or 'serving up' was used in the world of these young people, which refers to selling drugs. And like those that sell burgers and fries, street-level crack and heroin dealers, such as Marc and Tolu, are expendable and easily replaceable (Ruggiero and South 1995).

Selling drugs for Marc and Tolu was more profitable than burglary, robbery or theft (Fagan 1996; Robins 1992; Ruggiero and South 1995; Taylor 1989). The money made from selling drugs was enough for them to buy the items they desired, and neither of them committed other acquisitive offences when they sold drugs.

Marc estimated he sold £600-worth of heroin or crack every day, and was paid £150 a week for this. Tolu mentioned making 'about £500 a month' from selling £100-worth of heroin every day on the streets around the skatepark connecting Stockwell and Brixton. Tolu said selling heroin was 'easy money'.

Both Marc and Tolu said they played a small part in a larger 'business'. These two were given heroin or crack, told to go and sell it and then bring a specific amount of money back. Without their friends who supplied them with crack and/ or heroin, Marc and Tolu would not have had the opportunity to sell the drugs. Tolu, when comparing his position to that of his friends who sold heroin, said, 'I wasn't really as deep as them'. Marc also mentioned how he became involved in the street distribution end of selling crack and heroin:

> It's like, it wasn't my business. It was their business, you get me? I'm just working for them … They just give me [the crack or heroin], and say cut it out [weigh it up], you get me?

Marc, however, 'cut out' crack and heroin in a different way from his other friends who sold drugs. He and the others were told by those who supplied them to sell the crack or heroin in £20 bags containing 0.4 g. In a move to maximise profits with the amount of drugs he was given, Marc 'skanks' by offering the users less product for the same price, and sells what he called 'shorts'. Through doing this Marc earns an extra £150 a week, bringing his total profits to £300.

> But [my friends] don't know that, see? When the cats come, they [the bags of crack or heroin] come in shorts. Like, they come up with the £20 and you say, 'Blam, they're shorts', y'get me? I just take my money out of that. I just don't let them know that I would skank [steal] around the same, around £150 a week, but only £150 they would know about.

Aside from weighing the drugs and being told what prices to ask for them, Marc and Tolu did not talk about being trained or told how to sell crack and/or heroin. Rather, their initiation into selling crack or heroin on the street was a baptism of fire. These young men taught themselves certain skills associated with selling illicit drugs on the street. For instance, while dealing on the street Marc and Tolu needed to 'watch their backs' from police, and make sure not to get caught with several bags of crack or heroin on them. Tolu did this by not carrying the wraps of heroin on him at all times. Rather he hid them in a 'little hiding space'. Also, with all the money and crack or heroin they had on them, the possibility of being robbed by older, physically larger drug sellers or desperate addicts in need of a 'fix' looms. However, Tolu said roughly the same people approached him for heroin in Stockwell, and never troubled him. Considering Tolu is about 6'2" (1.88 m) and probably weighed 14 stones (89 kg), he would make a good adversary to anyone attempting to attack him.

Marc, on the other hand, was smaller. He was about 5'8" (1.73 m) and maybe weighed 10 stones (64 kg). Marc, however, did not sell drugs on the street. Rather, he had the users call him on his mobile phone. Norma, a detached youth worker, also mentioned the young men she worked with were selling heroin the same way. For Marc, selling heroin on the phone minimised the dangers in street level dealing, such as being arrested or robbed. He said:

> Yeah, all I have to do is when the phone rings, just meet them. So, I just go to them, get the money, and go.

Despite their involvement in selling, neither Marc nor Tolu used crack or heroin, and as we have already seen were dismissive of users, calling them 'cats'. Taylor (1989: 97) noted a similar stance for members of 'corporate gangs' in Detroit when he said, 'The no-drug use rule of corporate gangs is a serious, mature, business-based rule' (see also Fagan 1996). Like some of the other young people, Marc and Tolu frowned upon crack and heroin use and users. These two have had numerous encounters and dealings with crack and heroin addicts and have consistently witnessed the ill effects of habitual crack and heroin use. They dislike crack and heroin and those who use such drugs.

On the surface, there appeared to be something of a paradox in their value system: selling crack or heroin was acceptable, but using it negatively stigmatised. However, for Marc and Tolu, the distinction between using and selling crack and heroin was clear enough. Selling was viewed as a legitimate economic activity; using was foolish. This consideration made by these young people is significant, and suggests even those in my sample who sold 'hard' drugs had qualms about their use. This suggests that, once again, very fine distinctions were made by young people in my sample, in this case relating to illicit drugs.

Marc and Tolu were (and perhaps still are) making fairly large amounts of money for young people of their age and experience, and did this, apparently, with relative ease. They possess the connections, the know-how and the demand. More than anything, these two have profited from selling drugs, and may come to find that stopping all of this may be very difficult. For instance, others have noted that young people's involvement in the legitimate labour market is crucial in their desistance from offending (for example McGahey 1986; Pitts 1999; Sullivan 1989). However, Marc and Tolu mentioned not wanting to participate in this labour market. Marc is attending an off-site education unit in order to 'keep mum happy, init?', and that when he gets older he will 'do crime, init?' in order to earn money. At the time of the interview, Marc said he stopped selling crack and heroin because he got caught with a couple of bags of 'shorts'.

> *Did you ever realise how much time you could do getting caught?*
> That's what I'm saying, man. Because I was young, I knew I could get away with it, you get me? I did. I got nicked. I didn't go to jail, you get me? But I stopped now, init?

Tolu was still selling heroin, even though he said he stopped prior to the interview. Nonetheless, I have seen Tolu at the skatepark several times since our interview. He said he completed school and does not attend college. He also said he still sells heroin, but now also has others 'working' for him, and a couple of times at the skatepark, I witnessed younger guys on their mountain bikes make 'exchanges' with Tolu. For Tolu, the money to be made through heroin is much greater than any other job he could get based on his skills. He could be doing this for some time, as long as he does not get caught. Whether or not Marc desisted from selling heroin and crack is uncertain; the interview was the last time we spoke. Marc mentioned selling cannabis to make money. For both of these young people the opportunity to make considerable amounts of money selling crack or heroin was within their grasp. Opportunities to make comparable amounts of money in the legitimate labour market, on the other hand, were not as available for them, nor did they express they wished to make money this way. Furthermore, these two have not invested much time into ways of making money other than selling crack and heroin. Thus, they may come to consider selling drugs as their 'job', not only because this 'job' is the most profitable and readily available way for them to make money, but also the most feasible way to do so.

Selling cannabis

Marc, Quentin and Sonny were the only ones who said they sold (or still sell) cannabis. Again, this suggests those in my sample have two very different ideas of what it means to use this drug and what it means to sell it. While they apparently have no problem smoking weed, selling was a completely different story, as only 3 of the 31 in my sample did this. Within the worldview of these young people, sharp distinctions emerged between selling and using weed.

The three young people sold cannabis for different ways and different reasons. Quentin and Sonny discussed similar experiences and incentives, yet how and why they sold were significantly different from Marc and Tolu's operations. Marc, for instance, sold skunk cannabis much like he did crack and heroin: to others who called him on his mobile phone. He said he can buy an ounce (28 g) of cannabis for £130 from one of a number of people he knew. As Marc said, 'There is bear [a lot of] people that sell weed around this area'. Marc sold skunk in increments of £5, £10, £20 or 'anything you want'. For £10 Marc offered a twentieth of an ounce (1.4 g) of skunk, which he considered a 'much better deal' when compared to the others he knows who sold cannabis. He said his prices were more competitive.

Marc smokes skunk on a daily basis, and by selling it he reduces the amount he pays for it. However, Marc also mentioned saving up money earned from selling cannabis towards buying things he wanted. In order to do this, Marc sells cannabis 'every day, man'. He replaced selling crack and heroin with selling cannabis in order to achieve his objectives. Selling cannabis is his 'job', and he uses business-like practices in order to maximise his profits. Below he discussed how he recycles profits from cannabis sales into buying more cannabis, which, in turn, increases his profit potential:

> I'm on around two ounces and a half now [70 g]. Like, I don't spend nothing [any of the money made from selling cannabis]. [I] wait to like it's up to [I have

earned enough to buy] around three ounces – four ounces [84–112 g]. Then started spending [the money on those ounces]. [I] Go back down to an ounce [sell all but one ounce], spend all the money [earned from the cannabis on more cannabis], and then start off at an ounce [28 g] again [sell everything except an ounce]. I want to get my moped, you get me?

Quentin and Sonny discussed selling cannabis in different ways and for different purposes. The first time Quentin sold cannabis was when he traded a stolen laptop computer and a mobile phone for a half-ounce (14 g) of 'bush green'. Currently, he occasionally buys half an ounce of 'bush' cannabis for £40, and sells it for £5 for a 1 g bag and £10 for a 2 g bag. Quentin explained he sold cannabis in order to 'keep me smoking', and possibly to turn over a small profit. He elaborated:

Sometimes I smoke a little bit and then sell a little bit, but if I got a certain amount of money in my pocket and I want to spend a certain amount on herb [cannabis] then I buy that certain amount and still be selling, but at the same time smoking. But I'm not watching the profit, while at the same time while I'm doing whatever I'm doing. The profits are going to help my pocket, y'knowhatimsaying? Cuz I might go to a little party or a club or whatever. I got whatever in my pocket. So, if I get this and that I can sell this and that.

Sonny said he sold skunk and 'regular weed' a couple of times before, and did this because it gave him some cannabis to smoke, and 'to make a little profit'. While both Sonny and Quentin said they spent their money on fast food or raving or other small personal items, they discussed selling smaller amounts of cannabis in comparison to Marc. Marc's example of selling cannabis was much more systematic and mechanical, while Sonny and Quentin only sold cannabis from time to time. Furthermore, Sonny and Quentin did not interpret selling cannabis as their 'job'; they put little effort into 'serving up'.

Whereas Marc said he sold cannabis daily and ounces weekly, Sonny said he might have sold a couple of ounces in his lifetime, and Quentin said he occasionally sold bush weed, a less expensive cannabis. Also, Marc had a larger clientele who asked for cannabis. On the other hand, Sonny and Quentin said they *only* sold to others they knew, which turned out to be a select few. Their relationship with those they sold cannabis to was very different from that between Marc and those he sold drugs to. Quentin talked about selling cannabis to 'people that I know':

Who do you sell to?
It's mainly people that I know or people that I don't know is more of a like it depends on what circumstance that I'm, yeah, who I sell to.
Do you go out on the street?
No, no. I don't go hustling out there on the street. I hustle people that I know.

Sonny also commented on how he only sold cannabis to his friends or others he knew:

You only sell it to your own [friends]. Somebody [a friend] would just come up to you and say, 'Do you have anything?', and you say, 'Yeah. I got this.' They hand you the money.

The way Quentin and Sonny sold cannabis was much less risky than the way that Marc and Tolu sold drugs. The penalties for possession with intent to supply cannabis are less than for Class A drugs, such as crack and heroin.[9] Quentin and Sonny said they only sold cannabis to those they personally knew, and were not as visible as the young crack and heroin sellers. They sold cannabis 'behind closed doors'. This limited the possibility of them being caught by the police or robbed by others on the street. While Quentin and Sonny did not take as extreme risks selling cannabis as Marc and Tolu did selling crack and heroin, they also did not make as much money as these two. However, for Quentin and Sonny, making money selling cannabis was only part of their plan. They also expressed how selling cannabis allowed them to use it for 'free'.

Conclusions

In this chapter I attempted to tease out some of the distinctions in attitudes towards, and uses of, illicit drugs by the young people in the study. First, cannabis was easily the most popular drug used by them. Those more involved in offending, in the main, used cannabis on a more frequent basis when compared to the others, which was partly bound up in their involvement in acquisitive offences; ill-received money from such offences went towards skunk. Cannabis was not used as frequently amongst those less involved in offending. Overall, though, occasional, frequent or experimental use of cannabis by any of the young people was almost to be expected. In fact, I argued that cannabis use was somewhat 'normalised' amongst them, and to a lesser extent it appeared to be within Lambeth. This hinged on the large number of young people who said they tried it, the routine behaviour that accompanied their use of cannabis, the saturation of popular youth culture by cannabis-related references, the unanimous belief held by the professionals about the popularity of cannabis amongst young people they worked with in Lambeth, and the overall lack of stigmatisation of the drug within the borough.

And while cannabis use was acceptable amongst almost everyone in my sample, I suggested a different story for other drugs. The use of 'hard' Class A drugs, such as cocaine, crack and heroin, was condemned by almost everyone in my sample, and some went so far as to negatively stigmatise users. This suggests that these young people, and perhaps others with similar backgrounds in Lambeth, made concrete divisions between using cannabis and using other drugs, particularly crack and heroin. Within the moral universes of these young people, finely tuned attitudes emerged regarding the acceptability of different illicit drugs.

Likewise, I suggested these young people made huge distinctions between using and selling drugs. Only 4 out of the 31 of them said they sold drugs at some time. This, again, highlights the point that these young people's values regarding their illicit or illegal behaviour, in this case that which may generally be considered 'drug-related' behaviour, were extraordinarily and, perhaps at times, unexpectedly differentiated. In this case using drugs was generally acceptable, but selling was out of the question for most. And while this may be an ethical consideration, a 'moral' stance against selling drugs, the small number of young people in my sample who had sold drugs may be related to the differential opportunity to do so in the first place. Unlike offences such as shoplifting, robbery and burglary – offences that pretty much anyone could participate in – selling drugs requires the right connections, many of which those in my sample did not seem to have established.

In the final section of the chapter I suggested two distinct ways and reasons *why* four young people sold drugs. Marc and Tolu sold crack, heroin and/or cannabis, and made considerable amounts of money doing so. They hustled drugs on the street, using business-like calculations, saving their capital and building up their 'overhead'. These entrepreneurs occupied (and perhaps still occupy) a tenuous and dangerous position within the illegal drugs market, and they placed themselves at great risks to sell crack and heroin. To them, selling drugs was their 'job'. On the other hand Sonny and Quentin *only* occasionally sold small amounts of cannabis to those they knew, such as their friends who, like them, smoked weed. Unlike Marc and Tolu, these two primarily sold cannabis in order to use it without having to pay for it, and perhaps make some pocket-money. Sonny and Quentin did not take the great risks, nor generate the fat returns that Marc and Tolu did. For Sonny and Quentin, selling cannabis was something done 'on the side', and not a central activity within their lives.

5   Graffiti, joyriding, vandalism

What purpose does graffiti serve? Why do young people destroy public property? Do they joyride for any practical reason? This chapter aims to answer these questions by examining the young people's 'expressive' offences, or their non-violent, non-acquisitive offences, such as graffiti, joyriding and vandalism. The analyses focus on incentives, frequency, significance and the situational context in which these acts occurred. Patterns are sought between these themes and the different young people. The first section looks at the young people's graffiti and partially relates this to an appreciation of elements within hip-hop culture. The second section explores their vandalism and joyriding within the context of 'looking for something to do' in working- or lower-class environments. Finally, I attempt to explain *why* the young people committed their expressive offences by considering issues of masculinity and leisure.

Tagging and hip-hop art

Graffiti tags litter Lambeth. A tag (short for 'name tag') is the nickname or street name of a young person, quickly written with pens, markers or cans of spray paint. The tags observed were barely legible street names, at times accompanied by punctuation marks, stars and other symbols. In my sample only a couple of young people occasionally tagged their name, but some patterns emerged. For instance, three of those more involved in offending said they *still* tagged their name, whereas the others said they only tagged occasionally when 'younger'. Nevertheless, all of the young people who tagged attributed little significance to this: it was just a way of saying 'I have been here' (Barker and Bridgeman 1994; Klein 1995; Phillips 1999), and, to a lesser extent, of expressing their involvement in hip-hop culture (Coffield 1991; Ferrell 1993, 1995; Geason and Wilson 1990; MacDonald 2001; Phillips 1999).

Not much large, developed and detailed graffiti 'art' was observed in Lambeth. A notable and significant difference exists between the style and effort involved in this graffiti in comparison to the simple tags. Several researchers have noticed how young people distinguish between tagging and graffiti 'pieces' (short for 'masterpiece'), which have also been affectionately referred to as 'hip-hop art', 'hip-hop graffiti' and 'spray-can art' (Coffield 1991; Ferrell 1993, 1995; Geason and Wilson

1990; MacDonald 2001; Phillips 1999). Whereas the small, monotone tags were drawn rapidly, the graffiti art observed obviously took much more time to produce, some drawn with several colours, giving the graffiti a three-dimensional appearance. Larger graffiti art in Lambeth covered entire walls, and was easy on the eye. And where graffiti art was not as readily observed as tags were in the borough, so too was this a rare talent within my sample. Only one, Kenny, said he created graffiti art. For Kenny, designing this graffiti was significant because it allowed him a chance to express himself artistically, and by doing this he believed vacant space was transformed into urban aesthetic (Ferrell 1993; Geason and Wilson 1990).

Tagging your street name just because

While many of the young people interviewed had street names, only a small number, 8 out of 31, said they tagged their name, and an additional one did this and created graffiti art (see Table 5.1). Street names of these young people were generated in three distinct ways: something derived from their physical appearance ('Speck', 'Shorty', 'Jesus', 'Hi-Top'), something about their personal habits, tendencies or attributes ('Ninja', 'Cisco', 'Rhino', 'Lyrical') or something due simply to their preference ('Verb', 'Dread', 'Thug', 'Assasin';[1] see Schneider 1999; Vigil 1988). The street names were either adopted by the young people themselves, or applied to them by friends or family members, sometimes as a way to 'take the piss', something mentioned in interviews. For instance, Kwame, a youth and community worker from Brixton, discussed the origin of street names:

> Basically, you'll see something about a person, and you'll take the piss out of that person. It might stick, or it just happens, rather than some person trying to give themselves [a street name].

Most of the young people only offered short responses when asked about the origin of their street names, and in some of these cases only a short response was necessary.

For instance, Brian said he 'looked like' Jesus, Theo 'used to drink Cisco[2] all the time', and Nathan 'just likes the name [Assasin]'. One of the more elaborate explanations of a street name's origin came from Martin who is also called 'Joker'. Martin said his friends called him this because:

> I don't joke because if I say, 'Oh, I'm gonna climb in through the window' and they go, 'Oh, you are only joking'. And then I'm gonna climb into the window. I go on to go rob that car, and they go, 'Oh, you're a joker'. And I'll go rob the car.

Many of the young people interviewed had street names, but such names were not consistently used, and in some cases changed. For instance, Norman is known as 'Nugget' or 'Skunks', as he said, 'sometimes'. Tolu is 'Verb', but his friend Kellen thought his street name was 'Conniver'. Larry is known as 'Speck', 'Tich',

Table 5.1 Reported street names, type and frequency of graffiti by offending category

	Age	Street name	Frequency of graffiti
Severe			
Sonny	14	Steamer	
Quentin	17	(None)	
Travis	18	Dread	Tagged his name daily when younger
Marc	15	Thug	
Tolu	15	Verb/Conniver	Tagged his name several times before
Karl	14	(None)	
Heavy			
Martin	16	Joker	
Noel	15	Quest	
Tom	16	(None)	
Kenny	15	MC Lyrical	Tags his name daily. Also does graffiti 'art'
Norman	15	Nuggets/Skunks	Tags his name 'sometimes'
Theo	20	Cisco	
Keenan	15	Shorty	
Nathan	16	Assasin	Tags his name 'wherever we go'
Lenny	23	Hi-Top/Gangsta	
Moderates			
David	14	Ninja	
Kevin	15	Snakes	Tags when 'buzzing' on cannabis and alcohol
Todd	14	Envious	
Larry	15	Speck/Tich/Inches/Lil'L	Tags 'everywhere'
Brian	22	Jesus/Rimmer	
Darrell	16	(None)	
Jack	15	Rhino	
Terry	15	(None)	
Dabblers			
Betty	16	(None)	Tagged 'sometimes'[a]
Frank	13	(None)	
Kellen	15	Sly	Tagged 'sometimes'
Winnona	15	Rage	
Eric	16	Sparks	
Isaac	17	Congo	
Tracy	15	(None)	
Tim	16	(None)	

Note

a   Betty said she only tagged her real name a couple of times, while the others said they tagged their street name more times than they could remember.

'Inches' or 'Lil' L'. Terry also said his friends' tags 'are always changing. It's not something they were really into. They change sporadically.' According to interviews with professionals, this behaviour was typical of other young people from similar backgrounds in Lambeth. For instance, Tex, a youth justice worker, talked about how the street names would 'stick for a couple of months, and then it would be something else'.

Nine young people tagged their street names, but Betty tagged her real one. From analysing the incentives, context and overall significance of all of their tagging, a couple of patterns emerged. First, the tags were spontaneous acts completed quickly, perhaps taking less than a minute, and done alone or with a couple of friends. Also, the young people 'didn't go out of their way' to tag, and tagged walls, fences, utility boxes, and even the ground, en route to normal, daily activity. This is not to suggest they left their houses with neither the intentions nor tools to tag; rather, no evidence emerged to indicate they pre-selected specific targets. Finally, young people's reasons as to why they tagged their names were vague, at times seeming wanton and hedonistic because they expressed that tagging did not serve any tangible purpose. When asked why they tagged (or still tag) their name, all of them said either 'I don't know', 'because there was nothing to do' or 'to let others know I was there', reasons, interestingly enough, noted by other researchers (such as Barker and Bridgeman 1994; Klein 1995; Phillips 1999). For instance, Phillips (1999: 318) argued that:

> Tags are not so different from other types of popular graffiti, calling back the insignia of various ages from 'Ivan wrote this' to 'Kilroy was here'.

According to the young people in my sample who tagged, the functions of their tags were 'expressive', not instrumental. For instance, Betty and Kellen said they tagged their names 'sometimes'. Betty said she 'didn't know' why she tagged her real name, and Kellen tagged 'Sly' in 'some places … letting people know it's me, y'know?' Kevin and Larry also said they tagged. Kevin said he and his friends tagged their names in an empty block of flats near his home when 'there's nothing happening, nothing doing at all. No one's making no jokes. We just like, do anything.' Larry said he tagged one of his aliases, Speck, Tich, Inches or Lil' L 'everywhere' in order 'To show the people. To let others know.' Larry continued:

> [We tag] whenever we got spray pens in our hands. We never go out of our way to tag, if you know what I'm saying? Yeah, whenever we see something there we just go and tag it.

Three of those more involved in offending – Nathan, Norman and Kenny – said they tagged their name in more places and at a greater frequency when compared to the others. Furthermore, these young people said they *still* tagged their name, whereas the others in my sample mentioned not tagging any more. While Norman said, 'I tag in some places. I don't go out of my way to tag', Nathan talked about tagging his name 'wherever we go' and continued by offering a reason why he does this: 'It's like dogs peeing. You leave your mark, and that you've been there, init?'

Kenny mentioned similar reasons as the others when he tagged because 'you just gotta put your name about'. However, as will be explored shortly, Kenny was much more involved in graffiti. He tagged all the time, and will 'probably do a couple' after his interview finishes. Kenny showed me the large pens and markers he carries on him and tags with, which were much easier to conceal than the larger, bulky cans of spray paint (Ferrell 1993).

Two others more involved in offending, Tolu and Travis, like the other taggers, said something to the extent that they tagged for no other reason other than 'to put their name up'. For instance, Travis, 17, whose tag was 'Dread', said he once went out with his friends ACME, Crow and Drop around 'his manor' in Waterloo when 15 and 16, and tagged with spray paint. Likewise, Tolu, who was 15 at the time of the interview, said he once did some 'tagging on the wall' near his home, but that this was a couple of years ago. With the exception of Kenny, Nathan and Norman, tagging by the young people was something done when 'younger'. No one in my sample over 16 said they tagged their name, and most of the young people observed tagging at the skatepark looked in their early to mid-teens. In Lambeth it seemed that, even by 'young people's' standards, tagging was, for the most part, done by 'younger people'.

The graffiti observed in Lambeth, and, indeed, elsewhere in London, were completely dissimilar to US gang graffiti. Gang members, tagger crews and 'wallbangers' in the US use graffiti tagging to mark out their territory and/or to threaten rival gangs and other taggers (Klein 1995; Padilla 1992; Phillips 1999; Sanders 1994; Schneider 1999; Spergel 1995; Vigil 1988). Padilla (1992: 2), for instance, noted how:

> The most prominent method for communicating or displaying … symbols of gang cultural identification is through graffiti art painted on walls of buildings and car garages through the neighbourhood.

In my home town of North County, San Diego some North Side Bloods tagged 'NSB' and their street names in various places, or crossed out the names of rival gang members as a show of disrespect or as a way to advertise that individual was going to be attacked. The tagging by the young people in my sample was *nothing* like this at all, nor were any other 'gang-like' tags or graffiti observed in Lambeth, or throughout the city for that matter. Moreover, I specifically asked about the significance of graffiti tags and none of the young people or professionals interviewed mentioned tags in Lambeth being used to warn outsiders of entering a 'controlled' territory or as a way to communicate. And even while Nathan likened his tagging to 'dogs peeing' and thus marking territory, his tags did not serve to outline any particular area he considered 'his'.

Another reason the young people tagged (or still tag) their street names was, in part, due to their appreciation of hip-hop. Hip-hop is not just a genre of music, but also a culture complete with a distinct style, slang and other insignias, such as emceeing (rapping and singing), beat boxing (using your voice and body to imitate musical instruments) and break dancing (flips, spins and a variety of dance floor moves). Graffiti is another aspect of hip-hop culture. As such, one of the reasons those in my sample tagged may have been partially related to a desire to participate in this dimension of hip-hop culture (Ferrell 1993, 1995; Geason and Wilson 1990; Klein 1995; MacDonald 2001; Phillips 1999). Youthful cultural indicators include music, style and language (Brake 1985; Ferrell and Sanders 1995; Hebdige 1979). Tagging is an additional indicator of hip-hop culture. Along with listening to the music, wearing the clothing that the rappers are rapping about and using the language of hip-hop, the nine young people advertised their entrenchment in hip-hop culture by tagging their names.

Music, style, slang and tagging are all interrelated aspects of hip-hop culture. The more someone appropriates items and symbols associated with a culture, the more they express to others and themselves their 'belonging' to it. However, cultural particulars of youthful cultures have a tendency to die out, move on and evolve. For instance, where have all the DA haircuts and Edwardian suits of the teddy boys, the long hair, flowers and peace symbols of the hippies, and the over-sized white gloves and happy face signs of the early UK ravers gone?[3] These past fashions are primarily associated with youthful cultures from yesteryear. In this regard, tagging could be nothing more than a passing fad connected with a currently popular youth culture. This may also help explain why many of the taggers in my sample, even at ages 15 or 16, said tagging was something that occurred in their past. Maybe they grew out of tagging.

On a final note, generally speaking, graffiti was not an offence those in my sample really participated in. Less than a third of them tagged their names, and most of them attributed little, if any, significance to this. For the most part, tagging was discussed as something they 'just did' when 'younger', and was not considered a big deal. The young people who tagged are, like those who have not used any drugs, those who have used drugs other than cannabis, and those who sell drugs, a significant minority within my sample. So why is this? Why were only a few of these young people marginally and temporarily involved in tagging? What seems to be the case is that there appeared to be some sort of hierarchy of 'respect' the young people attributed to different offences. For instance, smoking weed was considered 'cool', but using other drugs, in the main, was not. In a similar vein these young people may have thought that tagging was something superfluous, something they were not 'into', something that was not 'cool', nor something they found 'fun'. In this sense tagging seemed to serve little purpose. The lack of tagging amongst these young people may be related to its lack of appeal and the fact that nothing seemed to come out of it other than 'letting others know I was there'. This suggests the young people's attitudes towards various offences contrasted sharply, and that some illegal behaviours were acceptable but others were not.

Graffiti as art

Graffiti art is in a completely different category from graffiti tags. Artistic graffiti is appreciated by a broad audience in many countries (Coffield 1991; Ferrell 1993, 1995; Geason and Wilson 1990; MacDonald 2001; Phillips 1999). I observed beautiful graffiti murals in US cities, such as San Diego, Los Angeles, San Francisco and New York, as well as European ones, such as Lisbon, Bilbao and, of course, London. Also, specialist magazines, such as *Graphotism*, dedicate their pages to pictures of stylistic, well-crafted graffiti from the USA, UK and other countries around the world. Whereas tags are seen more as eyesores, 'the colour, humour and vibrancy of some graffiti art have successfully titivated some dark and ugly corners' (Coffield 1991: 62). This appreciation, along with the obvious skill involved, in part, elevates this type of graffiti to the level of 'art'.

In Lambeth tags are relatively easy to find, but graffiti art was only found in some areas. For instance, the chest-high brick walls and smooth surfaced transitions in the skatepark were splashed with graffiti art. A playground in Camberwell once had an entire wall covered with a detailed spray-painted mural of Bob Marley. Also, some of the high-street stores in Lambeth had their security shutters decorated with graffiti art, something I observed elsewhere in London. Graffiti art is not the quickly scrawled tags that litter public and private property. On the contrary, graffiti art is appreciated by a wide audience, but only constructed by a select few proficient designers. This point was confirmed by Wendy, a NACRO worker, when she said that many of the young people in Lambeth she worked with 'like the quality pictures, but they're not particularly skilled to do that'.

Indeed, only one young person in my sample, Kenny, said he created artistic graffiti. Kenny was much more involved in graffiti than anyone else interviewed, and was even arrested for graffiti a couple of times. Aside from designing larger graffiti pieces, Kenny said he frequently tagged his street name 'Lyrical' in a variety of places. Even during the interview, he mentioned how 'I got my pens with me. When I walk home, I'll probably do a couple then.'

Several of Kenny's friends were also graffiti taggers and artists. Creating graffiti was much more significant for Kenny and his graffiti buddies when compared to the others in my sample. For Kenny, tags served as 'stylised markers ... components of written social interaction and identities' (Ferrell 1993: 58). He talked about knowing the tags of other young graffiti taggers in London, and how several of them tag on trains, a practice observed in other countries (Coffield 1991; Ferrell 1995; Geason and Wilson 1990; Phillips 1999). To be sure, at the time of writing (2003), travelling on any of London's trains and not noticing at least one tag is difficult. According to Kenny, many taggers have their own train, and he mentioned putting his tag on a train already tagged by someone he knows would be wrong. Kenny elaborated:

> These are the boys that travel around on the trains. They got their own line. Everyone has their own line going over London where they put all their grafs [tags]. And if I see them, like there's hundreds and hundreds of lines, but if I go on a line and see loads of dubs of Bonk [Kenny's friend's tag] I wouldn't bother doing that there cuz I know that's his line. So you just go on a train and find out where there's no, where it's pretty clear.

Kenny continued by telling me occasionally no time exists to properly scrawl his tag. When such occasions arise, Kenny said he draws his 'dub face', which is akin to 'throw ups' or quickly written graffiti tags and/or symbols, apparently common practices amongst graffiti artists elsewhere (Ferrell 1993; MacDonald 2001; Phillips 1999). Kenny explained what a 'dub face' was:

> Usually, it's just like a face that you can do really quick. Just to go up with your tag. So say if you ain't got time to put your tag up, you quickly put [the dub face] up and people know that it's you, y'know what I mean?

Aside from tags and dub faces, Kenny talked about spending 'hours' on his artistic graffiti, especially the big ones he created that might 'stay there for years'. He continued by explaining how his larger graffiti pieces were sometimes a collaborative effort involving several of his friends where they 'get some draw', and turn the creation of their 'graf' into a small social event. Doing these things was important to Kenny:

> I feel good after I have done it because I can stand back and look at it and say, 'I've spent hours on that. There's a chance that it's going stay there for years.' The cleaners, they're not bothered cleaning anything like that, but when they paint over it, I feel gutted.

Kenny's goal of designing graffiti art on the street was not one of malice. Kenny is not a vandal in this sense, but more an artist. Phillips (1999: 310) noted a similar point on graffiti artists when she suggested:

> it is not the main goal of hip-hop graffiti writers to destroy. People write hip-hop graffiti to represent themselves within an arena of hip-hop graffiti writers; they work to establish a name and position within that arena for reasons that are addictive and positive. Hip-hop graffiti is about creation, not destruction … Vandalism is what they wind up doing during the course of their work, but their main goal is generally not that of the vandal.

Kenny would feel 'gutted' if his 'grafs' were destroyed. For him, graffiti art was a significant outlet for his artistic expression, and an opportunity to turn a relatively mundane and unused part of his environment into an urban masterpiece. As Geason and Wilson (1990: 8) noticed, graffiti art 'can look better than what it covers up'. I think the graffiti art in Lambeth, to paraphrase Coffield (1991), has certainly 'titivated some ugly dark corners', and has made things simply look better. Moreover, in Lambeth, some of the larger graffiti art has not been removed by the cleaners, or tagged over by other young people, suggesting, in part, they attributed a certain respect to it by leaving it alone. This also suggests that, to an extent, graffiti art in Lambeth in general was respected and appreciated. For Kenny it certainly was, more so than anyone else in my sample, for, while others may share his love of graffiti art, Kenny was the only one in my sample, and perhaps one of a small handful in Lambeth, who was capable of producing such work. This graffiti was important in his life.

Joyriding and vandalism

Joyriding is essentially the theft of a motor vehicle committed simply in order to drive it around. Some patterns emerged between the frequency and significance of joyriding amongst the young people. More than half of those more involved in offending said they joyrode before, and several were still doing this. By contrast about a third of those less involved mentioned doing this in the past or continuing to do so. Regardless of frequency, joyriding provided these young people with 'free' entertainment. Joyriding was not something done out of malice, but because these young people were looking for something 'to do' (Campbell 1993; Downes 1966; Presdee 1994). For those who joyride there appeared to be a code the young people followed in terms of how far they were willing to let this offence go. For instance, almost all of the joyriders said they just dumped the vehicle when they were finished with it. Only a few of those more involved in offending mentioned doing other things with the vehicles they joyrode.

Interestingly enough, only a few young people discussed vandalism, a peculiarity which may be explained by the approach taken in the research. As previously discussed, the young people, particularly those more involved in offending, may have thought their involvement in serious offences overshadowed the importance of vandalism, and thus did not talk about it. They, however, were not prompted to do so. Nevertheless, some patterns emerged. For one, those more involved in offending who did vandalise property caused much more damage when compared to the others. Also, those arrested for vandalism were the only ones who expressed remorse. The rest said they 'didn't care'. Amongst those that vandalised, most said these things occurred when they were 'younger' (Flood-Page *et al.* 2000; Matza and Sykes 1961). Finally, for all of the young people who vandalised property, the decision to do this was spontaneous and opportunistic, and they primarily did such things with a couple of their friends for playful purposes (Barker and Bridgeman 1994; Cohen 1973; Corrigan 1979; Downes 1966; Geason and Wilson 1990; Matza and Sykes 1961; Miller 1958; NACRO 1989).

Joyriding for fun

According to interviews, joyriding, particularly mopeds, was an extremely popular activity in Lambeth. For instance, Kerry, a youth and community worker from Brixton, noted that joyriding mopeds, or to 'nick peds', 'seems to be the 'in' crime at the moment'. Quentin made similar comments when he said how joyriding mopeds 'used to be the "in" thing to do'. Indeed, joyriding was popular amongst my sample; about half of them said they had joyridden cars or mopeds, and some still did.

No major differences emerged between the young people in terms of frequency, context or incentive. Joyriding was discussed as a spontaneous activity these young people did with their friends. This is not to suggest the young people did not actively set out to find mopeds or cars to joyride, but rather such events had an air of opportunism to them in that the young people said they discovered or came across a moped or automobile they believed would be easy to start without the proper keys. Also, none of them expressed any remorse over stealing motor vehicles. They all said something to the extent of 'I don't care', and I genuinely got the impression these expressions were sincere. Finally, none of them talked about showing off the stolen vehicle to their friends in different parts of Lambeth or London, or about taking 'road trips'. Rather, these young people said they stayed around their immediate area, just 'drove around' until the petrol ran out and then dumped the vehicle. Keenan talked about joyriding.

> *What do you do with [the mopeds]?*
> We just ride them. Ride them all night. Most the time they get taken by the police. People that we stole them from call up the police and say this boy's on the moped over in this area.

I asked the young people how they started the motor vehicle. However, only two, David and Theo, mentioned knowing how to hot-wire cars or mopeds. The rest were with others who knew how to do this. For instance, Martin said:

> One of my mates, I'm not sure how he does it, but if we get in to the car, he'll do the rest. He'll hot wire it. I haven't the foggiest idea how to do it.

David and Theo, on the other hand, discussed being shown how to hot-wire cars, mopeds or motorbikes by friends, suggesting these skills were transferred by those 'in the know' (Gottfredson and Hirschi 1990; Hirschi 1969; Sutherland 1949; Sutherland *et al.* 1992). For instance, David, 14, who has been riding off-road motorcycles since he was seven, said he learned how to hot-wire motorbikes and mopeds from working as a motorcycle mechanic. Theo said he learned by 'watch[ing] my friends. I used to watch them when I was a little stealing boy.' He discussed his proficiency at breaking into cars and getting them started without the use of the car's proper keys:

> Bang off the door, get in there. No breaking nothing. We use a screwdriver for the whole job. You just bend the door back, unlatch it, bend the door back in the shape, pop off the dashboard. Bang! It depends on what car it is. If it's an old car or a new car we used to hot wire. Just hook the wires up to the ignition, starts, you are gone. Pop the steering lock, and you are gone. Or we used to do with the black box ones where you just go in, pop off under the thing, take off the black box, you get me? Pop the steering locks. The black box is one of those little things that you can just start. You can have your own key and put it in the starter and it would start. Simple as.

Not surprisingly, all of the young people said they joyrode because such behaviour was 'fun' (Campbell 1993; Downes 1966; Presdee 1994). For instance, Presdee (1994: 180) looked at joyriding in working-class areas, and said how this provided young people with 'a dramatic break from the boredom of being wageless and wealthless in a consumer society'. Likewise, Campbell (1993: 259) noted how young men stole and drove cars 'purely for pleasure; that was their only ideology and motivation'. Interviews with professionals confirmed that, for young people in Lambeth, joyriding counters routine boredom. For instance, Bill, a detective constable from Clapham, mentioned how joyriding 'pump[s] a little bit of adrenaline into a lot of those quite dull lives'. Fiona, a NACRO worker, said, 'mopeds, I would say [they get] a huge adrenaline rush'. Wendy, another NACRO worker, also commented on how much fun joyriding is for the young people she worked with:

> A lot of it's the thrill, that's for sure. They are classically trained young people who haven't succeeded in anything else. They're often bored beyond belief. They don't have any other sense of achievement or excitement anywhere else in their lives.

All of the young people interviewed said how much fun joyriding was and how it helped pass the time. For instance, David joyrode when he was 'bored' and he 'felt like a laugh'; Brian said 'I got a bit of a [adrenaline] rush out of it'; Martin, said he joyrode cars because 'it's boring really. We just have a laugh. Just for amusement'; Sonny said 'It's exciting. It's exhilarating to drive these things.' Theo talked about how much fun joyriding was:

> That was just fun! That was blatant joyride. I enjoyed that shit, you get me? I used to come check Andrew in my stolen car. We used to go for drives and shit … What was fun is the cars. We used to have fun. We used to have proper races. Bang up races! We used to have fun in the cars.

Noel, who estimated he stole anywhere between 60 and 70 cars, was akin to Campbell's (1993: 255) 'The Don' who 'got into cars because he simply loved driving'. For instance, Noel said:

> I just love cars. I love driving them … we just like drive them around and have a good laugh with them until the petrol runs out and just dump them.

Only one young person, Kevin, offered a reason for joyriding other than fun. Kevin said one time he and his mates stole a car so they could get home. This, too, was discussed as a spontaneous, opportunistic event, but this occasion had more practical purposes other than for pure amusement. Kevin explained:

> We nicked one other car as well. We proper nicked it. We walk up and we were stuck. We had no transport. It was about two in the morning and we was just walking and we saw a car – an old shitty car, a real old banger. And it had the key in the boot … so we flew in, grabbed the car and fucked off. We didn't do it deliberately. We just took it to get home, left it and that was it.

A distinction exists between a few of those more seriously involved in offending and the rest of my sample in terms of their behaviour when they joyrode vehicles or where the vehicles ended up. Nathan, for instance, stole mopeds on more occasions than he could remember. A couple of times he deliberately positioned himself in front of police cars in the hopes officers would chase him (Campbell 1993). During one of these incidents Nathan crashed a moped into some pavement bollards. When the police caught up with him, they arrested Nathan for stealing the moped, and charged him with several other offences related to trying to escape from the police on a motor vehicle, including reckless driving, endangering the lives of citizens, endangering the lives of police officers and others. After this incident Nathan explained how the whole ordeal was 'exciting'. Several professionals mentioned similar stories. For instance, Fiona, a NACRO worker, noted how young people she worked with wanted the police to chase them when joyriding:

> mopeds ... there's no way of basing their activities on something. So, the end of the scenario is that they run from the police.

Wendy, another NACRO worker, also noted how, for the young people she works with in Lambeth, 'To be chased [on a moped] by the police is the biggest thrill to them.'

Additionally, Martin, Nathan, Norman and Theo did not always simply abandon the cars and mopeds when they finished using them. Norman said he took the vehicle to a 'scrap yard' and exchanged it for cash. For Norman, joyriding was not only fun, but a profitable offence. Martin, Nathan and Theo spoke of setting fire to the cars or mopeds at times when they finished joyriding (Campbell 1993). Sometimes, these fires caused the vehicles to explode – exactly what the young people wanted to happen. For instance, Martin and Nathan both said how they placed a rag into the petrol tank of mopeds, set the rag alight and then waited for it to explode. Theo said he tossed lit fireworks into a car doused in petrol, and explained how this was 'big fun':

> You know what you were talking about earlier, about kids blowing up cars? We used to do that you know. We actually did it. We'd done it. We stole the car, revved it up, drove around and like when you get tired of it, like roll it around some back area and just doused it with petrol. And this must have been like fireworks day then times. So we put two rockets in it, closed up the windows, closed up the doors and it just went. Boom! It blew up everything. It was just like a proper film. Man, now that was fun. That was big fun.

But what kind of young person finds this activity fun? What do their interpretations of such events tell us about their values and how joyriding fitted in with the rest of their lives? Matza and Sykes (1961: 713–15) once asked 'What makes delinquency attractive in the first place?' The authors found many delinquents committed offences in pursuit of leisure, and suggested that as such, their values were similar to an aristocratic 'leisure class'. Overall, the authors suggested the value system of the delinquent is not necessarily deviant, but the way they expressed these values was. In other words, delinquents want to have fun just like anyone else, but sometimes end up breaking the law doing so. The same could be said about the young people interviewed and those in Lambeth with similar backgrounds who joyride. Where the 'leisure class' may be afforded the opportunity to buy their entertainment, the young people said how they spent nothing joyriding and blowing up the vehicles, which was 'exhilarating' and 'big fun'. Joyriding, blowing up mopeds and being chased by the police provided a brief rush of excitement from otherwise non-eventful times (Campbell 1993; Downes 1966; Presdee 1994, 2000). For instance, one of the respondents in Downes' study (1966: 203) noted 'We [joyride] for enjoyment, you know. There's nothing else to do around here'. Essentially, joyriding provided free entertainment for the young people, who did not necessarily view this activity as being harmful to others, but rather titillating for themselves. In this regard, that young people in Lambeth with not much money turn to joyriding to entertain themselves should be of little wonder. And, perhaps not surprisingly, none of the joyriders expressed remorse when they stole cars or mopeds, drove them around until their petrol ran out, and abandoned them when finished or set fire to them. For them, joyriding appeared to be acceptable behaviour.

The acceptability of committing these 'fun-generating' offences may be related to the general attitude within the community regarding them. Other researchers have noted the relationship between expressive offences, leisure and the parent-culture of the young people (for example Corrigan 1979; Downes 1966; Miller 1958). For instance, Miller (1958: 6) noted how 'lower-class delinquency' is characterised by a set of 'focal concerns' or 'a way of life'. One of these concerns is the search for 'excitement', where Miller suggested young people in lower-class communities typically seek 'situations of great emotional stimulation' (1958: 11). These situations are characterised by their 'thrill', 'risk' and 'danger', and countered the routine 'boredom', 'safeness', and 'sameness' that young people in poorer communities were thought to suffer (1958: 7). Likewise, Downes (1966: 268) noted how 'the bulk of … working-class male teenagers attain their leisure goals in ways that are frequently delinquent'. In this regard joyriding might be seen as something to be expected from the young people in my sample, and those with similar backgrounds in Lambeth, because it provides them with this much-needed amusement at a price nobody can beat. Joyriding is, perhaps, a 'coming-of-age' offence committed by inner-city youth adept and curious enough to operate a motor vehicle.

Unlike graffiti, joyriding was a very acceptable offence for these young people. Many of them joyrode, several more times than they could recall. Joyriding was not only widespread amongst my sample, but, apparently, amongst young people with similar backgrounds across Lambeth. Evidence also exists to suggest the presence of a code or set of rules nearly all of them imposed on themselves when joyriding. For instance, while none of them expressed that they cared about taking a vehicle not belonging to them, only a small number of the joyriders said they *destroyed* the vehicle after using it. The rest safely abandoned the mopeds or cars, giving their proper owners some chance of reclaiming them. The majority of joyriders only took this offence so far, suggesting these young people made significant normative judgements regarding their offending. For the most part, while stealing a moped or 'old banger' and cruising around the block or estate was acceptable, doing anything more sinister either to or with the vehicle was a different story.

Smashing bottles, breaking windows, setting things aflame

'Vandalism' encompasses a variety of illegal behaviours, and is used to describe graffiti on walls, busted-up telephone boxes and bus stops, smashed-out windows, and other damage to property. Vandalism is 'the most visible form of juvenile crime' (Muncie 1984: 67). Only about a third of my sample said they vandalised something, a surprisingly low amount given how common an offence vandalism has been reported to be (for example Coffield 1991; Flood-Page *et al.* 2000; Graham and Bowling 1995). Again, this peculiarity may be explained by the approach. As explained before, the young people were not read a list of illegal acts and asked whether or not they had committed them. Rather, the young people were asked a general question about what illegal acts they committed. Thus, a possibility exists that those more involved in offending did not discuss vandalism because they might have believed their involvement in more serious offences over-shadowed their vandalism.

As with joyriding, the young people who vandalised did this because they were 'bored' and thought breaking, smashing and destroying things might be fun. The relationship between vandalism, young people and play is well established (Barker and Bridgeman 1994; Coffield 1991; S. Cohen 1973; Corrigan 1979; Downes 1966; Geason and Wilson 1990; NACRO 1989). Stan Cohen (1973) developed a six-tiered typology to describe different reasons why people vandalise: acquisitive, tactical, ideological, vindictive, play and malicious. Other, more recent, social researchers studying vandalism have seen little reason to make amendments to this (for example Barker and Bridgeman 1994; Coffield 1991). Using Cohen's typology, my findings suggest those in my sample primarily vandalised for 'playful' reasons; the young people did not express being bent on destroying or misusing public and private property for malicious reasons, or that their vandalism was political or instrumental towards any end. Only one young person, Kevin, said that he vandalised a shop as a way to lash out against the shop owner. This might be considered a more 'vindictive' reason:

> *The criminal damage: what were you doing?*
> I went to get some fags and one day they wouldn't serve me. They knew I was underage. One day they'd serve me even drink [alcohol]. I got in the shop. I got served in there, but the next day just because they didn't want to serve me, they didn't serve me. So I thought that was taking the piss and I said something to the man in there. He called me a honky, so I said, 'Boy, I'm not taking that.' And I said some racist words to him and he tried to kick me out of the shop, like proper physically kick me. But he missed because I flinched and he kicked my

leg instead. So I turnaround and picked up my little scooter outside and threw it through the big shop window. Went through and picked it up and fucked off and got fags from the other shop across the road ... So I just sort of flipped out and I got nicked three days later for that.

The others only discussed vandalism in relation to play. Like Corrigan (1979: 121) who, when researching the 'Smash Street Kids', noticed how 'doing nothing' plus the injection of 'a weird idea' led to them 'smashing things', those in my sample who vandalised did so spontaneously, most with the reasoning that 'it was something to do'. Also, Corrigan (1979: 140) suggested that, with the Smash Street Kids, 'rules are not broken specifically because they are rules', but rather 'as a by-product of the flow of the activity engaged in by the boys' (see also Matza and Sykes 1961; Presdee 1994, 2000). Similar comments can be made about those in my sample. In the main, they associated vandalism as being playful and having fun, not being malicious or damaging property out of spite. This point was confirmed in interviews with professionals. For instance, Trevor, a youth and community worker from Streatham, reflected on why the young people he had worked with smash things:

> They're hanging about, want a bit of excitement, smash a window. It creates a noise. It impacts on their senses. It gets attention, y'know? It provides a play, an area of play within the group and people can show their, umm, I don't know. Whether it's their bravery or their sort of sense of, y'know, group position and sort of, y'know, excitement. So, it's not a big deal in that sense.

Comparably speaking, Quentin, Martin, Nathan, Kevin and Tom caused much more damage to property than those less involved in offending. For instance, Quentin talked about how he and two of his friends went and 'busted up' a BMW car near his home in Brixton. Tom said that he and a friend went to some portable offices near a building site and 'destroyed them' by throwing desk drawers and paper about, breaking furniture and spray-painting the offices. Martin mentioned how he and his mate, Danny, went and stole some chainsaws from workmen, and went and cut down trees on their estate. Nathan said he once broke into his old school and attempted to set fire to it. All of them said how the acts were 'fun' or 'exciting' and did them out of being 'bored'. For instance, when asked why they vandalised, Tom said, 'just for fun', Martin said, 'it was boring', Quentin said, 'it was exciting' and Nathan said, 'there was nothing else to do'. One of the respondents in Downes (1966: 205) made similar comments about vandalism in London's East End, suggesting young people did this 'out of boredom. They got nothing to do around here.'

Those less involved in offending discussed relatively tame accounts of vandalism, such as breaking windows or smashing bottles, but in some cases they vandalised more frequently than those who committed more serious offences. For instance, Darrell used to 'break windows'. Todd used to go out in his neighbourhood wearing 'dark blue, not black' and randomly break car windows. David was arrested ten times *in the same place* for smashing glass bottles against a wall on a rooftop on a 'closed-off area'. Terry discussed setting washing lines on fire, breaking windows on buses and going into empty garages in order to smash abandoned appliances. Tim also said he broke bottles against bus stops and smashed car windows a couple of times. While the contexts were different, the reasons offered by these young people are still related to leisure and play. For instance, David said he smashed bottles because he was 'mucking around', and Todd said 'we just feel like doing it, so we just do it'.

It is significant to note that the only young people who expressed any remorse over their vandalism were the ones who were arrested for it. For instance, David said he 'felt like a prat. Shameful.' after being arrested for smashing bottles. Tom said 'I just wish I hadn't done any of that now' after being arrested for destroying portable offices. Quentin, after being arrested for vandalising a BMW, said his 'pride, if you like, with my mum and Nan suffered'. During the interview, they mentioned desisting from offending altogether, and their repentance over such acts appeared genuine.

On the other hand, Nathan, Kevin and Martin were also arrested for vandalism, but failed to express any remorse. As Martin said after being arrested for the chainsaw incident, 'it didn't really bother me'; Kevin said, 'I didn't feel nothing'. These three also committed a number of other, more serious, offences, which they mentioned not caring about. Thus, it is little wonder they failed to express any regret over a relatively minor offence such as vandalism. Those less involved in offending who broke windows and other things, yet were not arrested for such behaviour, also discussed not feeling remorse after doing such things. For instance, Terry did not feel bad afterwards, and related this to the suggestion that smashing things was 'not a big deal' because such behaviour is just 'being destructive'.

> You might just like, what I was saying about those [empty, abandoned] garages. You might just go in there and just break things really. People don't bother to use them, so we go in and smash things up. Just being destructive really … this is like, you're walking around, you might see some other things, and you pick it up and throw it. It's not a big deal. It's just done.

From speaking with these young people, I received the impression they truly did not care about the times they vandalised property. Their expressions were, perhaps, anticipated because such events were relatively minor within their lives and were in the past.

Vandalism amongst those in my sample was something most did when 'younger' (Flood-Page *et al.* 2000; Graham and Bowling 1995). But why do young people stop vandalising when they get older? According to Matza and Sykes (1961: 717) 'delinquents' eventually 'pick up' on conventional values, which 'bind the delinquent to the society whose laws he violates'. The authors continued to suggest that as the 'delinquents' age and mature, they eventually 'bond with larger society' and desist from offending (1961: 717). Even at ages 15 and 16, all the young people in my sample who had vandalised, with the exception of Todd and Nathan, said they desisted from this behaviour, and thus, perhaps, 'bonded' with society to a larger extent. In other words, they grew out of vandalism, much like many of the taggers in my sample seemed to have grown out of that.

Asking why these young people did not walk down more conventional paths towards entertainment and amusement is important. What about legitimate, traditional forms of youthful leisure pursuits, such as sports teams and youth clubs in Lambeth? Part of the reason the young people were bored and found illegal ways to have fun may be related to the lack of updated youth facilities within the borough (Geason and Wilson 1990; NACRO 1989). This idea was suggested in interviews with professionals. For instance, Rudy, a detached youth worker from Brixton, said how joyriding 'cures boredom', and continued by noting that:

> To a large extent there's a lack of positive alternatives out there ... there is a lack of provision for them and ... they find their own excitement.

Ayo, a detached youth worker from Stockwell, concurred with Rudy when he discussed how a group of young people he worked with vandalised and joyrode because there was 'nothing for them to do':

> From what they've told me, nothing for them to do. They have the youth club which is NOTHING to them. They can just come in and play table tennis, y'knowhatImean? They need something more constructive, they want, y'know. They need something else, y'know?

Mick, another detached youth worker from Brixton, commented on the lack of facilities at the centre he managed for the past six years as a partial explanation why young people were not going there:

> One of the things that I've recognised out of this right let me tell you this now, it's not so much the young people are the biggest problem, it's us as adults that work with the young people that are the problem because a lot of middle management have a problem of changing or [accepting] new ideas. They are so used to setting kinda, 'This is what young people want. This is what we'll give them. This is the budget.' And if you sit down and say to them, 'But don't you think that young people find that stale now?' Take, for example, this is a youth centre. If you talk to a lot of those youngsters that are in those young offender institutes and you say to them, 'Why don't you go to a youth centre?', y'know what their first reaction will be? 'What's it got to offer me?' Let's be frank about it. Remember, I'm the manager telling you now right, and I reach the young people that are in those places. I talk to the parents. And the reason why a lot of those youngsters don't come in here and they find themselves on the street doing what they are doing because it's quick money and they need to look good. Places like here don't do that for them. It don't look good. If you turn and said, right, you've changed the whole of this youth centre into what young people want of the 90s, you'll have it flooded ... one of the things that's missing, like I'm saying to you right in the delivery of meeting young people's

needs, it's that this is a youth centre built for a 70s and 80s generation. It's not modernised for a generation of the 90s into the millennium. And you've got to realise young people want different things to do. And I think that some of us right that make the decisions that hold the budget strings are not to sure how to deal with that. Give [young people] what they want. And what you have is a big differential change from management that sit around and decide how the budget should be made to the practitioners on the ground that work with the young people. If they marry up then you can see how things can happen. Young people recognise that, and when young people recognise that it says that if you're not getting the support, why should I come?

It is difficult to say whether young people's alternative, illicit pursuits of pleasure were related to their perception of youth clubs or leisure schemes in Lambeth as inadequate or out of date. While the lack of modern youth leisure outlets may have encouraged other, illegal forms of recreation, such as joyriding and vandalism, additional considerations are important to address when determining the attraction to this. For instance, a few of the young people said how the illegal status of such acts heightened the intensity of fun associated with them. In this sense, joyriding and vandalism are 'forbidden fruits' and, as such, attracted these young people to this activity even more (Katz 1988; Matza and Sykes 1961; Presdee 2000). For instance, Terry mentioned this when he and his friends joyrode mopeds:

> I think people were scared of what might happen to them, but that was part of doing it. That was part of the buzz.

The fact that such acts are illegal may have added to the thrill or 'buzz' associated with them. In this regard joyriding and vandalism are not only fun in themselves, but also *more* fun because of their illegality. The point being the lack of proper and modern youth centres in Lambeth may actually have *nothing* to do with the young people's propensity to joyride and vandalise (see Rojek 2000). For instance, the process of joyriding mopeds, blowing up cars, cutting down trees with chainsaws and other vandalism, as well as the associated 'buzz' knowing that such acts are illegal, may have been regarded by the young people as producing more excitement than any modern youth and community centre ever could.

Like their other offences, the young people made normative judgements about their vandalism. These young people did not vandalise out of malice or spite, nor for political reasons. To them, vandalism was only a way to have fun, or, at least, was rationalised as such. Also, for the most part, these young people only targeted certain areas or things to vandalise, such as breaking bottles and smashing windows. For them, some things were off limits. These young people did not say that they defaced churches, or other religious institutions, or other people's houses. In fact the only establishment vandalised was the time Nathan tried to set fire to his school. Moreover, they only vandalised things to a certain degree. For instance, they smashed empty bottles on the ground, not at moving cars or people. Also, they primarily only broke one car window, and did not destroy the entire vehicle. So while they clearly vandalised for fun, the young people were only willing to take these offences so far, further evidence to suggest that these young people possess very precise distinctions within their value-systems regulating their illegal behaviour.

Crime, excitement and masculinity

So why did the young people joyride, smash things and, to a lesser extent, tag their street names? From looking at their responses and those offered by the professionals these offences were clearly committed for the purposes of amusement. Such behaviours were primarily acts of play, not those born out of malicious intent or a desire to cause harm and suffering. But what do these reasons tell us theoretically? A couple of considerations are important to address when attempting to explain this behaviour: masculinity and excitement.

Joyriding, vandalism and graffiti are offences perpetrated, in the great majority, by boys and men. Possibly, the young men in my sample who committed these offences were 'doing masculinity' (Messerschmidt 1993, 2000). In other words, when these young men smashed things, spray-painted their name, and cruised around on stolen mopeds they engaged in behaviour conforming to masculine expectations. These expectations, in turn, may be both locally and culturally informed (Messerschmidt 2000). For instance, in movies and on television usually a boy or man is depicted stealing the vehicle, being chased by the police, spray-painting graffiti or destroying property. Smash, chase, steal, destroy, nick: such verbs are masculine and mediated images associate them closely with behaviours primarily committed by men and boys. Furthermore, for young men in Lambeth, engaging in such behaviour may be viewed as 'boys just being boys', participating in activity that, while illegal and relatively censured, falls roughly in line with traditional forms of behaviour amongst boys and young men within the area. That young men within inner-city London have been joyriding and smashing things for the same reasons for many years seems somewhat clear (S. Cohen 1972; Corrigan 1979; Downes 1966). These actions may be 'gender and class appropriate forms of nonconforming behaviour' (Messerschmidt 1993: 41). As such, issues of masculinity are important to keep in mind when attempting to draft an explanation for these expressive offences.

The theoretical stance that seems to best 'fit' with my data on the young people's expressive offences is the 'crime as an act of transgression' approach (Katz 1988). Katz's theory, as the title of his book denotes, suggests a seductive nature of crime where there exist 'moral and sensual attractions of doing evil'. This general theory of crime attempts to account for all types of offences from robbery and murder, joyriding and violence, burglary and vandalism. Central to all of these behaviours, Katz argues, are emotions and morality, vitality and excitement. Katz claims that offending can be explained as a reaction, a lashing out against everyday rationality, of everyday existence, and that doing crime is a 'release', a process of moral transcendence, a dipping into an irrational world in order to resolve an insufferable moral condition in the rational world.

Katz's theory is not helpful in explaining all of the young people's offending behaviour, but it somewhat captures their expressive ones. According to Katz, much of contemporary social life is characterised by its routine banality, something certainly the case within urban, impoverished social settings, such as those within the inner city. Young people within these areas must be frequently swamped with feelings of 'nothing to do', of being 'bored', of looking for 'action'. Certainly my data suggested this. Young people need to do something in order to counteract these feelings. Outside of 'the street' young people have few if any arenas for play. These young people have no money and are not upbeat about conventional outlets for youthful leisure. As a result, the young people make do with what they have, literally creating 'something' out of 'nothing' (S. Cohen 1972; Corrigan 1979). Within this process, offences such as vandalism, joyriding and, to a lesser extent, tagging come into play. By behaving in such ways the young people were able to temporarily negate their 'boring' existence, and become caught up in the fantastic emotions that committing these offences brings. These acts produce 'sneaky thrills' not only in themselves, but also because of their illegality; a 'delight in being deviant' exists (Katz 1988: 312). In other words, the illegality associated with the acts actually heightens the pleasure received from them. For the young people in my sample, engaging in such behaviours allowed them to champion the routine mediocrity and monotony characteristic of much of their existence. To this extent, Katz's theory of moral self-transcendence seems relatively applicable.

In a similar vein Presdee (2000) discussed a 'carnivalesque' nature of specific offences. Presdee (2000: 11) informs us that the idea that crime may be enjoyable to some is 'difficult to grapple with', but how, within a culture that so revels in consumerism and consumption, 'crime itself has become a valuable consumer entertainment commodity'. Central to the consumer–commodity–consumption culture nexus is 'the heightened pursuit of pleasure, which has become the necessary lubricant of everyday consumer life' (2000: 27–8). Yet many people exist outside of this consumer culture, who, for lack of resources, are not able to fully participate within it. These individuals find other outlets for pleasure, pursue other avenues in their search for excitement. These avenues may lead them to committing certain pleasure-generating offences, such as joyriding and vandalism, and, to a lesser extent, tagging. As Presdee (2000: 30) mentioned, 'put simply, transgressing and doing wrong are for many an exciting and pleasurable experience'.

Presdee (2000: 8) discussed 'the second life', an alternative 'reality', an alternative 'rationality' 'where the majority of transgressions take place. Here, we find the genesis and rationale for behaviour that anticipates the ability to destroy, disrupt and dissent.' Presdee draws heavily from the work of Mikhail Bakhtin, particularly that regarding his conceptualisation of 'carnival' – the culture of laughter and reversal, where conventionality is thrown out the door or stood on its head. For Presdee (2000: 38–9) 'carnival licenses transgression and thus openly defies or mocks the values of the hegemony. The transgressor is thereby put in a position of power as the carnival society temporarily replaces the dominant one.' In this sense, joyriding, vandalism and tagging are acts of empowerment as they allow the young people to break free from conventional limitations on 'having fun'. Crime as a commodity 'enables us all to consume without cost as we enjoy the excitement, and the emotions … that crime often contains' (Presdee 2000: 58; see also Rojek 2000; Stanley 1997). This perspective seems very beneficial at capturing the reasons why those in my sample vandalised property, joyrode vehicles and, to a lesser extent, tagged their names. In other words the 'crime as an act of transgression' approach somewhat fits with the young people's explanations about their expressive offences.

Conclusions

In this chapter I explored and analysed the young people's expressive offences, such as graffiti, joyriding and vandalism. First, I looked at different types of graffiti, and suggested tagging was not a popular offence amongst these young people, but rather a sporadic act only a few did alone or with a couple of friends, for no other purposes than to let others know 'I was there'. I further suggested the graffiti observed in Lambeth (and London in general) leads to evidence to suggest something completely dissimilar from that of US-style gangs. Comments from those interviewed suggest parallel conclusions. Rather than ganging, tagging was an expression of hip-hop culture. This point was based on the fact that these taggers listened to hip-hop music, and how tagging and graffiti art are additional indicators of this culture. Regardless, tagging was primarily done by 15- or 16-year-olds, and even some of them said they only did this when they were 'younger'. For Kenny, the story was a bit different. He spent much time creating skilfully drawn graffiti 'art', a form of graffiti appreciated and respected by a much broader audience. And while this may be the case, graffiti, on the whole, was not really an offence these young people committed. It primarily lies outside of their 'culture of offending'.

Joyriding was a very popular offence committed by many of the young people. The reasons they discussed for doing this were not those driven by malice or spite for any one individual, but rather out of a desire to do 'something fun', behaviour which may come to be expected in lower socioeconomic areas such as Lambeth, where joyriding provides much-needed entertainment for young people at someone else's expense. Another point stressed about their joyriding was that there appeared to be a set of guidelines they followed regarding this offence. By this, I refer to how most of them only joyrode around their immediate areas, and then abandoned the vehicle relatively unscathed. In only a few cases did the young people destroy the vehicle or use it for purposes other than 'just driving around'. What these guidelines, this code, suggests is that, within the value systems of these young people, within their moral universes, limitations existed relating to this illegal offence. For the most part, they only took joyriding so far.

In the later section I argued when the young people vandalised that such behaviours tended to be opportunistic, spur-of-the-moment actions that normally took place amongst friends. I also suggested their reasons for committing vandalism appeared to be caught up in the desire to find things to do, rather than behaviour that should be interpreted as malicious or politically motivated. Like joyriding, vandalism was something these young people did for 'kicks', but, unlike joyriding, something that primarily occurred when 'younger'. This suggests they grew out of this behaviour; vandalism was an offence that they committed 'a long time ago', at least from the majority viewpoint. As with joyriding, I implied that while the perceived lack of youth leisure outlets in Lambeth may be a partial reason why young people vandalised property to cure their 'boredom', there seemed to be a thrill associated with the illegal acts which produced a 'buzz', perhaps one much stronger than these leisure outlets were able to supply; the point being that the absence of youth leisure facilities in Lambeth may have had little to do with the reasons young people vandalised or joyrode. As with many of their offences, these young people made specific, normative (moral) judgements about their vandalism, only taking them so far, and/or differentiating between what was and what was not acceptable during the course of their participation in such behaviour. Their acts of vandalism were not serious, but relatively petty – breaking bottles on the ground or knocking out windows. Places of worship, historic buildings, schools, and people's homes were generally not targeted. This, again, indicates that, within the value-systems of these young people, finite distinctions appeared to regulate their offending behaviour, something that may be considered a specific code.

Finally, I related the young people's expressive offences to concepts of masculinity and leisure. Here I suggested that – when attempting to draft an explanation for graffiti, joyriding and vandalism – it is important to keep in mind that the great majority of these behaviours are committed by young men. By behaving these ways, to some degree they 'did masculinity' – behaving in a way that confirms their status within their inner-city environment as a young masculine male. Furthermore, these young men, rather than attempting to 'do crime' or 'do wrong', seem to have committed these offences for no other purpose othan their desire for action, their desire for leisure, their desire to have fun. Ultimately, their pursuit of leisure resulted in them committing these expressive offences. What remains uncertain, however, is the extent to which they actively engaged in this behaviour simply due to its illegality.

6　Violence

Rates of violence in Lambeth have been relatively high for many years. British Crime Survey data (Kershaw *et al.* 2000; Mirrlees-Black *et al.* 1998; Simmons *et al.* 2002) show that inner-city residents, particularly young men, are included in those considered most at risk of being a victim of violence. This chapter looks at and analyses the young people's experiences of violence. Here, violence primarily refers to fighting, which was something most of the young people in my sample were familiar with. Almost all of them had been in at least one fight; many had been in several. The first section explores the context, frequency and reasons for fighting, as well as how the young people felt afterwards. My analysis relates these themes to issues of masculinity and working- or lower-class culture. Next, I examine the use of weapons and the young people's attitudes towards them. Lastly, I address the extent to which residential 'territory' was an issue in their lives. Specifically, I attempt to determine the degree to which the young people consider any particular area or space 'theirs', and relate their responses to issues of territory, such as that exercised by US-style gangs, in order to account for similarities and differences. Throughout the chapter patterns are explored between these topics and the different categories of young people.

Sparked, banged up, bruck up

'Sparked', 'banged up' and 'bruck up' are slang terms the young people used to describe fighting or throwing punches. According to the Youth Lifestyles Surveys, fighting is a common offence, particularly for young men (Flood-Page *et al.* 2000; Graham and Bowling 1995). In Lambeth, offences of violence among young people were relatively high in relation to other London boroughs.[1] Many in my sample talked about fighting, and *only 4 out of 31* mentioned never being in a fight. Table 6.1 illustrates the number of fights the young people were in by their offending category.

Analysing the frequency, motivation and context of the young people's fights threw up some interesting patterns. First, several of the young people less involved in offending said they either had *never* been in a fight or had only been in a couple. By contrast, all of those more involved in offending had been in fights, about half in more fights than they could recall. Regardless of frequency, the contexts of nearly all the young people's fights were similar: fights were of a one-on-one nature, and

Table 6.1 Reported frequency of fighting by offending category

	Age	Frequency of fighting
Severe		
Sonny	14	Too many to count
Quentin	17	Too many to count
Travis	18	Not that many
Marc	15	Not that many
Tolu	15	Not that many
Karl	14	Too many to count
Heavy		
Martin	16	Not that many
Noel	15	Not that many
Tom	16	Not that many
Kenny	15	Too many to count
Norman	15	Not that many
Theo	20	Too many to count
Keenan	15	Not that many
Nathan	16	Too many to count
Lenny	23	Too many to count
Moderates		
David	14	Too many to count
Kevin	15	5
Todd	14	None
Larry	15	Too many to count
Brian	22	None
Darrell	16	Too many to count
Jack	15	20
Terry	15	None
Dabblers		
Betty	16	Too many to count
Frank	13	1
Kellen	15	Not that many
Winnona	15	None
Eric	16	Not that many
Isaac	17	1
Tracy	15	Too many to count
Tim	16	2

young people fought those of the same sex and roughly the same age. Sonny, Karl and Travis, however, talked of how they and their friends simultaneously fought other groups of young people. Also, these three said they attacked others for amusement, an incentive noted in other studies (Katz 1988; Patrick 1973; Yablonsky 1962). The others *only* said they fought when they 'had to', and offered reasons for fighting, such as being insulted, 'payback' from a previous physical attack, being cheated in a transaction, or simply because someone looked at them 'wrong'. For many in my sample, and perhaps those with similar backgrounds in Lambeth, violence appeared to be warranted and expected in specific circumstances, particularly when their 'respect' was threatened. This stance has, perhaps, been the case with previous generations of young people in the borough, who probably fought for the same reasons (Anderson 1999; Corrigan 1979; Hannertz 1969; Matza and Sykes 1961; Miller 1958; Patrick 1973; Pearson 1983; Shover 1996). Fighting by the young men may also be linked to them 'doing masculinity' (Braithwaite and Daly 1994; Messerschmidt 1993, 2000; Stanko 1994).

Additional consistencies emerged surrounding the severity of violence employed by the young people during their fights, and their emotions afterwards. While the severity of the fights was similar amongst nearly all those in my sample, some of those more involved in offending, such as Sonny, Karl, Travis, Martin, Lenny and Nathan, offered relatively vicious and bloody stories of when they fought others. Also, these young people were the same ones who used violence in a more instrumental manner, such as in street muggings. Furthermore, while a few of those less involved in offending generally regretted fighting, in parallel with their emotions after many other offences, those more involved expressed no remorse over their fights. These emotional responses were perhaps somewhat predictable because expressing remorse is not congruent with being 'masculine', upholding 'respect' or being 'tough'.

The nature of fighting

By the 'nature' of fighting, I refer to the context and frequency of and the reasons for fighting. First, the context of all the fights of those interviewed were remarkably similar. The young people fought with others who were the same sex and roughly the same age. Young men did not fight with young women or vice versa. Also, the young people did not fight with the elderly or the very young, and only a couple of young people more involved in offending, such as Sonny, Karl and Travis, said they 'rumbled' with other groups of young people. These three, unlike everyone else, offered examples of when they and their friends 'ganged up on' and attacked either one or a couple of individuals simultaneously. The others only fought on a one-to-one basis.

Travis, Sonny and Karl are also different from the other young people in that they said they fought 'just because' (Katz 1988; Patrick 1973; Presdee 2000; Yablonsky 1962). Katz (1988: 103–4), for instance, when discussing the 'ways of the badass' suggested how some 'badasses' sometimes seem to attack others because they 'need a beating', and continued by noting some attacks may have 'no utilitarian purpose', but rather are 'treated exclusively as "fun"'. In this respect Katz (1988) may find Karl, Sonny and Travis to be a couple of 'badasses'. Unlike the others in my sample, they talked about how they *enjoyed* fighting. For instance, Travis mentioned how he and his friends used to go out after drinking to cause trouble with other youths from Holborn 'for a laugh'. Sonny and Karl antagonised people into fights by saying 'What you looking at?' Karl elaborated:

> Sometimes we just go round and make trouble. Just go wild say, 'What are you looking at me for?' … sometimes we start a little trouble, but we don't really start it that much. We just wait for it to come.

Another pattern could be discerned in the severity of the fights and more general levels of offending. For instance, several of those more involved in offending – Sonny, Karl, Travis, Martin, Kenny, Lenny and, especially, Nathan – offered brutal accounts of fighting when compared to the others. During our monthly meetings, Nathan went into considerable detail about how he punched and kicked others, at times into submission and unconsciousness, and showed me his scarred hands from throwing blows. Lenny also talked about some serious fighting and, like Nathan, has the scars to prove it. He pointed some of them out, and reeled off a list of how he received them: 'I've been stabbed, shot, hit with pieces of wood, hit with a baseball bat, burned with a cigarette…'

These scars stemmed, in part, from Lenny's previous 'work' as a debt collector for some older adults. For Lenny, violence was used as a means to either intimidate or coerce others into giving him money they owed to his 'bosses'. Lenny's 'job' required him to fight, and he 'messed people up' on numerous occasions. Lenny is, physically, the broadest young person interviewed. The vest he sported during the interview showed off his muscular arms and shoulders, as well as his tattoos and scars received 'on the job'. Lenny suggested that his size and training in Wing-Chung, a martial art, were seen by his bosses as being beneficial for his role as a debt collector. He mentioned being very effective at his job:

> Because of my size and my strength and what I used to do, because I trained, they [his 'bosses'] would say, 'Look, this geezer's giving me trouble. Go down there and sort it out and get my money.' [When I went down there] They'd give me the money almost every time.

Others more involved in offending also used violence in contexts outside of fighting, which distinguished them from the other young people. For instance, all of those in my sample who robbed others, except Marc, used force during this offence. Marc, on the other hand, said he just ran past and grabbed a purse or mobile phone. The others attacked or shouted at their robbery victims. For instance, Martin discussed how he robbed boys:

> Let's say I see a boy with a nice phone, and that I want it because everybody wants something. And some people are little gits. And I go, 'Excuse me mate. Can I look at your phone?', and he was like 'Fuck off! Leave me alone!', and I'm like, 'Who you talking to?', and he goes, 'Do you know who I am?', and I go, 'I don't give a shit!', and just lean into [start punching] them … [not] to an extent where it hurt him really bad … just until he gives us what I want and then leave him alone.

Table 6.1 also illustrates patterns that emerged in the frequency of the young people's fighting. The majority of them said something to the extent that they either fought 'more times than they could remember', or, alternatively, they fought 'not that often'. Only a few of those less involved in offending, such as Todd, Brian, Terry and Winnona, said they *never* fought. Others, such as Jack, Frank, Isaac and

Tim, were able to quantify their fights. With the exception of Jack, these young people were only in a couple of fights. Whereas those more involved in offending either were in 'hundreds' and 'loads' of fights, or, alternatively, 'not that many' or 'a few' fights, those less involved offered more precise amounts. The fact that they actually counted their fights suggests such events were comparably limited in their lives. In this sense, as with many other ways, those less involved in offending were distinct from those more so.

In the majority, fighting by those in my sample appeared to be *only* a reaction to others' wrongdoing. A major cause was insults, a recurring reason for fighting offered by many of the young people, even amongst those who only committed a couple of offences, such as Frank, Tracy and Betty. For instance, Frank said he fought another boy who 'cussed his family'; Tracy got into a fight with a girl who 'raised her mouth' about Tracy's mum; Betty said she fights if 'girls get rude to me or my friends'. Indeed, from my own work experience with young people either as a primary school teacher, child care worker or volunteer social worker, both in the USA and UK, insults, particularly about one's family, have often been the cause of fighting. Darrell also noted how often insults lead to fights, and summed it up quite nicely by mentioning that fighting was often the result of when 'someone said something to someone, or something like that'.

Larry and David also fought when others insulted them. Larry noted how 'some people can get a bit rude … like giving it all the big [mouth]', and that this may result in him fighting. David offered a similar reason for one of his fights:

> I beat up some boy because he was getting lippy.
> *Did he start saying something bad to you?*
> He just kept on cussing me … if someone keeps going and going and going, I'm not gonna stand there and let it happen. I'm going to fight back.

Those more involved in offending also mentioned insults as a reason for fighting. Nathan, for instance, said he fights with others who 'talk trash' to him or his friends. Kevin fought a boy who 'was coating me off [talking negatively about me] for months'. Others, such as Kenny, Theo, Martin, Keenan, Karl, Sonny and Travis also noted how insults were the source of their altercations.

Another recurring, perhaps more obvious, reason for fighting mentioned by the young people was that such behaviours were retaliations for a previous attack, or that they fought in order to defend themselves, their family or their friends. For instance, Eric said he fought when 'people start[ed] picking on me'. Kenny had been in 'loads' of fights and estimated it was in the 'hundreds'. Below is a paraphrased version[2] of an incident where Kenny received a charge of grievous bodily harm (GBH) when he attacked a 23-year-old young man for throwing something at his sister.

> Kenny said a 14-year-old boy threw something at his sister after she was being 'mouthy' towards him. Kenny went over to the 14-year-old to talk to him about what he was doing. As Kenny approached, the 14-year-old boy's older

brother, who is 23, came down and punched Kenny. Kenny then attacked the 23-year-old and knocked him unconscious. According to Kenny, he broke this boy's ribs, knocked one of his gold teeth out, and blackened both of his eyes.

Like Kenny, Noel hit his sister's boyfriend with a baseball bat after the boyfriend beat her up. Noel said he 'rarely' fights, but that because his sister was punched he wanted to 'shoot the bloke's head off'. Keenan also got into a fight when boys from another estate in Brixton came and gave him and his mates some 'trouble' over using a stolen motorbike. Tolu fought because a boy was 'messing about' with him. According to Tolu: 'I didn't want him to play me [push me around], and I dragged him out and he couldn't take it.'

'Bad' transactions, where the young people felt 'ripped off', had things taken from them, or where they believed someone owed them something, were also reported causes of fights. For instance, Isaac got into a fight when someone stole his bicycle. When Isaac noticed a boy ride past his house on his bike, he chased him and fought for it back. Nathan went and 'banged up' a boy who sold him some 'bunk' cannabis that tasted 'like dirt' and did the same to another boy who owed him money. Martin also said he fought a boy who was a cannabis runner. Because the weed the boy sold Martin was underweight, Martin went and beat up the runner, took back his money *and* kept the cannabis.

A final reason for fighting offered by the young people had to do with someone looking at them 'wrong', something referred to as 'screwing'.[3] Katz (1988: 110–12), in his chapter entitled 'Ways of the Badass', discussed the 'danger of eye contact' or 'visual bump', whereby a physical altercation may arise simply because someone is looking at another, perhaps in a threatening or provocative manner. Katz continued on how the phrase 'Whachulookinat?' was a way for 'badasses' to instigate fights with those who 'just look' at them. Indeed, from growing up in San Diego, I remember how mere glances at the 'wrong' person easily led to fights. Likewise, several young people mentioned 'looks' as a reason for fighting. I probed one of them, Larry, on how being 'looked at funny', or 'screwed', made him want to fight:

> See like most people, if you look at them, they want to fight you.
> *Really, most people who look at you, they want to fight you?*
> Well, some people are like that in Brixton. I know some people like that.
> *And it's just like that? They want to fight you?*
> Like, if they look at you in a funny way – if they screw you.
> *If they screw you, does that mean looking at them in a funny way?*
> Yeah.
> *And they just want to fight you?*
> Yeah.
> *And why is that?*
> They don't want to ask. They want to ask you, 'Why you screwing me?'
> *Why do you think they do that?*
> I don't know.

If someone looked at you funny, would you want to go up and knock them?
It depends on how big they are.
If they were about your size and they look at you would you go after them?
If they looked at me and said something then, yeah, but not if they just looked at me.
What if they were bigger than you?
I'd still do it, but I'd go up to them and say, 'Why you starting?'

Several of the young people, including Betty, Tracy, Nathan, Martin, Kenny, Sonny and Karl, also said they fought others who 'screwed' them. For instance, Sonny said he fights because 'people screw you' where they 'look at you like *that*'. Their reasons for doing this were very similar to Larry's. Perhaps, Katz (1988) would come to find that these young people, too, are several 'badasses'.

Generally speaking, looking at the reasons why the young people said they fought suggests these individuals were more antagonised than antagonistic. In other words, the majority said they fought in order to defend themselves, as opposed to attacking others. These reasons could be *post hoc* rationalisations, but, with the exception of a small handful of them, the young people who fought mentioned not finding pleasure in this behaviour, did not commit violent offences, and did not actively seek out and start random, purposeless fights. Rather, they mentioned something to the effect that they 'only fight when they have to'. Perhaps work by Miller (1969) best sums up the 'catch-22' suffered by most of the young people in my sample who failed to express they enjoyed fighting, but acknowledged certain situations where they *must* fight. Miller paraphrased what he suggested to be an average 'gang member's' stance on the use of fighting:

> We know perfectly well that what we are doing is regarded as wrong, legally and morally; we also know that it violates the wishes and standards of many whose good opinion we value; yet, if we are to sustain our self-respect and our honor as males, we *must*, at this stage of our lives, engage in criminal behavior.
>
> (1969: 23, original emphasis)

The reasons offered by the young people as to why they fought suggests they engaged in such behaviour in order to save 'face'[4] or maintain respect, something they interpreted as being significant. According to Cooley's (1964) 'looking glass-self', we see ourselves as others view us (see also Anderson 1999; Becker 1963; Goffman 1959). In this sense, self-image relies on the perceptions of others, suggesting that the opinions other people hold of us have much to do with how we view ourselves. Backing down when insults fly, being bullied or pushed around, letting others 'walk over you', and being 'ripped off' in a transaction were direct challenges to the young people's self-image, and responding to them violently may serve to establish and/or maintain 'respect'.

When attempting to explain fighting, it is important to highlight that these young people are, in the great majority, young men. And when discussing young men and violence it is important to bring up issues of 'masculinity' (Braithwaite and Daly 1994; Messerschmidt 1993, 2000; Stanko 1994). Issues of 'masculinity', of 'manhood' and 'coming of age' are bedfellows with violence and fighting. For instance, Braithwaite and Daly (1994: 189) suggested that 'violence is gendered: it is a problem and consequence of masculinity'. Stanko (1994: 43) also noted that the violent experiences of men 'are all too often attributed to their experiences of *normal* masculinity' (emphasis added). Is it then possible to view fighting amongst the young men in my sample as 'boys just being boys'? Are these violent responses to insults and injuries simply them 'doing masculinity' (Messerschmidt 2000)? This could be the case. As such, we should, perhaps, not find it too surprising that most of these young men said they fought. For them, fighting seemed 'normal', but only in particular circumstances. For the young men in my sample, being 'cussed', attacked, 'ripped off', and 'screwed' are challenges to their 'status', 'reputation' and 'manhood'. By fighting, they exhibited masculine qualities, such as 'bravado', 'hardness', 'physical courage' and 'toughness'. Fighting by them may thus be viewed as a normal response to threats to their masculinity, another valued commodity closely related to respect. As Anderson (1999: 91) suggested, respect and manhood in the inner city 'are two sides of the same coin'.

The acceptability of using violence as a means to maintain respect and a masculine image varies by social class (Anderson 1999; Kennedy and Forde 1999; Messerschmidt 2000). For instance, research by Kennedy and Forde (1999) suggested the legitimisation of violence differs between segments of the population, and Anderson (1999) suggested that middle-class men were *less* likely to resort to violence in order to maintain respect than those in the lower classes. In the world of the working- or lower-class male, maintaining respect 'on the streets' is of paramount importance (Anderson 1999; Hannertz 1969; Matza and Sykes 1961; Messerschmidt 2000; Shover 1996). For instance, Anderson (1999: 66) noted:

> In the inner-city environment respect on the street may be viewed as a form of social capital that is very valuable, especially when various other forms of capital have been denied or are unavailable. Not only is it protective; it often forms the core of the person's self esteem ... Given its value and its practical implications, respect is fought for and held and challenged as much as honor was in the age of chivalry.

Respect was a highly valued commodity amongst the young men in my sample, and, perhaps, to a greater or lesser degree amongst those with similar backgrounds in Lambeth. As such, fighting is something that should come to be *expected* when their respect is challenged, this being the young people's 'code of the streets'. Shover (1996: 91) has suggested a relationship between fighting, maintaining respect, and displays of toughness and courage amongst working-class males:

> These men are judged by how they respond to challenges of one kind or another. The ability to take care of oneself in a world where challenge and adversity are thought to be inevitable counts as a prime virtue ... In the world

of the lower-class males, respectful treatment by others is expected. When it is not forthcoming or worse, when one is insulted or 'disrespected', a violent response is condoned if not expected.

These culturally and gender-informed perspectives suggest that being respected and 'tough' have been 'traditional' concerns for young men growing up in lower- or working-class environments (Anderson 1999; Corrigan 1979; Hobbs 1988; Miller 1958; Patrick 1973; Shover 1996). For instance, Miller (1958) suggested 'toughness' and physical prowess were a cultural continuity or 'focal concern' amongst young men in lower-class US cultures. More recently, Anderson (1999: 70) noted how adults in the inner city verbally inform children they must 'watch their backs', 'protect themselves', 'don't punk out', 'respect yourself', and 'if someone disses [disrespects] you, you got to straighten them out'. Also, Corrigan (1979: 135), in his study of the 'Smash Street Kids' in the UK, discussed how 'the context of the fights tends to reflect, for the most part, traditional concerns of the [working-class] cultures that the boys grew up in' (see also Hobbs 1988). These cultural perspectives suggest that many generations of young people in lower- or working-class environments, both in the USA and UK, have fought, and continue to fight, for similar reasons: people taking what they perceive as 'liberties'. And as mentioned earlier in the chapter, rates of 'violence against the person' in Lambeth, which includes offences such as assault, actual bodily harm (ABH) and GBH, were relatively high in comparison to other London boroughs and have been for several years. In this regard, there appeared to be a 'tradition' of violence in Lambeth in that, since the 1960s, young people growing up in the borough have probably fought for the same reasons as those in my sample. To this degree, these young people, and perhaps those with similar backgrounds in Lambeth, were a continuation of this 'tradition' (Pearson 1983).

What these perspectives may also suggest is the existence of sanctions against those who *did not* fight when specific instances arose. According to many of the young people interviewed, fighting was primarily instigated by challenges that threatened their 'image' or attacked their personality, or by something that diminished their respect. Not to fight may have led to feelings of disrespect and humiliation, possibly interpreted as causing more damage to the individual's self-image than a physical lashing. Perhaps, if they fail to fight when challenged, these young people run the risk of looking like 'punks'. Hannertz (1969: 80) previously suggested this when researching in the inner city:

> You are not respected if you do not show some toughness; if people can step all over you and you do nothing about it, you are nothing but a punk.

It is also beneficial to address the concept of masculinity because it may help explain why the older people in my sample did not fight any more. Those more involved in offending – such as Quentin, Travis, Theo and Lenny – said they fought when 'younger', but at the time of our interviews were not fighting. These young men were all aged between 17 and 23, and mentioned not being troubled by others any more. Travis, for instance, had not fought with anyone in a 'long time' because 'people don't come and give me shit'. As these young people were older, perhaps they discovered other means to express their masculinity or prove their 'toughness' outside of violence, or maybe their desire to be violent subsided with age and experience (Matza and Sykes 1961). However, the most recent Youth Life-styles Survey (Flood-Page *et al.* 2000) showed those in their late teens and early twenties actually fought more than when they were younger.[5]

Given all of this, how do concepts of masculinity account for the young women's values and experiences with fighting? Two of the girls in my sample, Betty and Tracy, were in many fights, and they discussed fighting 'properly' using their fists in a one-on-one context. Overall, no differences emerged in Betty and Tracy's inter-pretations of fighting when compared to those of the young men. For instance, Betty said she had been in 'loads of fights, proper fights – not bitch fighting'. She continued to explain that 'bitch fighting' or 'cat fights' were fights between young women that involved 'scratching and pulling hair and all that'. Betty, on the other hand, talked about 'boxing their heads' when other girls 'get feisty' with her. In regards to fighting, Betty and Tracy were similar to Campbell's (1991) 'tomboys', and their attitudes towards and experiences with fighting were similar to many of the young men in my sample. In this respect, they perhaps held the same 'mascu-line' values as them (Campbell 1991), and, like the young men, these two appeared to use fighting as a way to 'campaign for respect' (Anderson 1999).

Emotions and reactions to fighting

Many of the young people said that they 'didn't care', or something to that effect, when asked how they felt after fighting. However, some interesting patterns appeared. For instance, a few young people – Frank, Isaac and Tim – were only in a couple of fights, and expressed concern over them. Frank said he felt 'terrible' after his only fight; Isaac felt 'stupid' after his fight; Tim felt 'shit scared, cuz of my old man' after being arrested for fighting. Others less involved in offending, however, did not express remorse. For instance, Kellen did not feel 'anything' after fighting. Likewise, Eric did not 'feel anything after the fights, just to see if I'm cut or something'. Being remorseful over fights was not tomboy behaviour either. Betty feels 'happy' if she wins and 'gutted' if she loses, wanting to fight again. Tracy offered similar comments when asked how she felt after fighting: 'Well, if the girl runs away crying, or is on the floor bleeding then I feel proud of myself. If she ain't got a mark on her, then I just carry on.'

For others less involved in offending, whether or not they generally felt 'good' or 'bad' after their fights was not so clear. Jack and Darrell, for instance, said that how they felt after their fights depended on their demeanour at the time or reason for the fight. Jack, who has been in twenty fights, talked about having 'mixed feelings' afterwards:

> Sometimes, like, I don't have no morals for person, like I wanted to kill them or something. After a while, when I had a good think, I said to myself, 'I wish I

could rewind that time and stop what happened because it shouldn't have happened'. And other times I think, 'I don't care'. So I've got mixed feelings. I wasn't sure if I should regret it, or just stay emotionless.

Darrel offered similar comments to Jack's, and said that how he felt after his fights was conditional. Darrel explained:

> It depends on who you're fighting. If I was fighting someone who had done something specifically then, then after I'll be like, 'Yeah, he deserved it'. But if it's just someone who's been just looking … I think that's a little bit of a liberty.

Others, such as Larry, did not say they felt bad over their fighting, and David went so far as to say he 'felt good' after punching someone who was being 'lippy' with him.

While those less involved in offending, overall, had mixed feelings over their fights, none of those more involved expressed remorse. Nathan, Theo, Quentin, Sonny and Tolu, for instance, all said something to the extent that 'if you disrespect us, you got what you deserved'. This position is similar to Sykes and Matza's (1957: 668) 'denial of victim', one of their 'techniques of neutralization'. The authors suggested that with the 'denial of victim' the individual is viewed as being 'punished' not 'injured'. Correspondingly, Kenny justified fighting a 23-year-old when he said 'he got what he deserved':

> [I felt] Nothing. He got what he deserved. He shouldn't have come down … I know my sister was being mouthy, but you shouldn't throw things at people, especially if they are younger than you. And secondly she's a girl. Now you don't do that to my sister. And I say doing that to her, that's liberties. She's 11 and he's 14.

As suggested earlier, the reasons those in my sample offered for fighting suggested these young people were saving face, defending and maintaining their self-image and being masculine. These young people were 'hard' and 'tough' and did not back down when challenged. For the most part, they expressed no concern, regret or remorse, emotions incongruent with being 'tough', proving your manhood, defending your self-image, earning respect and 'doing masculinity'. Furthermore, for many of those in my sample violence was acceptable under particular circumstances (Anderson 1999; Kennedy and Forde 1999; Matza and Sykes 1961; Messerschmidt 2000; Shover 1996; Wolfgang and Ferracuti 1967). And because the young people in my sample believed their use of violence was legitimate in specific instances, it should perhaps be expected they felt 'fine' after fighting.

Overall, what these interpretations suggest is that the young people made normative judgements about their fighting, similar to their other offences. Nearly all of them said they *only* fought with others for specific, justifiable reasons – reasons that were apparently shared by others throughout Lambeth. For the most part, their fights were not wanton or reckless, and they refrained from laying into others randomly. Moreover, when they fought, these young people did not beat people into pulps, and with few exceptions their accounts of fighting were not too extreme.

Rather, they fought in order to defend themselves, or redress insults, not to cause permanent damage to others. For them, fighting was something done in order to teach the other person a lesson, as opposed to being born out of a desire to cause severe harm. Within their moral universes, violence seemed to have an 'air of respect' about it, and certain situations warranted its use.

Choppers and other weapons

In comparison to the other boroughs in London, at the turn of the century, Lambeth had a relatively high number of offences involving 'weapons that discharge', such as genuine and replica guns, CS or pepper spray, and air guns that fire pellets.[6] Even more significant is that in November 1997 Lambeth police launched a month-long 'gun amnesty', which allowed those possessing a gun illegally a chance to hand it in without being prosecuted. The fact that this amnesty was one of the first times such an event took place in the country suggests the relative high presence of guns in Lambeth. However, the 'word on the street' was that the illegal gun owners turned in their older guns, while keeping more recent models.[7] This way both sides remain happy: the police have something to show for their efforts and the 'bad guys' keep their new guns.

Rather than guns, knives seemed to be an issue in London. When I first arrived in June 1996, I noticed several police posters warning about the severe penalties for being caught with a machete, referred to as a 'chopper'. Coming from Southern California, I often heard about guns, but never anyone using a chopper, let alone carrying one. However, during my time in Lambeth, I heard numerous stories about young people using choppers, such as Chang, who, according to some of the young people befriended while working at The Design, nearly 'chopped' a boy's wrist off. Also, David said his buddy's street name was 'Chopper' because 'he carries it wherever he goes'. David also said how one time he saw Chopper chop two fingers off another boy. As David said:

> He went *Bang*! And it was, like, gross … His fingers rolled off the table.

Other times I read about guns or knives in London or Lambeth specifically, including these four examples from newspaper clippings:

> In the grim litany of Brixton gun crime there is little left to shock, yet on a warm evening outside the Green Man public house in Coldharbour Lane last month the man who put 10 bullets in to 29 year old Devon Dawson did just that – by using a sub-machine-gun.
>
> (*Evening Standard* 27 May 1997)

> A London Underground worker was injured and scores of passengers left gasping for breath after a gang of teenagers threw a can of CS spray into a Tube carriage.
>
> (*Evening Standard* 9 February 1999)

> Death has come to the school gates with the ... conviction of a 16-year-old for murdering a boy from a rival school in a machete attack.
>
> (*Guardian* 16 September 1997)

> Some residents of the Osprey estate know but will not reveal the identity of a gang of murderers who battered to death a 17-year-old boy with snooker cues, baseball bats and cricket stumps – so violently that they shattered their weapons into shards of wood.
>
> (*Evening Standard* 1 December 1997)

Little firearm violence existed in Lambeth when compared to Southern California. Nonetheless, an aspect of gun culture has been imported from the USA on to the streets in Lambeth: the drive-by shooting. However, I only know of a couple such incidents during my time here, one particularly close to my home in Brixton. About two hundred yards behind my house, at the basketball court where I once coached, a drive-by shooting occurred in the summer of 1999. According to a leaflet produced by the volunteer group in charge of the playground, two men on a motorbike pulled up alongside the court and fired several shots at a couple of the players. No one was killed, but two youths were shot. Conversations with police officers in Brixton suggest this, and other incidents involving guns in Lambeth, were drug related, as the individual shot was thought to be involved at some level in an illicit drugs trade, and interrelated in that such a shooting was a 'retaliation' from a previous incident. To be sure though, firearms incidents in Lambeth were *nowhere* near as frequent as they are in inner-city areas in most major US cities (see Zimring and Hawkins 1997), and 'drive-by shootings' are certainly not a cause for a new moral panic in the borough or anywhere else in London.

Overall, despite the occasionally sensational tale from the interviews, my own experiences or those read about within the newspapers, the young people mentioned very little about weapons. Larry felt that 'guns aren't that big amongst young people here'. Only four of the young people even talked about using weapons: Noel, Nathan, Quentin and Karl. For instance, Quentin was in numerous fights, and was responsible for one of the more serious attacks recorded among my sample. He 'chopped' a man across the neck with a rusty chopper because the man owed him 'over £50'. Quentin said the man survived the attack and received nineteen stitches from his left ear down towards the collarbone. Noel also used a weapon once, hitting his sister's boyfriend on the head with a baseball bat. Unlike Quentin, Noel 'rarely' fights, and this incident was the only time he used a weapon. Nathan also said he occasionally used weapons. He showed me a leg from a wooden table that had his and his friend's tags on it. Nathan said he retrieves this wooden leg, which he hides under his bed, when 'trouble' arises. He also said how he once found an air gun that shoots pellets, which he carried with him for a while. However, Nathan did not say that he shot people with it. Karl, however, did. He talked about being a 'sniper' on the rooftop of his estate. Karl said he 'would sniper some people on the roofs' with one of his pellet guns, a source of excitement for him. However, Karl is the only one of the sample who used a weapon 'for fun'. The others wanted to cause great harm to their victims with their weapons, and perhaps even permanent damage.

While rumours about the rise in 'gun culture', and how much like the USA Britain is becoming in this respect, may swim in the media, guns were not really an issue with the young people interviewed. None used a real gun, and most have never even seen one, nor do these young people know anyone who has one. However, Sonny and Karl once saw real hand guns, and continued by saying they could 'get a gun' through others they know. Furthermore, Karl and Nathan both discussed using air pistols or air rifles, but only for recreational purposes. Overall then, for these young people, no gun culture existed.

Some evidence emerged to suggest the reason why the young people did not carry weapons stemmed, in part, from the probability of them being randomly approached by the police. The young people's relationship with the police will be discussed more in depth in the next chapter, and is brought up here only to suggest that not carrying any type of weapon was a conscious decision made by some of them who felt that doing so might lead to negative police intervention. For instance, Travis said:

> Weapons is shit. I get pulled [stopped by police] too often.

Steven, a detached youth worker from Stockwell, agreed:

> Most of the [young] people don't carry no weapon because it's too, it's too dangerous to be walking around because they all ... get searched.

A couple of others mentioned being in trouble with the police for carrying what could be used as a weapon. Darrell, for instance, said how the police found a fishing knife on him that his dad gave him. Darrel was bringing the knife to his friend's house to show him, and was not carrying it for 'protection' or for any other purposes. Likewise, Lenny was stopped once by the police who found a pair of scissors and shaving shears on him, and questioned his genuine use of the scissors for cutting hair. Neither Darrell nor Lenny was arrested for carrying offensive weapons, but they were stopped, searched and questioned by the police. Their examples, however, highlight the real risk young people in Lambeth who carry anything that resembles a weapon may face. Generally speaking, reasons for not carrying a weapon due to their fear of police detection appear to be well-founded.

Fighting over territory

Due to my interest in street gangs, I specifically asked the young people if they 'protected' any area, considered it 'theirs', had any 'rivalries' or something of that nature in order to provoke a discussion on how they defined territory, whether this was relevant in their lives, and, more specifically, if they ever fought over it. Territorial violence has been a common theme explored in research on juvenile-delinquent and criminal street gangs, and in some cases is considered a prerequisite for their existence (see Cloward and Ohlin 1960; Decker and Van Winkle 1996; Fagan 1996; Hagedorn 1988; Jankowski 1991; Keiser 1969; Klein 1971, 1995; Moore 1991; Padilla 1992; Sanders 1994; Spergel 1964, 1995; Taylor 1989; Vigil 1988). Interviews with the young people and the professionals, however, suggested nothing really like this existed in Lambeth. The few reports offered by those in my sample of 'clashes' with another group of youths were absolutely *nothing* like territorial gang-related violence in the USA, a point in line with other UK research (for example Corrigan 1979; Downes 1966; Parker 1974; Willmott 1966). Interviews also suggested no evidence of long-standing rivalries, tit-for-tat violence, gang 'rumbles', 'gang-banging' or territorial disputes. A couple of reports were mentioned of rival groups called the 'Twenty-Eight Posse' and 'The Untouchables' (also mentioned in Graef 1993) who existed in the late 1980s and early 1990s, and, reportedly, lived all over Lambeth.[8] However, in my six years in Brixton I never saw anything like gang rivalries akin to those in the USA, nor heard reports of them. Comments from Rudy, a detached youth worker in Brixton, support this:

> I don't think that you will find that there's a demarcation, like you don't cross over this line. You don't have people that wear red or blue or whatever to protect a certain territory. But in saying that, although there is not a clearly defined territory as such, there is this kind of 'know where to be based'. It's not to say that people can't come in and out; you can come in and out. There is no problem with that. There ain't no statement out there that you don't come into the estates. [Young people] are just based there. I can't really say there's even any inter-gang warfare or rivalry or argument or contention that would give me some type of sense.

Overall, very few accounts emerged about the young people 'protecting' or 'controlling' areas and 'territorial rivalry'. Many young people, regardless of offending history, mentioned some aspects of territory, and no clear patterns emerged on this theme. Rather, the responses about territory all had a similar nature to them. They talked about 'their' area that they 'protected' and 'took care of', and how 'no one could run us out' of 'our manor'. Their 'code of the street' demanded that others could not 'disrespect' them by coming into 'their' area and pushing them around (Anderson 1999; Hannertz 1969; Hobbs 1988; Miller 1958; Shover 1996). All of the young people in my sample seemed to suggest: 'Do not come into my neighbourhood and start trouble, which in this case refers to insulting or illegal behaviour, because if you do we may attack you.'

The comments offered by those in my sample suggest that territory and defending space were enforced primarily to prevent outsiders or those not living in the immediate area from causing trouble within the young people's home environment, apparently for a couple of reasons. One was practical in that by keeping other young people with the intention of committing offences out of their area, those in my sample took up preventative measures to ensure offences were not committed against their friends and acquaintances. Also, by keeping others bent on offending out of 'their' area, these young people reduced their chances of being approached by the police for offences that did not concern them. This, however, is not to suggest those in my sample did not commit offences in their immediate neighbourhoods. Rather, by aiming to deter those not from the area from committing offences the young people reduced the risk of being apprehended for crimes they did not commit. For instance, David offered this reason when asked why he 'protects' his area:

> *Is there any area or territory that you protect or consider yours?*
> I protect my block.
> *When you say protect what do you mean?*
> If anything goes wrong, I'm always there to sort it out, cuz me and my crew we're always there. Like, if someone's nicking a car and we don't know that person, we go down and beat the shit out of them, tell them to put everything back in the car, and one of us goes up to the block we know, tells them and the bloke comes down and beats the shit out of them – the person that owns the car.

Martin offered similar reasons:

> If anyone come on my estate and I don't know them, I fuck 'em off. I go, 'Look, you can't skin up on the stairs. Go away!' And if they cause trouble, then I just get on my phone and call my bredrens, and they will come over and they will help us get 'em off the block.

Kenny also said he keeps 'trouble' off of his 'manor':

> Mostly because boys come around and start like, 'This is *our* manor'. If they come round that's all right, but when they come around, I know stuff that goes on. Yeah, if they come around the area and start saying stuff, like you can't let that happen … because they're boys from other areas come in and like mugging and robbing us or robbing the houses around. They're mugging boys around the area, and the minute anything happens around there the police are gonna come around there and arrest us for doing it.

Another reason offered by the young people about defending space stemmed from their neighbourhood pride. Several from different offending categories said 'this is *our* area'. To them, estates or streets are areas they grew up in and in which they 'belong'; these areas are their 'manor', their 'neighbourhood'. This stance reflects a desire held by the young people to protect and defend 'their' area, 'their' space. Perhaps, they believed it *belonged* to them. It seemed as if, for these young people, thinking outsiders could bully, insult or commit offences within 'their' space was unfathomable. Travis mentioned this when asked about 'protecting' his 'manor':

> *Was there any area or territory that you considered yours or protected?*
> Waterloo. That's our manor … that's what we used to call it, our manor.

How did you protect it?

If pricks come into our area and try to give it some then it would kick off, init? We wouldn't go walking down the street going, 'Yeah, yeah'. But if some boy was walking down the street and there was some next boys that wasn't from Lambeth and start going to us like, 'What you looking at prick?', we wouldn't have it. So, y'know, at the end of the day, if they did bang us over, a phone call away, they would get fucked. There would be some bone heads [crack addicts] looking on their asses boy … if they were from the area, it wouldn't be like that.

Marc expressed similar sentiments:

Yeah, no boys can come on that estate and run me out.
Why do you feel that way?
Because it's our estate, init? No one can come around there like they're bad. They'd get done over, you get me?
What do you mean by done over?
They just get done, man. You can't come walking around at other people's estate.

This reason was echoed in interviews with professionals. For instance, Ayo, a detached youth worker from Stockwell, mentioned this when discussing territory and a group of young people he worked with:

Do they claim or protect a certain area or territory?
Yeah, the Moby Estate. It's theirs.
So if another crew or group came into the Moby Estate would they attack them?
I think there would be some sort of argument or confrontation.
Why do you think they do that?
The Moby Estate is theirs! The same way that anybody would claim a territory. It's theirs. They grew up there.

With a few exceptions, the examples of territory present the young people, once again, as defenders and not attackers. Only Sonny, Travis and Karl discussed specifically going into other areas to look for trouble. However, these young people did not discuss a group of people they consistently fought with or specific area they persistently went into. For the rest of my sample who discussed being attacked in their neighbourhood, the attacks seemed few and far between. Overall, the interviews suggest that if groups of young people were simply passing through or even playing or hanging around in an area that was not 'theirs', they ran little risk of being attacked or confronted by a group of similarly aged young people from such areas. Furthermore, no evidence emerged of any long-standing or serious rivalries between groups of young people from different areas. Examples where groups of young people deliberately set out to cause trouble with other groups of similarly aged young people from different areas over a consistent period of time were unrecorded. No evidence emerged from any of the responses to suggest that a rivalry torch was passed on to a younger generation whereby those from Estate A never get along with those from Estate B.

The UK has exhibited little history of territorial disputes similar to those amongst gangs in the USA. Fighting amongst young people and adults from different areas in the UK has had other outlets outside of ganging. One such outlet is football hooliganism where supporters of one team fight supporters of another, some of which has been known to be somewhat organised before and/or after football matches (Armstrong 1998). Indeed, during my time here I heard much about hooliganism, particularly amongst two London-based football teams, Millwall and Chelsea. However, unlike US-style street gangs, fighting amongst football hooligans erupts not over differences in where people live, but rather which teams they support. Thus, football hooligans supporting different teams may come from the same area. Likewise, football hooligans supporting the same team may come from different areas. In these respects, football hooliganism is distinct from ganging.

Conclusions

In this chapter I discussed the young people's attitudes concerning violence. To start, I attempted to show that, for the most part, they appeared more as defenders and not attackers, in that it always seemed to be that 'someone else' instigated their fights. While their responses could be *post hoc* rationalisations, these fights were primarily discussed as a reaction, a response to what these young people perceived as someone else's wrongdoing. Fighting served as a way to redress 'liberties' they felt were taken with them. This fighting, in turn, served to protect the young person's self-image, their 'rep', and helped them to maintain respect – all very powerful and significant commodities, particularly for lower- or working-class young people with limited opportunities to garner status amongst their peers, and where such behaviours and consequential attitudes may be considered a 'tradition'. As such, fighting for these reasons in areas such as Lambeth should come to be expected. Furthermore, fighting by the young men may be seen as customary masculine behaviour, or as the emulation of such behaviour in the case of the two young women. Perhaps it is to be expected that they would not express any concern or anguish, let alone regret, over their fighting because such feelings are inconsistent with being 'tough', 'hard', and other broadly conceived masculine images. 'Doing masculinity' not only entitles 'doing violence', but also expressing indifference, if not righteousness, over such acts.

In the second section I discussed the young people's use of weapons, and suggested that, for nearly all of them, weapons were not an issue at all; the young people did not use them. I argued that the overall lack of desire to use or carry weapons seemed to stem from a fear they would be stopped by the police and questioned about their weapon, a fear that appeared to be justifiable given their examples of similar occasions. What this distance the young people keep between themselves and the use of weapons suggests is that they made very fine distinctions regarding their violent behaviour. As I attempted to show earlier, not only was it evident that within their value-systems there exists a certain code they seemed to have adhered to, which regulated their 'justifiable' reasons for violence, but this code, these rules, also applied to their use of weapons, or rather their lack thereof. Fighting may have been acceptable in certain circumstances, but the use of weapons, for the most part, was clearly not.

Lastly, a couple of of suggestions were offered about territory and whether the young people fought over this. Young people in my sample were in no way similar to US-style gangs on this point, and issues of territory were primarily absent within their lives. Rather, some made mild claims about the immediate area they grew up in, and 'protected' it only to the extent that they attempted to keep those not from their area from committing their offences, and they didn't let others 'run them out' or 'tell them what to do'. This suggests that, for these young people, not only did they attribute a certain respect, a particular love, for their neighbourhoods, areas they affectionately referred to as 'our manor', but these young people were willing to defend 'their' area with the threat or actual use of violence. Attempts by others to cause trouble in the young people's neighbourhood were met with the same response as other threats to their self-image: violence. This indicates once again that these young people made distinct normative judgements about their illegal behaviour, in this case their violent behaviour.

7 Style, group behaviour, interactions with the police

The previous four chapters addressed the context and frequency of, and attributed reasons behind, the young people's offences, as well as how they felt after committing them. A major shift in focus occurs in this chapter. Rather than exploring what offending meant to these young people or how it fitted in with the rest of their lives, the aim of this chapter is to offer a picture of them by considering their style, group behaviour and their interactions with the police. The first part of the chapter analyses the overall style of the young people, which refers to the clothing they wore, music they listened to, and other cultural miscellany. Next, I look at the activities the young people and their friends did on an 'average' day, and compare this behaviour to that of US-style street gangs. The final section explores the young people's interactions with the police in Lambeth, and why the young people were stopped and searched by them.

The young people's style, group behaviour and interactions with the police are three completely different subjects, but are grouped together in this chapter because they constitute 'cultural' aspects of their lives. 'Culture' has many definitions, including 'knowledge, beliefs, values, codes, tastes and prejudices that are traditional in social groups and that are acquired by participation in such groups' (Cohen 1955: 12). The last four chapters each explored and analysed a different classification of offence the young people committed. One analysed their acquisitive offences, another their expressive offences, a third their drug-related offences, and the last chapter their violent offences: such topics were the 'themes' of the chapters. To this degree, the 'theme' of this chapter is to examine and analyse the mentioned cultural signifiers of those in my sample.

Thus far the criminological significance of my aims have been fairly self-evident: to analyse the young people's offences. But what is the significance of looking at their mentioned cultural signifiers? For one, doing this adds depth and colour to the portrait of young people who have offended in Lambeth. Examining these signifiers is examining the 'culture of crime', what others have referred to as 'cultural criminology' (Ferrell and Sanders 1995; see also Brake 1985; Hall and Jefferson 1976; Hebdige 1979; Katz 1988). When examining and analysing the young people's style, group behaviour and their interactions with the police, the overall aim is to find out what (and if) these aspects of their lives tell us about their illegal or illicit behaviour, and to investigate the common ground between culture and crime as it pertains to these young people.

Style and homology

Generally speaking, while the young people's offending differed markedly, culturally, in terms of style, many similarities were evident. I wrote down descriptions of the clothing they wore during their interview and the other times we met, and noticed all of them followed the same fashion. I also specifically asked them about what music they listened to, and again found similarities. Finally, I watched how the young people interacted with one another, and noticed they all strutted, greeted each other with the 'touch' of their fists, and showed their disrespect or contempt by 'sucking' their teeth. This suggests that, while clear differences existed between the young people based on criminal aspects of their lives, it would be impossible to distinguish between those more or less involved in offending in my sample based on what they looked like walking down the street together, how they interacted with one another, or the music they listened to.

In the first part of this section I analyse aspects of their fashion by looking at the clothing they wore and assess its significance. Here, I suggest all but a few of the young people in my sample placed a lot of emphasis on looking 'good' and wearing the 'right' clothing – very significant characteristics in their lives. Because their fashion consisted of sportswear with relatively expensive popular labels, such as Nike and Adidas and other designer clothing, the young people, through wearing these clothes, were able to somewhat distance themselves from their lower- or working-class environment. Their clothes gave off an affluent impression, in contrast to the overall inner-city urban Lambeth environment. Furthermore, these young people seemed to be trend followers not trend setters in terms of fashion; the clothing they wore was packaged and manufactured specifically for them and comprised the latest youthful fashion. By sporting this fashion the young people bettered their chances at being viewed as 'hip', 'cool' and respected, very important commodities in their worlds (Anderson 1999; Campbell 1993; Jacobs and Wright 1999).

The music the young people listened to is also examined in this section. Several of them, regardless of offending history, said they felt a certain connection with their music, particularly 'hard-core' hip-hop and jungle. In other words they believed what the artists were rapping about mirrored actual events that had happened to them, or they felt the theme and tone of this music accurately reflected their personal experiences or lifestyles. Other miscellaneous cultural signifiers of the young people explored in this section include the way they talked, the way they walked, and their overall demeanour. In the final part of this section I look at all of the elements discussed that make up the young people's style and suggest the existence of a homology (Willis 1978) or 'sameness' that interwove throughout this style, their personality, their attitudes and the overall lives of many of them, particularly those more involved in offending.

Looking cris

In the world of the young people, to look 'cris' means to look good, fashionable, to give off the desired appearance. Clothing was very significant to those in my sample; clothing gave them the look of affluence. All of those in my sample, except Tom, Frank and Tim – 'T-shirts and jeans' young men – placed a great deal of emphasis on wearing the 'right' clothes like sportswear items, such as trainers, sweatshirts, fleece wear, tracksuit bottoms, 'puffa'-style jackets, hooded tops, sports jerseys of athletic clubs and T-shirts. This sportswear was not ordinary, but consisted of designer labels such as Nike, Adidas, Reebok and, to a lesser extent, Ellesse and Kappa. Karl, Larry and Martin were so passionate about sportswear they said they once shaved logos, such as the Nike 'tick' or the Adidas 'leaf', into the back or sides of their hair. The young people also wore some expensive, designer clothing, such as Calvin Klein, Armani, Dolce & Gabbana, Moschino, Versace, Fubu, Tommy Hilfiger, Helly Hansen, Mecca and Pelle Pelle. What tended to be the case with them was that they predominately wore sportswear, but had a couple of pieces of clothing made by the high-street designers, such as an Armani jacket, Dolce & Gabbana sweater, Versace trousers or Tommy Hilfiger jeans. Also, they tended to be well presented in their clothing, and did not wear torn or tattered clothing or trainers; not to say their clothing was immaculate, just fairly clean. Again, no differences in fashion emerged between different young people. On the surface all of them looked similar.

Other fashion accessories the young people wore included modest numbers of gold or silver rings, bracelets or necklaces. Headgear, such as baseball hats, 'woolly' hats and 'skullies' – nylon caps worn snug on the head – and baseball hats made of cotton with long ear warmers, all with a visible sportswear name or insignia on them, were also popular. Mobile phones, or just 'mobiles', were another necessary accessory, as nearly all of the young people had one. Observations suggest this fashion was not exclusive to those in my sample, but rather part of a general youthful fashion observed in Lambeth and other parts of London.

The clothing the young people wore was packaged, advertised and marketed specifically towards them. Where others have suggested that inner-city youth cultures eventually become absorbed and incorporated into mainstream popular culture (for example Hebdige 1979; Melly 1970; Muncie 1984), the impression received from those in my sample is one of them following rather than generating fashion. Their fashion was influenced by, if not directly appropriated from, mainstream popular culture. In other words, the young people were wearing the 'latest fashion'. I observed many advertisements in Lambeth and throughout London with models posing in clothing the young people wore, including popular sports celebrities and hip-hop and soul or rhythm & blues musicians. Such images seemed to be very influential in terms of what the young people wore, a point confirmed in interviews with professionals. For instance, Ayo, a detached youth worker from Stockwell, briefly commented on how young people wanted to wear what their favourite artists were wearing:

> If you watch a Jay Z [hip-hop artist] video and you're gonna think, 'Wow! Look what Jay Z's wearing!' Then, like a couple of weeks later, you gonna be wearing the same thing.

In twenty years or so perhaps the hyper-loud Versace and Moschino trousers, tight-fitting 'skullies', baggy jeans at least two sizes too big, expensive trainers and the rest of the clothing worn by the young people will be remembered as what was fashionable in the late 1990s on into the early parts of the new millennium. In this sense, their fashion deserves a place within the continuum of Britain's youthful fashions, such as the Edwardian suit of the teddy boys in the 1950s, the anoraks and leather jackets of the mods and rockers in the 1960s, the braces, safety pins, and Doc Martens of the skinheads and punks of the 1970s, the big hair and pegged trousers of the new romantics or new wave, and the day-glo, extra-large-sized clothing and 'happy-face' T-shirts of the ravers in the early 1990s.

By wearing designer clothing many of the less affluent young people in my sample, particularly those more seriously involved in offending, were able to mask their economic situation. At first, I found it peculiar that many of them lived in public-sector housing with one parent who worked at a low-income job (if at all), *and* were still able to afford relatively expensive clothing. Brenda, a youth justice worker, also mentioned this in relation to some of the young people she has worked with:

> They might not have a house. They might not have a roof. You go to the house that they lived in and it's the basic necessities or it's squalor. But they've got the most expensive [clothing]. So their priorities, it's like, I wouldn't say they're wrong, they're just out of sync if you like. They've got it the other way around.

This observation was something I noticed about others throughout Lambeth, such as my co-workers, neighbours and some of the other young people I met during my time in the borough. For instance, two co-workers at the clothing shop on Coldharbour Lane, Heidi and Theresa, both lived on an estate, and both dressed themselves and their children in brand-new designer clothing. I wondered how they and those from similar backgrounds could afford such clothing.[1] Wearing designer clothing seemed so important to them. But why was this? Overall, it appeared that amongst a section of Lambeth's less affluent population looking 'good' through the appropriation of relatively expensive clothing was highly significant, something certainly the case with most of the young people in my sample. These young people placed much emphasis on presenting themselves in approved, fashionable attire. For them, Heidi, Theresa and perhaps those with similar backgrounds in Lambeth, designer clothing allowed them to look like they possessed more money than they actually did. Sporting this fashion also told others that, despite growing up and living in a lower- or working-class borough, they 'made it', that they managed to rise above the poverty that continually surrounds them, and that these young people were amongst 'people going places' (Campbell 1993: 272). Campbell did some research in the inner city, and suggested young people placed a great deal of importance on designer clothing. She (1993: 272) said:

> The passion for the label suggests aspiration and ambition rather than rebellion, and yet within that style strategy they are breaking the boundaries of work and leisure, respectability and relaxation – the very frontiers that these

same commodities would have asserted for another class who move in everyday life between home and work, public and private, those spaces which are defined by dress code: people going places.

Fashion was a feasible way for the less affluent young people in my sample, and others in Lambeth with similar backgrounds, to transcend the poverty they suffered on a daily basis. For them, their self-presentation in the public sphere was highly significant (Anderson 1999; Finestone 1957; Jacobs and Wright 1999; Katz 1988; Shover 1996). Fashion creates a façade that suggests if these young people could not match the riches of those in the middle or upper classes, they at least could appear to have done so. Fashion allowed these young people to be visually on a par with the more affluent, and, as such, was very important to them.

Music

I asked the young people what music they listened to and, generally speaking, they mentioned liking hip-hop, jungle, drum & bass and garage, and, to a lesser extent, reggae, and soul or rhythm & blues. All of this music is somewhat related in that the music is bass heavy, similar themes are 'rapped' about within all of them, and various musicians and lyricists from these different categories of music have been known to collaborate (such as reggae or soul artists singing with hip-hop rappers; hip-hop rappers on jungle or drum & bass tracks).[2] In this regard, these classifications of music are different branches from the same tree, and are somewhat related to one another.

Hip-hop refers to music as well as culture. Hip-hop cultural signifiers include graffitti, break dancing, emceeing, DJing and rapping. 'Rap' and hip-hop are often thought of as being the same thing, and generally speaking this is the case. But rap, in the context of hip-hop culture, refers specifically to the way the lyrics are spoken or sung within a song, and 'rappers' are hip-hop lyricists.

Hip-hop music styles vary, but the young people said they primarily listened to 'hard-core' or 'gangsta' hip-hop groups or rappers. Lyrics in hard-core hip-hop music often surround violence, drugs, and other stories of inner-city neighbourhoods and their inhabitants. Reynolds (1997: 1) referred to hard-core hip-hop as being 'the music [with] a sonic simulation of the city-as-warzone ... tension-but-no-release'. In hard-core hip-hop music, men are frequently referred to as 'niggers', 'gangstas' or 'playas', women are 'bitches' and 'hos', and profanity is used in nearly every song. Hard-core hip-hop's bad mouth and its violent, misogynist and drug-related themes caused a 'moral panic' in the 1980s and 1990s in both the UK and USA, and some artists and record companies were charged with obscenity (see Ferrell and Sanders 1995: 8–11).[3]

Jungle and drum & bass were also popular with those in my sample. While these are technically different categories of music, similarities exist between them. The beat in jungle and drum & bass is essentially a hip-hop beat with the tempo considerably sped up, combined with the conglomeration of other electronic sounds looped throughout. Jungle does not always feature a lyricist, but is rather characterised by its rapid-fire, deep bass grooves and hooked 'samples' – previously recorded sounds – scattered throughout the songs. The speed of drum & bass is similar to jungle, but often has a jazzy, upbeat tone to it. Also, lyrics are not as uncommon in drum & bass as in jungle. Drum & bass and jungle albums may also contain a mixture of each type of music whereby some songs on the album are similar to jungle, and others akin to drum & bass.

Garage, like jungle and drum & bass, has a very quick beat. Lyrics within garage music are to be expected, and the rhythm is upbeat and the tone not as 'dark' as that commonly found in jungle. Another characteristic of garage is the way an emcee (MC) will 'chat' or rap throughout the song. The rapping associated with garage music is distinct from that found in hip-hop. Because the tempo of the raps tends to coincide with that of the music, the rapping in garage is usually faster. Nonetheless, the lyrics are often similar to those found in 'gangsta' hip-hop (for example money, self-aggrandisement, drugs, violence).

Many of the young people also said they listened to soul or rhythm & blues. Contemporary soul or rhythm & blues is similar to lighter, more melodic forms of hip-hop. While the beats in soul or rhythm & blues may sound similar to those produced by hip-hop artists, lyrics centre around themes of money, clothing, sex and, most of all, love and relationships. As Lawrence, a NACRO worker suggested, 'R'n'B is about the opposite sex'. Furthermore, the lyrics within soul or rhythm & blues are, for the most part, sung rather than rapped as they are in hip-hop, and the tempo is adjusted accordingly.

Reggae was also popular, but much less so than the other kinds of music discussed thus far. Reggae has various classifications, but the young people talked about 'ragga', also known as 'dancehall' reggae. In Brixton ragga and other reggae can sometimes be heard pumping out of stores along Coldharbour Lane and throughout the Brixton marketplace (a 'reggae car' painted the colours of the Jamaican flag, with speakers strapped to the roof playing reggae, has been observed in Brixton numerous times). The beat in ragga music is very bass heavy, and the lyricists often sing with a thick Caribbean patois.

Reasons for listening to any one particular music will obviously vary, and attempting to understand why those in my sample prefer one music over another is difficult given the approach. However, when asked, several of them mentioned having 'no idea' why they listened to their music. For instance, Kevin, when asked why he listened to garage, replied 'I ain't got a clue, mate. I just like it.' Some, however, offered reasons why they enjoyed their music. Marc and Travis said they liked the dark and brooding tones of jungle. Marc, for instance, said he listened to jungle because the music is, 'Aggressive, ya get me? Scary and rowdy, ya get me?' Travis listened to jungle because 'it's dark … evil … crooked':

> It's dark man. It's evil man. Evilness in the jungle man. It's crooked. When the MC starts chatting man about sucking bones [smoking crack through a pipe] Yeah, man, crack heads, shit like that. When you go to jungle raves, all rudies are bunning [smoking] joints filled with crack and all that.

Others, such as Kenny and Sonny, said they listened to garage because they enjoyed rapping to it. Kenny said he liked to MC to garage music and called himself 'Lyrical' because:

> I'm a lyrical miracle. I don't know. I'm just good with words … when I chat. When I MC.

Sonny also said he preferred jungle, drum & bass and garage music because he likes to

> MC, like to jungle and stuff like that.

As mentioned in Chapter Five, Kenny created graffiti pieces and tags – dimensions of hip-hop culture. Kenny's involvement in hip-hop culture extended beyond this, though, because he emceed and DJed on a 'pirate' radio station. Kenny said he owned 'a pretty good transmitter' that cost him £70, which he sometimes placed on the roof of his estate and connected to an amplifier, a set of record turntables and a speaker. This mini radio station allowed Kenny to broadcast over a limited distance. When returning to the youth centre for additional interviews, he told me he gave a 'shout out' on his radio station by saying something like 'Big up and respect to Bill from America over in Brixton'. Many radio DJs and listeners calling in give 'shout outs' or 'big ups' to others on stations playing hip-hop, rhythm & blues, jungle and/or drum & bass music. Such a practice is to be expected in such situations.

Regardless of offending history, one recurring response the young people offered when asked why they listened to their music was a 'connection' felt between their lives and what was being 'rapped' within hard-core hip-hop. For instance, Brian said that he felt particular hard-core hip-hop musicians were 'keeping it real' especially for those 'in the struggle' like himself. Quentin said hard-core hip-hop music expresses 'the rawness, the realness' of experiences similar to his own. Isaac said hard-core hip-hop 'tells you what's going on in life'. He elaborated:

> Sometimes they [the rappers] tell you what's going on in life … I listen to the ones that's street life, that know what's going on … people like Eminem [hip-hop artist]. He wrote a song about, like his girlfriend tried to take away his daughter and things like that. He had to go through custody and things like that. Things like that are true, so I just listen.

Kellen said hip-hop artists rap about 'real life':

> The words they talk is not bullshit; it's like real life. They're not making it up. They're talking about real stuff, like what's happening.

Likewise, Larry said hard-core rappers 'chat sense':

What do you like about the Wu-Tang Clan?
They chat sense.
When you say they chat sense what do you mean?
Just the style. They rap about how it is growing up in the wild side and all that.
What do you mean by wild side and all that?
Well, it [Brixton] isn't exactly a posh area now, is it?

This 'connection' felt by these young people was confirmed by professionals who said young people in Lambeth from similar backgrounds that they worked with had offered similar comments. For instance, Lawrence, a NACRO worker, found that young people in Lambeth 'identify with' hip-hop music. Ayo, a detached youth worker from Stockwell, talked about how hard-core hip-hop was about 'expressing yourself', and how lyricists rap about how they 'see it'. He explained:

> I think the thing about hip-hop is why I like hip-hop is that some songs are about expressing yourself. Like, you know expression: How you feel; what you've seen; what you think [is] gonna happen; how easy things [are] in general. It's just about expression … At the end of the day, if what you see like, say you come out of your house and you don't see no green and all you see are bare blocks and concrete playground and everything and what you gotta say? You see men getting shot and everything, that you have to rap about it. You can't rap about what you can't see, y'get me? … Part of it is how you see it really, y'get me?

Rudy, a detached youth worker from Brixton, discussed how hard-core hip-hop artists were 'representing' the 'ghetto type':

> I think that, I mean what the artists are representing, I think that what the artists themselves represent the social condition where they're coming from, y'know, coming from the ghetto type. I think they [the young people] identify with that. I think that some of the symbolism of success, y'know i.e. the car, the girls, these kinds of imagery. They're buying into that kind of image, and I don't know how financial secure or if their career plan is to get to those points, but you know that very much is kind of the symbolism that is all around them.

That many of those in my sample, and young people in Lambeth with similar backgrounds, said they felt a 'connection' with their music should not be surprising. The experiences of working- or lower-class inner-city inhabitants are often themes in hip-hop, jungle, garage, drum & bass and reggae, and the lyricists rapping in these categories of music often claim to be from such environments. By rapping about what they see these artists deliver 'reality lyrics', which discuss a social condition these young people can identify with. In this regard, the music they listened to was culturally compatible with the rest of their lives. The young people would seem out of place if they listened to country and western music just as a cowhand or farmer from the 'heartland' of the USA would seem listening to hard-core 'gangsta' hip-hop.

Offences such as selling drugs, robbery, burglary and car theft are common fodder for hard-core hip-hop rappers, and to a lesser extent jungle and garage lyricists. Furthermore, the consequences of being caught and arrested for these offences – such as dealing with the criminal justice system, life in and out of jail and the repercussions of life after prison (for example stigmatisation as an ex-convict, problems finding legitimate employment) – are also frequently rapped about. In some cases the distinctions between being a hard-core hip-hop artist and being a real gangster or thug are blurred. For instance, two gangsta rappers very popular with those in my sample, Notorious B.I.G. and Tupac Shakur, both rapped about guns, violence and 'thug life'. In September 1996 Tupac was shot dead in a gangland-style execution; Biggie met the same fate about half a year later. Other hip-hop artists popular with those in my sample who have criminal histories include Snoop Dogg, who was in court on murder charges; Ol' Dirty Bastard from the Wu-Tang Clan who, at the time of writing, is on remand for probation violation; and 50 Cent, a former crack seller, who once reportedly drove himself to the hospital after being shot several times at point-blank range. Garage musicians who rap about similar themes found in hard-core hip-hop have also been in legal trouble. For instance, in 2002, Asher D from the garage collective So Solid Crew was found guilty of possessing a loaded gun, and sentenced to 18 months in a young offenders' institution. For all of these artists such events, no doubt, reinforce their credibility as 'gangstas from the street', and are testament that their accounts of 'street life' are authentic. For several of those more involved in offending, and perhaps other young people with similar backgrounds in Lambeth, the connection felt with this music is even tighter because it discusses offences they committed and other experiences with the police and courts they may have had. In this regard, gangsta hip-hop, jungle and garage was the theme music to their lives.

Cultural miscellany

Another cultural indicator of the young people was the way they walked. Observations suggest they exhibited a sway or swagger, what they referred to as 'bowling', rather as if the young people were not just walking, but rather bouncing or strutting, similar to what Anderson (1990: 178) called 'the quasi-military swagger to the beat of "rap" songs in public places' (see also Katz 1988). Each of those in my sample had their own signature stride, which was somewhat distinct from what may best be described as a 'standard' walk. The young people also greeted each other in a particular way. Instead of shaking hands, many gently knocked their closed fists together, in what was called a 'touch'. Also, the young people showed their disrespect towards someone or contempt of something by 'kissing' or 'sucking' their teeth. Teeth kissing varied in length – some made the teeth-kissing sound quickly, while others drew it out for effect. These cultural indicators, however, were not particular to those in my sample, as these behaviours were observed amongst many young people in Lambeth and elsewhere in London.

Several of the young people mentioned how they 'hung out' with their friends, and tested their skill at 'taking the piss' out of one another (Anderson 1999; Katz

1988; Schneider 1999). For those in my sample, the intentions of these sessions were not to threaten or harm; rather, these 'battles of verbal wit' were done amongst friends in an overall light and humorous environment. For instance, individuals within a group might exchange insults, among which lewd comments about mums seemed to figure prominently, and the success of each cuss or slur was gauged by the responses of the others in the group (cheers, jeers, and so on). Kevin talked about doing this with his friends, what he called 'the raw deal':

> Like, when we're all together, the amount of jokes they come out, the amount of the things that are so funny. They just give you bear [many] joke, like when you with them just bear. I mean like proper jokes. It's like, if we're all sitting there one minute it will be switched around to someone else, but like we take the piss out of all of us. Like we call it 'the raw deal'. Let's say one night I might get it. They'd give it to us hard, right. Just terrorise you, everything you got on. Say your collar was sticking out – they'd make a joke about that, a good one. They wouldn't say it unless it was a funny joke.

Culture, behaviour, homology

The concept of homology is borrowed from Willis (1978), who discussed a 'homological' level of cultural analysis when conducting research on 'hippy' and 'biker' youth subcultures in England. Willis (1978: 191) suggested that the homological analysis focused on how 'particular items parallel and reflect the structure, style, typical concerns, attitudes and feelings of the social group'. Willis's (1978: 4) argument linked the 'particular relationship' between the motorbike and rock-and-roll lifestyle with the bikers, and drug taking and the 'progressive' musical tastes with the hippies.

A homology existed between many of the young people in my sample, particularly those more involved in offending, and cultural aspects of their lives, such as their style and music. In other words, for these young people, a consistency emerged between their experiences, attitudes, music and style – a 'particular relationship'. For instance, several mentioned they felt a 'connection' between their music and their lives in that they could often relate to what was being sung or rapped about in the music. The rappers rapped about events or experiences the young people had been through themselves. Also, as discussed earlier, gangsta rappers and jungle and garage emcees also often rap about serious 'street' offences, such as drug selling, street robbery and burglary – offences committed by some of those more involved in offending. For these young people, the homology seemed even stronger.

The celebration of cannabis and disgust at crack and/or heroin use amongst those in my sample was also reflected in their music. Likewise, tagging, graffiti art, being verbally witty, 'sucking' teeth and greeting acquaintances with the 'touch' are other behaviours associated with their music – behaviours the artists rapped about. Finally, physical prowess, maintaining respect through fighting, not being taken advantage of, and the importance of clothing and wearing the 'latest' fashion are themes in hip-hop, garage, jungle, rhythm & blues and soul. Following suit, the young people in my sample placed a similar emphasis on defending their self-image, being 'respected' when out 'on the street' and looking 'good' – very important things to them. Even their overall demeanour went hand in glove with their music and style. Their laid-back walk, the 'cool' touch of the fists and how they ended sentences with a cocky, self-assured 'y'know?', 'yaknowhatImean?' or just 'init?': for many in my sample, and perhaps other young people in Lambeth with similar backgrounds, this behaviour is to be expected when out 'on the streets' in order to 'keep it real'. This 'tough/cool' demeanour was congruent with their 'tough/cool' music. Overall, for those in my sample it is pretty clear that a particular relationship existed between their style, attitudes and behaviour. For those more involved in offending, this connection was even tighter.

That a homology exists between the style of those in my sample and how many lead their lives is, perhaps, not surprising. For instance, the music they listened to was largely performed by artists who claimed to have been brought up in similar environments to those in my sample: the 'rough' inner city. In this sense there appeared to be a reflexive relationship between the young people and their music – an excellent example of culture as both a product (music about the inner city) and a process (growing up in the inner city). This is not to suggest that their music influenced them to commit certain offences or behave in a particular way, rather that the lyrics within a lot of the music they listened to reflected and possibly reinforced the lifestyles many of them led, particularly those more involved in offending in my sample, and other young people in Lambeth growing up in similar circumstances going through similar experiences.

Young people and their friends

Analysing the group behaviour of the young people has sociological significance because much can be learned about them by looking at what they and their friends got up to. Furthermore, looking at this group behaviour is also important for criminological purposes because these young people said they committed their offences with their mates, a point consistent with much research (such as Downes 1966; Klein 1971; Reiss 1986; Sullivan 1989). Looking more closely at their social groupings may thus offer additional information related to their offences.

In the beginning of the book I explained that my initial interest in coming to London was to determine if US-style street gangs existed. So I attempted to make it clear that no one in my sample nor the professionals really talked about gangs, that the graffiti by those in my sample was dissimilar to US-style gang graffiti, and that no evidence emerged to suggest they or other young people in Lambeth with similar backgrounds fought over 'turf' or had long-standing rivalries characteristic of US-style gangs. Nonetheless, during my time in England the use of the word 'gang' itself seemed to be used liberally within the mass media. For instance, from the newspaper clippings collected, it was obvious that journalists defined 'gang' in a very loose way. Some examples include:

Juvenile gang rape is a new and horrific crime which is on the increase the

length and breadth of the country. Kids barely into their teens are being sent
to jail for sex crimes that are unthinkable to most of us.

(*The Voice* 16 November 1998)

Heroin gang jailed.

(*The Guardian* 28 April 1998)

Gang members acted as lookouts and gave signals to warn of police, allowing
dealers to melt into the crowds.

(*Evening Standard* 15 March 1999)

The appeal committee heard how a gang of pupils 'became a mindless mob'
and brought shame on the school as they punched and kicked their victim to
the ground.

(*The Guardian* 13 October 98)

How Police Have Beaten Knife Gangs.

(*Evening Standard* 22 July 1997)

Gangs, especially American Crips and Bloods, get huge media exposure but
the true extent of the problem in British schools and how much violent fantasy
is in danger of becoming a reality here are in dispute.

(*The Guardian* 16 September 1997)

These clippings suggest 'gang' referred to 'a group of people'. However, as the
last clipping from *The Guardian* noted, the presence of US-style street gangs appears
'in dispute'. With my sample of young people, very close attention was paid to their
group behaviour, and I asked them questions about the friends they 'hang around'.
More specifically, I asked if the young people were 'initiated' into their groups, if
they used group names, if any roles or statuses existed in their group, and the extent
they offended with their friends. All of these questions aimed to determine if the
group behaviour of those in my sample was similar to that of US street gangs
(Decker and Van Winkle 1996; Fagan 1996; Hagedorn 1988; Jankowski 1991;
Keiser 1969; Klein 1995; Moore 1991; Sanders 1994; Spergel 1995; Taylor 1989;
Vigil 1988). However, I found that, as far as these points were concerned, those in
my sample were *nothing* like the US gangs. Likewise, none of the professionals said
the groups of young people in Lambeth that they worked with were similar to
gangs in these respects.

Analysing the group behaviour of the young people threw up some interesting
patterns. First, all but two of them, Frank and Tom, said they spent the majority of
their free time in small groups of between four to eight others who were roughly the
same age, and, for the most part, same sex. Evidence suggests these groups formed
naturally, and that the young people 'hung out' with others for companionship,
because they shared similar interests, and for protection as they expressed how they
felt 'unsafe' walking around Lambeth on their own. Additionally, it appeared that,

overall, in terms of group behaviour, *all* of those in my sample were no different from groups of young people from the inner city previously researched (for example Downes 1966; Foster 1990; Parker 1974; Willis 1977; Willmott 1966).

What my findings also indicate is that, as with their 'style', the group behaviour of all the young people, regardless of offending history, was remarkably similar. In other words, when the young people were *not* committing offences, they discussed doing similar activities with their friends and shared similar interests. Those more involved in offending, for the most part, did the same kinds of activities as those who committed relatively fewer offences. In terms of group behaviour, distinguishing between those more and less involved in offending would be almost impossible.

Hanging out, meeting up, being known

According to gang researchers, many US-style street gangs regenerate by initiating young people in their neighbourhoods (Klein 1995; Spergel 1995). I asked the young people in my sample how their groups formed, and queried them on any initiation procedures, such as doing a 'daring' feat or fighting another young person already part of a group. *None mentioned anything like this.* Rather, the young people mentioned being friends with those they met through consistent interactions and associations stemming from residential proximity, attending the same school, and sharing similar interests. Complementing these similarities were other activities that served as a social glue, naturally binding the young people together in small groups. Such activities included school, youth clubs, activities and other youth-oriented programmes (such as community sports teams). In this regard the young people were similar to Parker's (1974: 64) 'Boys', described as a 'network of lads who've grown up together and are seen around together in various combinations ... a loose knit social group' (see also Downes 1966; Foster 1990; Robins 1992; Willis 1977; Willmott 1966). Interview material from the professionals also suggested that US-style gangs were not in Lambeth. For instance, Kerrie, a youth and community worker from Brixton, made the following point:

> I think because I've had experience working in America, I would define gang very differently in America from what I'd define gang here as. I don't think it's as organised or structured as it is in the States ... In England I would define the term 'gang' as a group of people who hang out together and I think it's as simple as that.

Rod, a drugs squad officer from Brixton, agreed:

> The gang situation here is a lot different to that in the States ... In London it is much more loose ... there are loose groups that operate together, but they won't necessarily operate as a traditional gang. They will run for a while then not exist any more ... They're really more groups or associations of people rather than gangs.

Even one of the young people, Eric, mentioned the dissimilarity between his group of friends and US-style gangs.

> *Are there any clothes or colours or signs that distinguish your group from any other?*
> Nah. This ain't America.

Residential proximity, companionship and sharing similar interests and activities were the general reasons why all the young people, regardless of offending histories, 'hung out' with each other. For instance, Kenny, who was more involved in offending, briefly discussed how he became friends who those he 'hangs around'.

> *How do you decide if someone's in your group?*
> I suppose they're like with us all the time.
> *How are they with you all the time?*
> When I'm out there, they're there most of the time … and they usually like to come to the places, like, that's with us and they like.

Eric, who was less involved in offending, mentioned something similar.

> *Why do you hang out with these guys?*
> They think like me and they understand things that I go through cuz like we go through the similar things like, and I see them. We go to the same school and live in the same area and we go and pump weights.
> *How do you decide if someone is a part of your group?*
> Well like I said, you either make friends naturally or you don't make friends.

Professionals concurred. For instance, Lawrence, a NACRO worker from Brixton, said young people did this because:

> It's just an association. I think every human being needs friends and people that you know. We just like to associate. We're just social animals and that's basically it. And the fact that they have an identity with each other and are close to each other … Young people have a tight bond with their friends that they develop from school or the local estate. And the fact is they're so close to each other and they see each other frequently and it's the frequency of it which gives that type of bonding, yeah? … It's that frequency of contact which gives it that special bond.

Ben, a youth and community worker from Clapham, mentioned something similar:

> I think it's a group, y'know, in any other group for some of the same reasons. You'll find it gives them a sense of belonging, a sense of identity. The people they associate with generally are on average from similar cultural backgrounds, have similar types of social experiences. They're also the same gender. Umm, they have similar kinds of interest in terms of music, dress

codes, what they each sort of, umm, subcultural vocabulary, y'know? I think it's those sort of things that bind them together.

Other, perhaps more practical, reasons were expressed by the young people as to why they 'hung out' with their friends, namely protection (Anderson 1999). Many in my sample expressed feeling 'safer' with their friends when they travelled in Lambeth, and how venturing out on their own was 'dangerous' due to the perceived risk of being attacked. These young people said that their friends 'had their backs', meaning they would help if any of them was attacked or threatened. For instance, Kenny said his friends provided him with 'security'. Tracy discussed how her friends acted as 'back-up'.

> *Why do you hang out with those guys?*
> Because, one they are my friends and two you gotta have back-up when you need it.
> *Back-up for what?*
> If a bunch of people try to trouble you.

This point was confirmed in interviews with professionals. For instance, Steven, a detached youth worker from Stockwell, mentioned how 'protection' was a reason he believed young people he worked with coalesced in small groups. Lewis, a CID officer from Clapham, also mentioned 'safety in numbers' as why he thought young people he worked with 'hang out' together.

> *Why do you think they hang out together?*
> Again, it's just safety in numbers. They just feel secure with their numbers. It's almost as if they get picked off when they go and do something on their own. They hang about in that estate in a number. Very seldom do we see one or two together on their own.

Tommy, a youth justice worker, mentioned a protective aspect about the group:

> If you walk on your own and there's a group of five kids at the other end of the street, it's a good more likely to, y'know, that you'd get bullied, that you'd get robbed or anything. [But] if you walk down the street and there's five of you … then it's likely that the group will let you go by … it's not safe to be one on your own.

In terms of their group behaviour all the young people had much in common, and no differences were apparent between those more or less involved in offending in terms of what they said their 'average' days were like. In other words when, for instance, Marc was not selling drugs or committing other offences, he engaged in similar activities to the rest in my sample, even, for instance, young people like Kellen or Tim, who committed relatively petty offences. In terms of daily activity outside of school (for those attending) 'average' days for the young people in my sample consisted of sitting around with others and chatting, playing football or other athletic activities in parks and playgrounds, playing on 'the computer' (for example the Sony Playstation; Nintendo 64), 'checking' or looking for and talking to young people of the opposite sex, smoking cigarettes and spliffs and generally 'nothing' or just 'hanging around' the immediate areas they lived in. Overall, these young people, like gang members in the USA, spent the majority of their time *not* committing offences (Klein 1995; Spergel 1995; see also Matza 1964). Some examples of replies to the question 'What do you and your friends do on an average day?' from Terry, Kenny, Keenan and Jack respectively, are below.

> Just typical day? Just like hanging around in the estate, walking up and down. Just looking for something to do really.
> Sit down. Bun [smoke cannabis]. I don't know. We're just hanging.
> Just hang around on the estate, listen to music.
> Just hang out, smoke (*Smoke?*) Cigarettes or sometimes weed, and just hang out, smoke, muck about, talk to girls. Just that stuff.

Many of the professionals also discussed how young people spent a great deal of their time simply 'hanging out' with friends. Excerpts from interviews with Declan, Tommy and Barry (three youth justice workers), respectively, about what they thought an 'average day' was like for young people they worked with are below.

> They hang out together … chat to girls. If they could go to a friend's house who was old enough to let them and listen to music. Just hang out mainly.
> They would get together and listen to music at one of the parents' house where it was allowed. They would sit around in the house. They did used to go to youth clubs … They would go along and play pool. They would stay for an hour and then move on. They would hang around outside of pubs … Just hang around on corners.
> They get up late, come together. Depends upon the funds available to go shopping. Or hang out and smoke, play computer games, watch television, listen to music until the evening time … Go to some other houses, meet girls, get some drink maybe, then some [cannabis] would get used. Maybe go to a dance.

Group names were also relatively absent amongst my sample, and only a few of the young people said they or their friends had one. For instance, Kenny and Darrell were part of a larger collective, who lived on an estate in Kennington, who called themselves the 'No Rules Crew'. According to Kenny, a couple of the boys in this group had 'NRC' shaved on their heads, and others have tagged 'NRC' alongside their tag or graffiti piece. Also, Nathan and Larry are brothers who lived in Brixton. One of their friends was Sonny. The three of them were part of a larger group of about eight who called themselves 'The Brookside Bombers', named after the Brookside Estate in Brixton where some of them lived. However, according to them, the name Brookside Bombers has changed a couple of times. These young people have also called themselves 'The Brookside Massive' or 'The Brookside Posse', as Larry said, 'sometimes'.

Later, they stopped referring to their group by any of these names. Like the No Rules Crew, none of the other young people interviewed who lived within their area nor any of the professionals had heard of them. The purpose or function of these group names appeared to be amusing, not practical, and the group names did not serve to establish the young people as a recognisable collective. In this sense these group names were applied in a similar way to the young people's street names: inconsistent, temporary and likely to change. On this point, these groups of young people differed from US-style gangs, as street gangs often have a name known by many throughout their neighbourhoods (for example Klein 1971, 1995; Spergel 1995).

While specific group names were the exception, 'mans' was a generic term used by some of the young people to describe other groups of young people. For instance, they discussed 'Streatham mans', 'Brixton mans', 'Stockwell mans' and so on. However, no other distinguishing characteristics of each group of 'mans' emerged other than being associated with the area (no colours, insignias, tattoos, and so on). Kenny succinctly made this point when he said:

> Basically, if you live in Streatham and you're that age, you're a Streatham man.

Sonny made a similar point:

> It's where you live. That's what makes you with a different mans. It's just where you live.

Getting in trouble together

All of the young people discussed committing their offences with at least one other person, and said that, for the most part, they committed their offences with those they normally 'hung out' with. Several of the professionals offered parallel comments when discussing how the young people they worked with normally committed their offences with others and sometimes in small groups. For instance, Danielle, a youth justice worker, mentioned:

> Generally, young people that we work with always will do most of the offences in groups. They don't do offences on their own. It's more unusual to come across someone who has committed an offence on their own, you know, a burglary or whatever on their own. It's usually in a group.

Karen, a youth and community worker from Brixton, also talked briefly about young people offending together:

> I know young people that commit crime and tend to do it in groups rather than individually.

For the most part, those in my sample discussed committing offences with others from their group. The only exceptions came from Norman, Kellen and Tolu. These young people are in different offending categories, but were all close friends. While Kellen did not commit acquisitive offences, Norman said he burgled with several people he normally did not associate with. Also, Tolu said he sold heroin on the streets with others who, according to him, are not his 'regular' friends. While the majority of the time Kellen, Norman and Tolu 'hung out' together, particularly at school and at the youth club, Norman and Tolu did not commit offences together. Their good friend Kellen was not even sure if they committed offences at all. He speculated:

> I think some of them have done a little drum or a little dealing or something like that. But I'm never with them when those things happen cuz I would tell them not to do it cuz, y'get me? I don't make those things happen. I try to stop them things from happening, y'get what I'm saying?

The young people were also asked about any 'roles' within their groups, such as leader, war counsellor, second in command and others, as these have been observed US-style street gang characteristics (such as Keiser 1969; Vigil 1988). Again, *nothing* of this nature was revealed by any of the young people or professionals interviewed. Some evidence, however, emerged to suggest that different statuses existed amongst the individuals within the group, with some, for instance, being more influential over the group's activity. Ben, a youth and community worker from Clapham, mentioned 'dominant figures' within the groups of young people he worked with.

> They're more dominant figures ... Those who sort of, umm, tend to influence the group's decision. Whether that's the same thing on the street I wouldn't know, but I would be inclined to think, from what I know and what I've encountered in working with them in the youth centre, when certain individuals in the group agree to participate in the programme, the others seem to show a similar willingness. When they show reluctance the others seem to conform. I would say that that's a pattern that's the same out in the street as well.

While none of the young people interviewed mentioned specific roles within their groups, some said they took up specific positions in their groups in the course of offending. These statuses were based on size, strength, skills and nerve or courage of the young people. For instance, Travis talked a bit about nerve when offending:

> Some people were better at what they did and other people weren't, if y'understand what I'm saying ... when it comes down to whatever, what was happening, some people would shit it more than others. Basically the ones that wouldn't were the ones that were more smart, init?

Size seemed to have played an important and practical part in determining status within the course of offending within the young people's groups. For instance, some were physically bigger and stronger than others within their group.

If strength was required in the course of an offence, say to break down a heavy door, then the physically larger young person within their group might be called into action. For instance, Theo recalled how in the process of a burglary his friends would 'like get me, use my strength to open one of the doors'. Also, joyriding was discussed as a group activity, yet not everyone knew how to hot-wire the vehicles. Indeed, only two of the young people interviewed, David and Theo, knew how to do this. Thus, they may have taken up the role of 'the hot-wiring one' within their group as they attempted to joyride motor vehicles.

No gangs in Lambeth

I attempted to show that interview and observational data suggested Lambeth did not have a problem with territorial, inter-gang violence. The young people in my sample congregated in groups, not US-style street gangs, nor posses or yardies. The word 'gang' itself seemed foreign to some of the young people. For instance, Jack mentioned:

> When you say gang, right, to me it means something different, like something organised, like people going out to do something.

Furthermore, none of the professionals described the groups of young people as gangs, or suggested they possessed gang-like characteristics, such as specific group names, colours, tattoos, symbols, leadership, role allocation, initiation procedures or persistence in time as a collective. Also, words such as 'posse' or 'yardie' were, for the most part, not used amongst the professionals to describe groups of young people who offend in the borough. Finally, some of the most compelling evidence relating to the absence of US-style gangs stemmed from the fact that *nothing* was observed which resembled such a collective around the streets of Lambeth.

The picture of young people in my sample, and perhaps in Lambeth more generally, was one of them in small groups of between four to eight others roughly the same age, and, for the most part, same sex. These young people knew each other because they grew up together and shared similar interests. As well as doing most things together, they also committed their offences together. In these regards, their groupings were probably no different from previous groups of young people in Lambeth growing up in similar circumstances. In other words the young people in my sample most likely did the same things as the young people who grew up before them. To this degree, young people across generations in Lambeth have been going through the same experiences (Foster 1990; Willis 1977). Those in my sample were just the latest group of 'kids in the neighbourhood', not gangs.

Much can be gained from comparing the group behaviour of those in my sample to that of US-style street gangs. For one, an importance lies in *not* classifying the groups of young people in my study as 'gangs'. The terms social scientists use to describe groups of young people can have powerful and profound effects on them, both practically and theoretically. 'Gang' is a loaded word that does not merit casual application. If the groups are not addressed as gangs, the young people are not demonised or stigmatised as being akin to US-style gangs. Rather, those in my sample seem more of an extension of Britain's 'history of respectable fears' (Pearson 1983) in terms of the nation's definition of groups of young people who have offended.

Why were no street gangs found? Downes (1966) asked a similar question after his study in London's East End failed to find evidence of delinquent subcultures, of which the term 'gang' was synonymous at the time. Downes (1966) suggested that the absence of gangs in Stepney and Poplar had much to do with full juvenile employment in the boroughs, both boroughs being ethnically homogenous, and the idea that young people accepted their working-class situation rather than aspiring beyond it. More than twenty years later Downes (1998) noted how these conditions have been flipped on their head. Generally speaking, in many of England's inner cites juvenile unemployment is high, multiculturalism is the norm and Thatcher's long reign as prime minister gave rise to a new sense of individualism and consumerism, breaking down 'traditional' cycles of work and leisure within Britain's lower- or working-class communities (Downes 1998). Nonetheless, even holding for all these conditions in Lambeth, my data still fail to suggest that gangs existed.

Another possible reason why no US-style street gangs existed in Lambeth has to do with some obvious historical, cultural and structural differences between the USA and the UK. However, if Lambeth were in the USA, it would probably have gangs. Lambeth was very similar to areas in the USA where gangs exist – densely populated, inner-city environments where crime and unemployment are high. Also, the image of a gang member is primarily a black or Latino one, a point based on empirical evidence (see, for example, Klein 1995; Spergel 1995) and general media portrayals, such as those seen in movies. Latino- and African-Americans, like Afro-Caribbean people in Lambeth, have parallel experiences of housing segregation, employment discrimination and prejudiced policing. Thus, by searching for gangs in Lambeth, the aim was to look in the 'right' area – an area with a somewhat similar history and demographic make-up to those in the USA where gangs are found.

Essentially, the main difference between the groups of young people in my study and US-style street gangs had to do with aspects of territory or 'gang-banging' – claiming a particular area and deliberate and consistent violence with one or more rival gangs (or groups) from different neighbourhoods. These aspects are *defining* cultural indicators of US-style gangs.[4] Those in my sample mentioned nothing like this and no evidence of it emerged elsewhere in Lambeth. No one I came across in Lambeth even *talked* about anything akin to 'gang-banging', let alone gangs. Outside of gang-banging, however, those in my sample did the same things as US gang members: offend, chat up the opposite sex, drink alcohol, use drugs, fight and more than any of these behaviours 'hang out' and do absolutely *nothing*. In these respects, the groups of young people in my sample and US-style gangs *seemed more alike* than different.

Aside from some general socioeconomic differences between the USA and the UK, additional significant reasons for the apparent absence of gangs in Lambeth are important to consider. For one, the UK has no *history* of US-style street gangs. Since the mid-twentieth century researchers have continually shown findings that do not support the existence of juvenile or criminal street gangs (see Downes 1966; Foster 1990; Mays 1954; Parker 1974; Pearson 1983; Scott 1956; Willis 1977; Willmott 1966). In other words, the UK has no *tradition* of gang-banging.

Cultural differences between the USA and the UK may also account for the absence of gangs in Lambeth. For instance, the history of ethnic diversity in the USA is a significant basis for the formation of street gangs. From Fredrick Thrasher's (1927) arduous and ground-breaking work on *The Gang* through more contemporary pictures of street gangs in the USA (Klein 1995; Spergel 1995), research suggests gang members from the same gang often have the same ethnic background. Indeed, this situation is present in San Diego (Sanders 1994), and generalising where gangs of a specific ethnicity are to be found is possible (for example black gangs around downtown, inner-city San Diego; Latino gangs in the south-east; Asian/Filipino gangs in North County). And while ethnic diversity is intrinsically woven into the fabric of US history, such diversity is a much more recent development in the UK and, as such, may help explain the apparent absence of US-style street gangs in Lambeth.

Two additional cultural differences between the USA and the UK may also help explain why my data fail to support the presence of gangs: drugs and guns. In the 1980s a 'crack epidemic' occurred in the USA, which contributed to the rise of crack-selling street gangs (Klein 1995; Spergel 1995; Taylor 1989). In the UK such an 'epidemic' has not (yet) transpired, which, in turn, perhaps removed the basis for the rise of such gangs. On a related point, no gun culture exists in England. As with ethnic diversity, firearms have been a part of US history since its inception. The American people, generally speaking, highly value their 'Bill of Rights' written into the country's Constitution, of which the 'right to bear arms' is one. The belief in this right, has, in part, contributed to the fact that in the USA lethal violence due to guns is *astronomically* higher than any other industrialised nation (Zimring and Hawkins 1997). The recent (2002) Oscar-award-winning documentary *Bowling for Columbine* pointed out that in a year there were about 70 firearm-related deaths in the UK, but more than 11,000 in the USA. Guns in the USA have allowed gang members to enforce territorial claims with deadly violence, which, in turn, increases the potential for tit-for-tat retributions. Due to the relative absence of gun culture in Lambeth, and Britain more generally, ganging is thus further hindered.

Finally, a simple reason for the absence of this behaviour amongst the young people in my sample could be that ganging did not make any sense to them. Why bother with all the group names, tattoos, bandanas and rivalries with other groups of young people? As mentioned earlier, most of the time the young people did the same things as US-style gangs: hang out and do 'nothing'. Surely to take it one step further and appropriate a 'uniform' and have ongoing 'battles' with groups of other youths is to imply the young people must make additional efforts. Some in my sample did get into fights with other young people from different areas based on that difference alone, but their ferocity with rivalries and the resulting violence amongst them was nowhere near that of US-style gangs. Furthermore, gang-banging is surely going to bring unnecessary and unwanted police intervention. Travis, for instance, mentioned this:

> To go around, in my personal thought, to go around and just like hutting your-self up [making your presence be known], cuz that's what it does, hutting your-self up, baiting yourself up, y'knowwhatImean? When you go around and say I'm a [so and so] boy, because then the police can observe the group and then they can see what's going on. To call yourself in a certain group, just, I would never do that cuz, I would never go around and go 'Yeah, Yeah, I'm a Borough Man'. And all of that shit is immature.

I relate to what Travis said. In San Diego the gang members were easy to spot: such individuals were the ones 'flying their colours' and 'throwing up' gang signs. In this respect, that these young people were going to be breaking the law eventu-ally was apparent. These gang members may as well wear targets on their shirts or print 'Going to Offend Soon' on them. In Lambeth the lack of gang 'uniforms' makes it more difficult for the police to pick out who is likely to commit an offence. Also, by having sworn enemies the young people just make more trouble for them-selves. Who wants to constantly 'watch their back' for fear of being attacked by a rival faction? Again, such practices are extra efforts. In these respects, for those in my sample, and perhaps young people in Lambeth with similar backgrounds, ganging just did not make any sense. Where ganging is more of a tradition in the USA amongst inner-city youths (and seemingly becoming one with suburban young people) ganging was, perhaps, simply disadvantageous for those in Lambeth.

Interactions with the police

The final cultural aspect I address concerns the interactions of the young people in my sample with the police in Lambeth. Out of the 31 young people, 29 mentioned being stopped and searched by the police, several more times than they could recall. All of them said they were stopped because the police said they looked 'sus-picious', a significant point. The young people referred to this as being 'pulled on a suss'. Once again, as with their style and group behaviour, no differences appeared in their interactions with the police amongst all the young people. In other words, those more involved in offending mentioned being stopped and searched by the police for the same reasons as those who have committed a fewer amount of (rela-tively minor) offences.

Stop-and-search procedures and the question of selective policing was certainly topical in London given the findings of the Macpherson Report (1999) on the Stephen Lawrence murder, which, among other things, found London's Metro-politan Police to be 'institutionally racist'. The findings of this report are, perhaps, not too surprising because since the 1970s the relationship between police and black people in Britain's inner cities has been less than amicable (Gilroy 1987; Hall *et al.* 1978; Jefferson 1993; Pryce 1979; Robins 1992; Solomos 1988). Furthermore, the differential treatment of black people by a police force run predominately by white men *not* from inner cities has been discussed in much research (such as Britton 2000; Fitzgerald 1998; Gilroy 1987; Hall *et al.* 1978; Jefferson 1993; Pryce 1979; Solomos 1988). Since the 1980s, relations between the police and the 'black community' in Lambeth have also been 'poor'[5] (Burney 1990; Scarman 1981; Spencer and Hough 2000).

In this section I argue that, while ethnicity is undeniably important to consider when looking at why young black men are stopped and searched by (predominately) white police officers, other considerations are important to explore when addressing *why* those in my sample were 'pulled on a suss'. These include their style and their group behaviour, as well as their age, sex and the fact that they lived in the inner city. In the minds of police officers in Lambeth, these characteristics were, perhaps, cultural indicators of 'the criminal Other' (Jefferson 1993) – young people likely to be 'up to no good'. In other words, police in Lambeth probably figure that groups of young people, mostly young men, walking around in designer clothing or expensive sportswear were probably breaking the law or about to. This suggests, in part, that the police's impression of young offenders in the borough may have been influenced by specific cultural indicators. In this sense, 'the meaning of criminality is anchored in the style of its collective practice' (Ferrell and Sanders 1995: 5; see also Brake 1985; Hebidge 1979; Katz 1988).

Pulled on a suss

Those more involved in offending were pulled over by police officers more in comparison to those less so. However, on the whole, for anyone in my sample to get stopped for 'looking suspicious' was not so uncommon. Although stopping someone for 'looking suspicious' is not formal police procedure, a long history of police using 'suspicion' as an incentive to stop and search exists, and other researchers have noted that young people in the inner city have been stopped for similar reasons (for example Foster 1990).

That those more involved in offending were, generally speaking, stopped more by the police in relation to the others is not surprising. These young people were arrested more times and thus *known* by police in their area. For instance, Kenny, Martin, Nathan, Travis, Quentin, Marc and Tolu said they and some officers were on a first-name basis, and that officers have routinely stopped them. Also, these young people may have been approached more by officers because they 'hung about' outside of mainstream education, and were thus more likely to have drawn attention to themselves. For instance, with the exception of Tolu, these young people said they attended off-site educational units, which would mean such individuals did not wear school uniforms and had hours different to those from a mainstream school. If these young people were 'hanging out' after their school hours, yet before mainstream school had been let out, this could be interpreted by police as a groups of kids skipping school, which, in turn, could lead to cops wanting to have words with them.

Many of the young people mentioned being were 'pulled on a suss' frequently. Just looking 'suspicious', however, is not an adequate reason for a police officer to stop someone, let alone search them. Two young people, Karl and Kevin, were aware of this. Both of them mentioned not allowing the police to search them if the officers did not have 'reasonable grounds'. Karl briefly talked about his understanding of this:

> For a long time they stop me and search me and all that saying, 'Where do I live?' see if there's any warrants out for me. I say, 'What grounds are you searching me on?' If they can't say any grounds, I just walk off.

Kevin also mentioned a similar technique that he and his friends applied when approached by the police:

> *What did they stop you for?*
> They just say for a routine check. You cannot argue with it, but around our area we're sort of clued up. We know what they got to do and what they don't have to do. Like, if they pull us up that they got to read us this thing on their shoulder, and they have to tell you their names and what reasons they're pulling you for, and that's why we don't say nothing to them. As soon as they don't do that, we say that to them. Sometimes they leave us alone because they know we're clued up. Like, a couple of days ago I got pulled up and I knew it was just a general routine. They weren't like picking on me or anything because I've never seen this policeman in my life and they were new policemen from Streatham. Like, they pulled us up, me and my mate, and we waited for them to slip that like. We were waiting for them to own up and shit and show us their cards and everything like that, but they don't always do that. Sometimes they just say, 'What are you doing around these parts of the area? What are you walking around for quietly?' Not quietly, but suspiciously.

Regardless of frequency, all of the young people were pulled over for looking like someone who committed an offence in the area. This response was so common that being 'pulled on a suss' could have been an ad hoc rationalisation used by officers in Lambeth to justify why they stopped young people. The stories by the young people went something like this: the police stopped them and told them an offence had been committed in the area, and that they matched the description of the perpetrator. For instance, Martin mentioned this:

> *How many times have you been stopped by the police, just stopped by them?*
> I've lost count. I've really lost count. [He estimated 100 times.] … [Once] I got pulled three times in a row. I went to the shop, I got pulled. I came back, I got pulled and I got pulled straight outside my house. I have completely lost count. I got pulled up for just coming to school a few weeks back.
> *When they stop you what do they say?*
> They're just like, 'What, what you doing? Where you going? We've had a complaint. Two boys have kicked the door in' or 'Someone's been climbing

over a fence fitting your description'. And they radio in. They take my name. They ask for the description. They tell them what I'm wearing and then he comes back and he goes, 'No this is not him. Take his name'. And that just in case, so they take my name, they search me and that's it they send me off.
Does that happen each and every time, the same thing?
Yeah, no matter what. If they don't ask questions they will search me.

Brian offered a similar story:

> *Have you ever been stopped by the police?*
> Yeah, yeah … I used to get stopped like quite regularly.
> *What did they stop you for?*
> Basically, looking suspicious.
> *What do they say to you when they stop you?*
> They say yeah, 'Excuse me. Where you going? What are you doing?' They just ask you where you going. If you've got a bag they say, 'What's in the bag?' and you just ask them, 'Why are you searching me?'
> *Do they search you?*
> Yeah, they search you and they say, 'We had a report of a burglary and you fit the description.'

Tom felt others who looked like him committing offences were roaming around Lambeth:

> For four to five years it's [being 'pulled on a suss'] been going on. There's supposed to be suspects that look like me and all that running around with the same clothes. I'll say one thing: I don't got a twin brother.

So why did these young people get 'pulled on a suss'? A couple of them suggested that the police had been 'racist' towards them, and offered their own personal experiences from which hostile feelings grew. For instance, Lenny who described his ethnicity as 'part Jamaican, part Guyanian, part Chinese' told me how one time he felt racially harassed by two undercover police.

> One time I was on the bus and for some reason that day I threw away my ticket. Don't ask me why. And that day an inspector came on the bus and it just happened that there were two undercover policemen on the bus. They stopped the bus, took me off, started asking me questions. One was really sarcastic. He asked me my name, where I lived. Asked me my dad's name. I said, 'My dad's name was Ron.' He looked at me and said, 'Is your dad a white man?' I said, 'What?' He said, 'Is your dad a white man?' He was looking for a reaction from me and I goes, 'Do I look white?', and he was stumped because he thought I was going to react to it and you could see that in his face. And he said, 'If you're going to cause a problem, come back to the station.' I goes, 'I'm not going to cause a problem.' Two people got off the bus and stood behind

me and said, 'He never caused a problem. We saw him throw his ticket away. There's no problem here.' For some reason they just decided to pick on me.

According to Lenny, things like this happened to him 'everyday, every other day' during his teenage years, and his story is not isolated. Quentin, whose dad was originally from Sri Lanka and mum is English, said that four police officers chased him, caught him, and then hit him 'untold' times. Quentin said the officers thought he robbed somebody, but that he, in fact, did not. Quentin saw these officers yelling and chasing him, so he ran. At the end of his story, Quentin told me he thought that the officers hit him because of his Asian ethnicity. He said, 'I hate the police forever.' Likewise, his brother Nathan also mentioned being 'roughed up' by police when arrested, and believed the officers treated him harshly because of his Asian background. I talked to Nathan's mum and she confirmed that Nathan had several large bruises on his abdomen and stomach, apparently caused by police batons after he was arrested. Marc also talked about how much he hated the police. He said he once unknowingly burgled a policeman's house, which made him feel 'good'.

> *How did you feel about the burglaries afterwards?*
> I felt good, man, because one time I must have burgled a policeman's house. It felt good.
> *How do you know it was a policeman's house?*
> Because he had his hats and pictures of him like getting awards and stuff, you get me?
> *Did you take his hats?*
> No, cuz if you get caught with the hat, it's over, you get me? Just take liberties. Pissed up on his TV. Stuff that we can't take, piss on it, and tear up his house because he's a police.

Relations between the police and black communities in Lambeth have been strained for over two decades, and experiences of 'harassment' suffered by black people at the hands of the police have been well documented (Burney 1990; Scarman 1981; Spencer and Hough 2000). While only a few young people said they outright hated the police or had bad experiences with them, additional evidence emerged that some held the belief that police in Lambeth had been racist. Several detached youth workers and youth and community workers had personally experienced what they believed to be blatantly prejudiced policing, or felt the police used excessive force on young black men who came into their youth centres because of their ethnicity. For instance, Samson, a helper at a youth centre in Brixton, offered a story of how officers grabbed him and laid him face down in the gutter with their feet on his back after he said, jokingly, 'Ya got a flat' to the officers in their stopped police car. Jacob, a detached youth worker in Brixton, talked about how once, outside of his youth centre, a young man said 'fuck you' to passing police officers, which resulted in the entire youth centre being surrounded by officers, and the young man being physically struck while handcuffed on the ground.

Oscar, who runs The Design in Brixton, said that when he grew up in Lambeth in the 1970s, officers made him part of what they called a 'black-man sandwich'. According to Oscar, this incident occurred several times where, after being arrested by officers, Oscar was taken to an empty room at one of the stations, had cushions placed in front and behind him with police dogs at his side, and then was beaten repeatedly through the cushions with batons. Apparently, the cushions were used so no marks or bruises would be left by the baton blows, and the dogs kept Oscar from trying to 'escape' out the sides of the cushions.

Other professionals interviewed discussed being weary of the police. For instance, Wendy, a NACRO worker, mentioned:

> I don't really deal with the police because I can't afford to really. I've dealt with them a lot because I've often gone out and got them [the young people I work with] out of jail ... I wouldn't want to be a copper around here ... I think that we would risk credibility of our young people if we had a meeting with some of the police.

Tanya, another NACRO worker from Brixton, said:

> One time I was at an estate and there were a bunch of kids just sitting on a wall and the police rolled up and started harassing them, for no reason. I told them that I was with NACRO, and then they lectured the kids a bit and then left. If I had not been there, you don't know how far they'll go.

Even a couple of the police officers interviewed recognised a general ill-feeling towards them coming from young people and others in Lambeth. For instance, Barney, a CID officer from Clapham, commented on how:

> There is a lot of anti-police-kind-of-cause-troubles. Police officers stopping them. Doing this and [people saying that we are] Babylon.

Chris, a detective inspector from Brixton, thought this feeling was more 'anti-authority' rather than 'anti-police':

> I don't think it's anti-police, but just anti-authority and the police are just representatives of that. I don't think they are out to get us. Although there is this ill-feeling [towards police in Lambeth].

Given the recent findings of the MacPherson (1999) report, which found that the Metropolitan Police were 'institutionally racist', it would be wrong to suggest that racism within Lambeth's police force did not exist. The incidents reported by some of my respondents are also alarming. Ethnicity is important to consider when looking at the roots of differential policing, if only because black people are a visible minority (for example, Fitzgerald 1998; Keith 1993; Marlow 1999). There may also be labelling processes occurring within the borough whereby prejudiced police officers associate blacks, particularly young black men, more so than young white men, as being perpetrators of crime. Such labelling processes, in turn, can have detrimental effects upon a young black person to the extent that may come to see themselves as 'criminal' and act accordingly (Becker 1963). The combination of differential policing combined with these labelling processes may help explain the disproportionate amount of young blacks arrested in Lambeth and London more generally.

Additional aspects of these young people's lives are important to consider when addressing *why* such individuals were 'pulled on a suss'. These concern where these young people live, their age, their 'style' and the fact that these young men 'hang around' with several friends. Generally speaking, young men in Lambeth in their mid-teens to early twenties, wearing sportswear or designer clothing and congregating in small groups were prime suspects for being stopped and searched by police officers in Lambeth. This is not to deny that ethnicity is important to consider when addressing police and community relations in Lambeth. However, the salience of ethnicity, in establishing who police in Lambeth were likely to stop, was, perhaps, equal to other conditions, such as being a young man in an inner-city environment (Jefferson 1993). For instance, British Crime Survey data have consistently shown that inner-city areas are 'hot spots' for street crime (Kershaw *et al.* 2000; Mirrlees-Black *et al.* 1996, 1998; Simmons *et al.* 2002) and that young men between the ages of 15 and 24 commit a significant number of these offences (Simmons *et al.* 2002). As such, young men living in Lambeth within this age range might be considered more suspicious by police when compared to others. Such young men are the one that the police need to keep their eyes on.

The young people also said they congregated in small groups, which may have contributed to them being suspicious in the minds of the police in Lambeth. Evidence from interview material suggests this. For instance, Kevin said:

> if you are walking around in a group like that. They [the police] think you're mischievous and other sorts or something like that.

Larry made similar comments:

> When we're walking in like a group, we're more likely to get stopped because they [the police] think you're doing something. They'll stop you on a suss, a suspicion, like carrying drugs or burglary, something like that.

Sonny also mentioned how walking in a group makes the police suspicious:

> When we're walking in a group, we're more likely to get stopped because they think you're doing something. They'll stop you on a suss, a suspicion like carrying drugs or burglary, something like that.

Even a police officer, Chuck, a retired special police constable in Brixton, talked about how groups of young people in Lambeth aroused police suspicion:

If you're a young police officer and a you've come from, like most police officers, from a very so-called middle-class background and you live all your life ... out in the sticks and suddenly you've got this desire to join the police force and you end up in the borough of Lambeth. You are not used to seeing groups of people about, and your immediate reaction when you see a group of people talking loudly and shouting and hollering is that there must be some sort of disturbance going on, there must be something happening or something is going to happen ... you're a young police officer [and] that is the first thing. He's inexperienced. He doesn't understand. But also when you put yourself in a situation that you think something is going to happen you actually feel fear of what might happen, so you then go the opposite way and become aggressive to cover up your actual fear, so you find that a lot of young officers tend to be a little over the top ... a little bit over the top with attitude. Say you suddenly find all of a sudden the bloke [police officer] will pull himself up to his full 5 foot 8 inches and becomes almost aggressive, but it's fear. It's not through an attitude of like 'I'm going to sort these bastards out! And you know this is my general way of doing my job.' It's fear, but you can't explain that to a group of kids on the start of the tarmac, because all they see it is the aggression or whatever.

Another important aspect to consider when addressing how suspicious these young people appeared to police in Lambeth concerns their style. Style is a significant visual identifier, and several researchers have noted how youthful styles in the inner city have been criminalised (for example Anderson 1990; Brake 1985; Ferrell and Sanders 1995; Hebidge 1979; Katz 1988). In other words the police may associate 'style' with 'crime'. One of the young people in my sample, Todd, commented on how his clothing made him look suspicious:

I know I look suspicious because of [what I wear]. I just like it.

As discussed earlier, the fashion of the young people was in contrast to their financial situation and the overall aesthetics of Lambeth's inner-city environment. Thus, officers policing the borough may come across a group of young men in designer clothing or sportswear and think: 'Where did they get the money to buy those clothes?' This may arouse their suspicion because, for them, it might seem culturally inconsistent to come from a 'poor' background and wear expensive clothing.[6] This suspicion may be compounded by other 'menacing' qualities about the young people, such as their aggressive, 'wicked' inner-city-street-life music about drugs and crime, nonchalant and carefree stroll, and use of slang words and phrases the police may not understand and, perhaps, interpret as hostile. While many of those in the borough with this overall style are unlikely to be offenders, it appeared to have been associated with a 'coherent deviant aesthetic' (Katz 1988: 90) in Lambeth, and as such may have brought about negative police attention to those who sport it.

Overall then, in terms of who police in the borough view as potentially suspicious, issues of age, gender, location, style and whether these young people are alone or in small groups are important to consider. Young men in the inner city who adopted the aforementioned style and pal around in small groups seem to be high on the list of who police consider suspicious. Ethnicity is an additional, significant aspect to address, yet accurately assessing its salience and ranking amongst these other considerations is difficult. Given reports of institutional racism throughout the Metropolitan Police, it probably ranks high in the minds of the police. As such, young black men in Lambeth are probably more likely to be stopped and searched than young white men. Consequently, those most at risk of being stopped and searched in the borough due to being seen as suspicious by the police are young black men in small groups wearing 'fresh' sportswear and/or designer clothing. The prospect of race being very significant within the minds of police in Lambeth in terms of who they consider 'suspicious' may help explain differential policing, and black people's frustrations of being needlessly stopped and searched (Spencer and Hough 2000).

The style and group behaviour of those in my sample were, according to interviews with professionals, typical of young people in Lambeth with similar backgrounds. This point raises an important question: how can the police differentiate the great majority of young people in Lambeth who do *not* commit offences, but who share the same cultural indicators as those who do? In principle this may help to explain why even several of those who committed only petty offences, such as shoplifting and the occasional fight, were stopped by the police many times. Such a principle may also help to explain an officer's claim that the young person they stopped 'matches the description of an offender in the area' because many young people in my sample and in Lambeth more generally actually *did* wear similar clothes.

As mentioned earlier, evidence emerged from those in my sample and the professionals to suggest that young people 'hang around' with others for 'protection'. That these same groups seemed to draw more police attention than a lone youth walking around is thus slightly ironic. A young person walking around on their own in Lambeth may not be noticed by the police as readily as a group of them, but the loner may be exposed to threats posed by other groups of young people wanting a 'challenge'. Either way these young people faced a dilemma: walk around the borough on your own and risk getting attacked; walk around with a group and risk being stopped by the police.

Even if the young people were not actually committing any offences, simply by walking around Lambeth it appeared likely such individuals were going to get in trouble with the law if stopped by the police. While those in my sample mentioned being stopped by police because they 'fit the description of someone in the area who had just committed an offence', many of them often *did* carry something on them that could have got them in legal trouble, mainly cannabis. As explored in Chapter Four, about half of those in my sample, mainly those more involved in offending, said they smoked cannabis daily. They also said they carried it on their person, which could get them in legal trouble. For instance, Nathan said how one time he and his buddies were stopped by police and that all were searched. Nathan's friends gave him the cannabis, and Nathan hid this in his pants (underwear) where the officers did not search. However, during another incident Nathan hid cannabis in his jacket, but this time an officer found it. David also mentioned how often he carried cannabis:

> I've always got something illegal on me ... puff most of the time.

Aside from cannabis, a few others said they occasionally carried pocket knives. Tom mentioned being stopped out of 'suspicion' and then arrested when police found 'the old rusty pen knife that I've had for years'. Darrell talked about being pulled over for looking suspicious, and that the police found a fishing knife. Darrell was arrested for carrying an offensive weapon.

> They [the police] said that someone had just burgled a car and we fit the description ... I generally liked the knife. I use to go fishing with my dad and I really liked it. It was gold rimmed, like gold plated. It was small though, an inch and a half, but it locked, so they said it was offensive because it locked.

While the young people talked about being pulled over for looking like the perpetrator of a burglary, robbery or other offence in the area, their encounters with the police placed them at great risk of being searched and found with something illegal. Kevin felt the police actually thought this way, and that they randomly pulled young people over because of the likelihood of finding *something* illegal on them. Kevin said:

> They [police officers] ... go 'Let's give him a pull. He's bound to have something on him.' Or 'He's bound to have done something.'

Because the young people were getting pulled often by the police they needed to be careful when carrying items they might get arrested for if searched. By carrying weapons, particularly knives – whether for protection purposes, transportation from one location to another, or just because the young person likes them – they placed themselves in a precarious situation due to the frequency with which they were stopped by police. Looking suspicious or fitting the description of someone in the area who has just committed an offence were, according to those in my sample, justifications offered by the police in order to search and determine if a young person was actually violating the law somehow. Finding a knife or cannabis only confirmed their initial suspicion. Being 'pulled on a suss', and consequently searched, increases the chances a young person may get arrested for something relatively minor. While some police within Lambeth may think that cannabis use in the borough is 'no big deal', a young person may still be arrested, cautioned and processed through the criminal justice system if caught with some. In situations like these a relatively law-abiding young person becomes unnecessarily dragged into the criminal justice system alongside many others who are *real* offenders (Becker 1963). This, in turn, can have a serious impact on many aspects of their lives.

Conclusions

In this chapter, when analysing the overall style of the young people – which refers to their clothing, music and other behaviours and idiosyncrasies – I argued several points. For one, I suggested the young people seemed to have adopted the latest fashion, one which was marketed directly towards them, not something they started, but one they followed. I also tried to demonstrate that these young people, in the majority, placed a significant emphasis on 'looking good' because it provided them with an affluent image, allowing them to visually rise above the urban degeneration that encompassed them on daily basis, and enabling them to give the impression to others that they had 'made it'. I also argued that many of the young people felt a particular connection between hard-core hip-hop and/or jungle because this music discusses or accurately reflects the lifestyles many of them have led or their experiences, particularly for those more seriously involved in offending. From here, I suggested that a homology or 'sameness' existed between these cultural aspects of the young people and how they led their lives. In other words a particular relationship, a consistency between their attitudes, style, behaviour and life experiences existed.

I then examined the daily behaviour of those in my sample and their friends, and made several points. For one, evidence indicated the young people's groups formed naturally through neighbourhood proximity, attending the same school, and/or sharing similar interests, and that they congregated in groups of between four to eight others, all roughly the same age and, for the most part, same sex. In the majority no differences emerged between the young people on this point; all of their daily behaviours and general activities seemed to be very similar. I further indicated that they 'hung around' with others for no apparent reason other than because of things in common, and that they expressed feeling safer in numbers when travelling around Lambeth. In this section I also compared the overall group context and behaviours of those in my sample to US-style street gangs. Here, I endeavoured to illustrate that, in many ways, the groupings of young people were completely dissimilar to gangs. For one, the young people did not possess gang-like characteristics, such as colours or a distinct hierarchy of membership, nor was there any evidence of them being initiated into their groups. The major distinction between those in my sample and US-style gangs, I continued, had to do with 'gang-banging' or ongoing rivalries with other groups of young people from different areas. While ganging is more of a tradition amongst young people (and adults) in the USA, I pointed out that significant historical and cultural aspects of the UK – such as the absence of a ganging tradition, shallow history of ethnic diversity, scarcity of guns, and relative absence of a crack epidemic – may have hampered the rise and persistence of US-style gangs.

In the final section I argued a couple of points relating to the young people's interactions with the police. All of these young people, regardless of their offending history, were stopped by police because they looked 'suspicious', what was referred to as being 'pulled on a suss'. I suggested that the young people's affluent style clashing with Lambeth's lower- or working-class aesthetics, combined with the likelihood of them 'hanging around' in small groups, may have drawn the police's attention towards them. Police in the borough perhaps figured these groups of young people with no jobs living in public-sector housing must be 'up to no good' to afford such clothing, and, as a consequence, stopped and searched them. And while institutional and overt racism may exist within Lambeth's police force, potentially resulting in black people's over-representation in criminal statistics and their general distrust of the police, I further suggested that other considerations about the young people, such as their sex, age, style and group behaviour, *not their race alone*, were potential reasons for being 'pulled on a suss'. And although it often turned out that these young people were *not* the ones who the police were initially looking for, because they discussed possessing something illegal, primarily cannabis, I continued to point out that this possession could lead to them being arrested and processed through the criminal justice system. A dangerous result of this could be that a relatively law-abiding young person becomes surrounded and influenced by those much more seriously involved in offending.

One of the most surprising and perhaps significant findings was that, in terms of the discussed cultural indicators, all of the young people were *very* similar. This holds true for how they looked, what music they listened to, how they walked, how they greeted each other, and other specifics related to their style. Likewise, no clear differences emerged in their overall daily group behaviour and interactions with the police. Young people, regardless of offending category, pretty much reported doing the same things on 'average' days, and nearly all of them were stopped by the police at least once in their young lives for the same reason – looking 'suspicious'. What this suggests, what aspects of their culture tell us about their crime, is that, outside of offending, distinguishing between those more seriously involved in offending and those less so would be very difficult. In these respects, these young people appeared to have more features uniting them than separating them.

8 The moral universes of young people who have offended

This book has explored what might be thought of as the 'moral universes' of a small sample of young people in the London borough of Lambeth in terms of how offending fitted in to their lives. 'Moral universe' here refers to a worldview, a viewpoint, the way someone sees things, or, in more sociological terms, a set of normative judgements. So what exactly has been learned about the young people's offending, and what has been learned about 'young offenders' in the borough? In this chapter I attempt to address these questions. First, I review the fine distinctions young people made (or were still making) about their offending behaviour. Next, I examine what the young people said about offending in the future, and explore how they viewed legitimate, 'conventional' employment. Then, I talk about what my data are able to say (and not able to say) about young people who have offended in Lambeth more generally.

The latter half of the chapter addresses the theoretical implications of my data. Here, I bring up the questions that prompted this research: What do we know about young people who offend in the inner city? What does this behaviour mean to them? How does it fit in with their lives? To begin, I address some major theories of crime and delinquency in order to assess their utility in adequately explaining or capturing the young people's offending behaviour. This discussion is not aimed at testing or proving any one criminological theory, nor at offering an exhaustive review of them, but rather to see how (and if) some of the more general ones 'fit' with my findings. From here, I offer my own theoretical views.

Observing the code: young people's normative judgements about crime

So what has been learned about these young people? What I attempted to illustrate in each of the chapters that directly discussed the different classifications of offences they committed is that all of them, including those who committed (or were still committing) relatively serious offences, all made (or were still making) normative judgements related to their acquisitive, expressive, violent and/or drug-related offences. Findings indicate that these young people were only willing to commit certain offences against particular individuals or targets to limited degrees or levels of severity. Throughout the courses of these illegal behaviours, the young people seemed to follow a set of guidelines. For them, 'rules' existed even within the arena of breaking the rules ('crime'). In terms of offending, the young people did not have an 'anything goes' mentality: these behaviours were regulated; their offending did not occur within a normless or valueless vacuum. Rather, they appeared to have followed certain ad hoc 'laws' or 'guidelines' – a 'code' – when behaving illicitly or illegally. For the 31 young people in my sample, the observation of this code seemed to be an intrinsic aspect of these behaviours.

So what were these 'rules', these normative judgements woven into the fabric of their behaviours? Many emerged, which applied to a variety of offences but not to all the young people; not everyone in my sample committed all of the offences discussed. Generally speaking, the relatively serious offences (burglary, robbery, drug selling) were primarily committed by those more involved in offending, while those less involved in this behaviour, in the main, only committed relatively minor offences (shoplifting, vandalism, 'light' drug use). Also, on the whole, those more involved in offending committed a larger number of offences when compared to the others, suggesting, in part, they employed these 'rules' with greater frequency.

To begin, those more involved in offending made subtle distinctions about acquisitive offences, such as robbery and burglary. For instance, when they robbed someone on the street – a very serious and personal offence – the young people had ideas of who to rob. For one, they avoided the elderly and young children: these people were 'untouchables', not to be victimised in such a way. None of those who robbed others said they targeted these people. In fact, Norman went so far as to say: 'It's not like I'm knocking off old ladies or anything.' Even though both the very old and the very young might be seen as 'easy pickings' by a street robber, these young people felt they should not rob them.

So why was this the case? Ethical reasons for this may be present, such as the idea these young people may have felt it 'unchallenging' or 'unfair' to rob such individuals because they either 'did not know any better' or were too weak to defend themselves. However, more concrete practical reasons were expressed by them in their choice of targets that may help explain why the elderly and the very young were not targeted. As mentioned in Chapter Three, the range of potential street-robbery victims selected by these young people had a lot to do with visible valuables, and who was probably going to be carrying such valuables with them in the public sphere. The presence of visible valuables seemed to be a significant consideration taken by these young people when determining who to rob. Seemingly, they chose not to rob the elderly or the very young because such individuals were *not* likely to be in possession of visible valuables – Walkmans, mobile phones, jewellery – and were less likely to have large amounts of money or goods on them, particularly young children. In other words, the potential robbers may have thought, quite logically, 'Why bother robbing those who may not have what I want?' As such, these normative judgements regarding street robberies may have stemmed from more practical and instrumental grounds as opposed to ethical or moral considerations. Also, the supposed exclusion of the very young and very old may also stem from the idea that these are 'types' of people that young people do not frequently come across in their daily activity. Young people are likely to come across other young people. For many of those in my sample who committed street robberies, the victims were other young people. This coincides with recent British Crime Survey data, which indicated that just under half of all robbery victims were aged between 11 and 20, and just over half of those who committed robbery were aged between 16 and 20 (Simmons *et al.* 2002).

Burglary was a common offence amongst those more involved in offending, and several of them committed many of these acts. Still, the young people did not have an 'anything goes' mentality when behaving this way, but rather made distinctions regarding *which* establishment to burgle. When choosing somewhere to burgle, these young people seemed to have followed an unwritten law: do not burgle houses from those in the same economic situation as you, but everyone else can afford it. They appeared to take pride in *not* stealing from those who they believed could not afford it, a significant distinction made regarding this behaviour, which served to legitimise such acts, at least partially (Foster 1990; Sykes and Matza 1957). These distinctions were the 'code' that conditioned their burgling.

Two possible reasons emerged as to why the young people made (or were still making) such distinctions about burglaries. One is practical in that by burgling more affluent addresses the young people bettered their chances at making a good 'score'. Richer people are more likely to have expensive, easily disposable gear to pilfer and trade, such as portable electronic items and jewellery. If these young people were going to take risks as large as burgling someone's home, then it paid to make the effort worthwhile; burgling a house belonging to someone with more money was more practical. Another reason why the young people did not target those in similar, relatively less affluent, economic positions as them may have to do with ethical considerations. The young people might have felt that burgling the houses of those who, like them, were not financially well-off, was 'liberties' or 'taking the piss'. Kenny mentioned this very point when he said:

> There's the people who can't afford it. They're in the same position as you. If you're taking it [burgling] off them, that's liberties.

For these young people, burgling 'the rich' was acceptable, but to do the same to those in similar financial positions as them was apparently not.

While this distinction about who to burgle may have stemmed from ethical considerations – that within these young people's moral universes an affinity, an empathy, was felt with others in similar economic situations to their own, so as to exclude such 'poor' people from the list of potential places to burgle – it may also, once again, simply have been practical. For instance, research generally suggests young people primarily commit offences in their own neighbourhoods (for example Gottfredson and Hirschi 1990; McGahey 1986; Pitts 1999). In neighbourhoods all around Lambeth, young people were spoilt for choice in terms of houses to burgle; I found wealthy pockets throughout. In this respect these young people could *afford* to make claims of not stealing from their own. Lambeth is economically diverse; affluence seemed to reside literally right alongside poverty. For those in my sample who burgled (or were still burgling), walking a couple a minutes from their estate or council flat presented them with the opportunity to burgle the residence of someone in a much better financial position than them, and thus increased their chances of a profitable burglary. So while these young people said burgling the homes of those in like financial circumstances was ethically unsound, a true test of how stringently such individuals would adhere to this dictum needs to take place in an environment where everyone is in the same economic position, or rather, where everyone is in the same position as them. As it stands, it seemed rather convenient for these young people to mention not burgling 'the poor'.

Next, I attempted to illustrate how young people's attitudes towards drugs were sharply differentiated. These young people did not treat the use of all drugs in the same way. Cannabis use was very acceptable: almost everyone had tried it at least once, and those more involved in offending used it frequently. Their overall nonchalant approach towards cannabis use was, perhaps, congruent with the current social atmosphere. The ubiquitous cultural references to weed, particularly those in the mass media, suggest its popularity in society, not least with young people. But while cannabis use was liberal and not considered a 'problem' by *any* of those in my sample, they felt very differently towards the use of 'harder' Class A drugs, particularly crack and heroin. Not only had none of them ever tried such drugs, but several went so far as to negatively stigmatise those who did and called them derogatory names. Within the moral universes of the young people, the use of cannabis was acceptable and in a completely different category from the use of other drugs. Little tolerance was held for illegal drugs other than cannabis. Even those most seriously involved in offending avoided 'hard' Class A drugs, such as heroin and crack, and only used other ones, such as ecstasy or powder cocaine, on the rare, festive occasion. In this respect, the young people were very different from persistent 'young offenders' previously researched who used 'harder' drugs more frequently (for example Audit Commission 1996; Hagell and Newburn 1994; Newburn 1998).

Moreover, these young people, in the majority, did not *sell* any drugs, not even cannabis. In fact, only 4 out of the 31 said they sold drugs at all. This suggests that, within their value systems, the use of cannabis and perhaps experimentation with 'other' drugs was acceptable, but clearly selling drugs, any drug, was a completely different story. And while these young people may have believed that selling drugs was 'wrong' and not acceptable behaviour for them, the limited number of drug sellers in my sample may hinge on the differential possibility of being able to sell drugs in the first place. Drug selling is unlike other offences in that in order to sell drugs, a 'connection' to supply them is needed. No connection is needed to, say, forcefully take something off someone in the street, take a chocolate bar from a newsagents without paying for it, or smash and destroy public property. These offences are ones *anyone* could commit. And while most of the young people knew someone or somewhere that sold drugs, primarily cannabis, this knowledge does not necessarily imply that their relationship with these 'associates' was close enough for the young people to have been offered the chance to sell drugs. So, overall, for the majority of those in my sample, while the stance on not selling drugs may be justified on moral grounds, it may be the case that such behaviour was simply impractical or unfeasible for them. Perhaps the young people have been denied the opportunity to sell drugs.

Another reason why those in my sample did not sell 'hard' drugs, such as heroin and crack, appears to have stemmed from their complete and total rejection of such drugs, a stance that, once again, seemed to reflect more general attitudes towards these drugs in Lambeth. Generally speaking, crack and heroin were, in my experience, negatively stigmatised throughout the borough, and indeed elsewhere in London. While I have heard and seen many positive cultural references to cannabis, such as in music and fashion, the same references to crack or heroin were absent. In Lambeth the overall impression seemed to be that crack and heroin were *the* drugs considered most harmful and most scorned, and, consequently, drugs the vast majority of people in the borough distanced themselves from.

Regardless of this general attitude, two young people within my sample, Marc and Tolu, sold 'hard' Class A drugs. However, even they made distinctions about their drug 'business'. For instance, while Marc and Tolu had no problem selling crack and heroin, they, like the others in my sample, did not use either drug, and treated those that did with little, if any, respect (see Bourgois 1995; Jacobs 1999). Indeed, the edict of drug sellers not getting 'high on your own supply', which may be defined as not using the drugs that you sell, is one that hip-hop artists, such as N.W.A., Notorious B.I.G.,[1] and many others have rapped about since the 1980s. Likewise, it was a decree these two drug sellers tenaciously adhered to. They happily peddled crack or heroin, but *never* used them. To a degree, that Marc and Tolu had no problem selling drugs whose use they held in such contempt was ironic. Nonetheless, this distinction was part of a code they followed when behaving this way.

Graffiti was an offence that lay fairly outside of the young people's culture of offending. Only a few did this, and their accounts of graffiti were minor. The young people did not deface religious institutions, houses, cars, or historic buildings, but rather tagged their names on fences, walls, utility boxes, street bollards, the ground, and other places they came across within the course of their daily activity. The few times the young people did scrawl their names with spray-paint cans or large markers were done for playful purposes, to let others know they were there. The code observed in relation to graffiti regulated both the location of and reasons for their tags. Even for those who committed many other offences, graffiti did not play a big part in their lives. Likewise, those who committed relatively fewer offences were not too bothered with graffiti, and no evidence emerged to suggest they 'graduated' into more serious offences. For the most part, the code associated with graffiti seemed to be *not* to do it.

A different story emerged for other expressive offences, such as joyriding and vandalism, as these offences were committed by many, particularly those more involved in offending, several of whom had joyridden cars or mopeds more times than could be remembered. That only a couple of those in my sample talked about joyriding and vandalism was, perhaps, somewhat peculiar, since vandalism is a very common offence committed by young people (Coffield 1991; Flood-Page *et al.*

2000; Graham and Bowling 1995). However, as has been explained throughout the book, a possibility exists that these young people did not talk about such offences because they may have thought their involvement in other, more serious ones overshadowed the importance of this. Alternatively, that they simply found joyriding and vandalism impractical or not worth their while could be the case because these offences were not going to bear the fruit – money or goods – they sought. For many of those less involved in offending, though, their lack of involvement in these expressive offences was consistent with their lack of involvement in offences more generally.

Overall, and perhaps predictably, a few of those more involved in offending who *did* vandalise property caused much more damage when compared to that committed by everyone else. Furthermore, only a few of them talked about taking joyriding to extremes, such as setting fire to the vehicles or using them to lure the police towards them, in the hope they would give chase. In these respects, these young people took these offences to a level that the majority of those within my sample seemed unwilling to go. This, however, is not to say these young people did not impose limits on such behaviour. Rather, as with other offences, all of the young people who joyrode or vandalised made normative judgements about these behaviours. For instance, no one talked about trashing houses, throwing rocks at church windows, or destroying local primary schools. It seemed these places were off limits. The most common forms of vandalism comprised of them randomly breaking windows or playfully smashing empty bottles. Also, in the majority, joyriding was something done for recreational purposes, and not out of a desire to harm or cause great damage. For the most part, the young people who joyrode did not go far from their immediate areas, nor did they destroy the vehicle afterwards. Rather, they stayed within earshot of their homes, let their mates 'have a go' driving the vehicle, and then safely abandoned the vehicle when it ran out of petrol or they became bored with it. Again, this suggests very finely graded distinctions were made about their offending in terms of the levels of severity the young people were willing to execute during such offences.

Thus far, that those in my sample did not have uniform attitudes towards or experiences of all of the offences discussed is apparent. However, nearly all of them made distinctions about their offences; they regulated this behaviour to an extent. Regarding fights, it seemed the young people all had parallel experiences and adhered to a specific code. By this I refer to how the majority of them noted how the use of violence was legitimised *only* in specific conditions that might arise in their lives. For these young people, events where others were calling them names, attempting to 'rip them off', had previously attacked them, or had caused them some sort of trouble in 'their' area were those in which these young people may have responded violently. In the main, fighting was 'allowed' when such occasions arose; for them, fighting was acceptable *only* in certain situations, not in all of them. Furthermore, carrying weapons was interpreted as something that might cause them great problems with the police, and none of them did this. In fact, only a couple of them really talked about weapons at all. These stances on fighting and not carrying weapons seemed to be codes that regulated their violent behaviour.

An overall theme emerging from the data concerns the finely tuned distinctions these young people made in terms of their willingness to commit certain offences, their choice of particular individuals or targets, and their limits or levels of harm or destruction caused. In other words, the young people exhibited certain guidelines or followed a specific code that regulated their offences. To them, offending was not something that was wanton, reckless or normless behaviour. Rather, within their 'culture of offending', self-imposed dos and don'ts were associated with it. This code seemed to be based on practical and instrumental grounds, as well as moral ones. To this degree, they must have asked themselves: what will I gain out of this? (is it worth it?) and how do I feel about this? (is it right?). This suggests that, like all of us, the young people made numerous, often very specific decisions about what they would and would not do.

These normative judgements are largely based on young people's responses. What the young people say and what they actually do may be two entirely different things. For instance, several of those who burgled houses said they never did this to someone who was 'in the same situation' as them or 'poor'. This distinction is not necessarily supported by other empirical data. For instance, recent British Crime Survey data (Simmons *et al.* 2002) have suggested that, in inner-city environments such as Lambeth, those most at risk of burglary include the same type of people these young people mentioned *not* burgling from – the 'poorest of the poor', the unemployed or low-income residents living on council estates. Other distinctions, such as their exclusion of the very young and very old from the range of potential robbery victims, does seem to be supported by this data, and their celebration of cannabis and rejection of 'harder' drugs seems to be supported by interview material from the professionals and observational data. So while the distinctions the young people made regarding their offending may not hold up in practice, such distinctions are, nonetheless, reflections of how they imagine themselves behaving, and are 'fallible evidence' of their 'realities' (Maxwell 1996; Wengraf 2001).

Future plans: we want what everyone else does

In this section I examine what the young people said they wanted to do with their lives in terms of employment, compare these aspirations amongst the young people, and then explore if their future plans were very different from those of other young people who might generally be considered non-offenders. Overall, I highlight that nearly all of those in my sample viewed their offending as something temporary, and they primarily saw themselves leading 'normal' lives in their futures, such as working at conventional jobs and having families. In this respect they seemed no different from 'average' young people who do not offend from more typical social, economic and cultural environments. In other words, the value systems of those in my sample were, in many ways, not too distinct from everyone else's. For the most part, these young people appeared to be relatively well-integrated into the dominant society. Moreover, in the main, their ideas of what they wanted to do with their lives were very probable; a likelihood exists that the young people will get the jobs discussed based on the resources and skills they possessed or those available to them. In only a few examples offered by those more involved in offending did future aspirations seem unrealistic or improbable.

Towards the end of the interviews I asked the young people what they wanted to do with their lives in terms of employment. All of them, except Marc who saw himself doing 'crime' until the end, had legitimate plans for their futures. This suggests that, as with some cultural aspects of their lives (such as their style, group behaviour, and interactions with the police), all the young people shared similar characteristics.

The likelihood of the young people getting the jobs they talked about is another story. While practically all of them said they wanted 'real' jobs, only some of those more involved in offending discussed future aspirations that were unrealistic. The others seem highly likely to eventually procure the kinds of jobs they wanted because these young people had more concrete future plans, such as being enrolled in school or on a vocational training scheme, or, alternatively, they already had these qualifications. For instance, David had been working with motorcycles for seven years and, at 14, already had a job as a mechanic; Theo, 22, had been cutting hair at a salon since he was 16 and reported being paid between £5 and £25 a haircut; Kevin, Tom and Martin all wanted to be painters and decorators and were pursuing NVQs in carpentry. Martin even said, 'I've got some work lined up already'. Several young people – such as Betty, Frank, Darrell, Kenny, Terry and Tim – wanted to be in the armed forces, and were in a Territorial Army Cadet programme. Whether or not their involvement in this programme was at all related to their offending was difficult to assess; young people with various offending histories attended. Overall, though, that many of these young people wanted jobs similar to those their parents had, or jobs that were roughly of equal status is interesting to note, and consistent with other delinquency research in England (for example Downes 1966; Willis 1977; Willmott 1966). Two of the young people in my sample even expressed wanting to do *exactly* the same thing their parents: Lenny was following his mother's footsteps by working as a traffic warden, and Todd will take over the pub business from his parents, if his professional football career does not take off.

For several of those more involved in offending, the story was a bit different. For instance, Marc figured he was going to be doing some sort of offending throughout his life to make ends meet. Tolu said that he wanted to go to college or 'open my own business. Something like that.' If selling heroin on the street by having others do the 'work' can be considered his 'own business', then Tolu has already reached his goal. Several talked of legitimate jobs in the future, but discussed plans that did not seem solid. They spoke of jobs on television or as a 'graphic designer or artist' due to being 'good at drawing'. These expectations are more fantastical because these young people were not pursuing any means to achieve these goals. For instance, Travis does not have any qualifications for a job as a 'graphic designer', and Karl, Sonny and, especially, Nathan are not putting too much effort into pursuing any art or design courses at the off-site units they attended. In other words, the roads these young people were currently travelling on did not lead towards the jobs they wanted. This suggests that, for many of those more involved in offending, aspirations were likely to outweigh expectations. They all wanted 'good' jobs, but had done little or nothing towards making them a reality. Several of the professionals discussed this very same dilemma faced by the young people they worked with. For instance, Rudy, a detached youth worker from Brixton, mentioned:

> Yeah, they've got aspirations. Some of them have aspirations, you know, professional kind of aspirations. One is interested in being an accountant. They spoke to me about being an accountant. Someone else spoke to me; he liked the idea of law. One of them spoke to me about politics, which was quite interesting. There are those ideas about … Some of them have talked about those jobs. On the whole, there seems to me to be a bit of a vacuum around what's next. So even though they have those ideas of professional career, or a lot, say, middle-class type occupations, there's a kind of lack of understanding of how you get there.

Steven, a detached youth worker from Stockwell, also talked about young people's aspirations about future employment:

> Just like me, they all had ideas. It wasn't specifically right, like y'know, 'I want to be a doctor', or anything, but y'know, like people don't even know what it is. 'I want to be a businessman, I want to be working in an office.' Y'know, but you don' t actually know. You just want to be in the office because that's what seen as a good job, but you don't actually know what is done in the office. That's basically what people were thinking at that point.

Fiona, a NACRO worker, discussed the careers that young people have spoken of, and the challenges they faced attaining them:

> [Plumbers, electricians, builders] Those sort of jobs … Very hands-on jobs, but in an unrealistic sense because I think there's an attitude of plumbers making, I don't know how much it is, but it is a very handsome job. But to be a plumber these days you have to go to college and you have to be an electrician. That's why I'm saying it's a bit unrealistic in their attitudes towards it … They still have to get a piece of paper [certificate] … Some of them haven't got the skills, they haven't had enough [school]. They've been out of school for two–three years.

The unlikely prospects these young people face in terms of getting the jobs they talked about when they become 'older' suggests, in part, that such individuals may not desist from offending quite as easily as the others. Finding legitimate employment has been suggested as playing a key role in a young person's desistance from offending (for example McGahey 1986; Pitts 1999; Sullivan 1989). Thus, if these young people do not make any practical moves towards these jobs and never get them, their offending may drag on. Also, committing offences is something those more involved in offending were particularly 'good' at. In other words these guys *did* make money through acquisitive offences or selling drugs, more so than they might have been able to make legitimately. The question then becomes: how were these young people going to stop offending and find a legitimate job when they earned a substantially larger amount of money through crime? Perhaps Marc, at 15, understood this completely when he assumed he would be committing crime his whole life to provide for himself. In his case we might want to ask *why* Marc would be bothered to stop this behaviour. This same question was brought up by a couple of detached youth workers from Brixton who talked about how some of the youths they worked with who sold crack or heroin, or committed a lot of burglaries or robberies, were faced with this dilemma. They mentioned how the rewards from these offences are, perhaps, too attractive to these young people, particularly when looking at other available employment possibilities. For instance, Rudy, a detached youth worker from Brixton, discussed this:

> What seems to come up with them is this whole thing of if they stop certain things, and this type of activity that we're talking about, is it financially viable? So what I'm saying is that the fundamental shifting in lifestyle: I mean, I stop doing this, how do I get, how do we continue to get the money that I'm used to getting? ... This is the dilemma as a youth worker. 'If you take it away from me what are you prepared to replace it with? Can you give me lifestyle? Can you give me a career?' So, they are very aware of that kind of reality, that for them they would either have to make a fundamental shift in lifestyle that they haven't got ... this whole thing of go to school, good grades, go to work, get a good job, have your kids and live happily ever after – they ain't buying that. They ain't buying that formula, right? So when you dialogue with them, we are coming up against quite regularly is this thing of, 'If I don't do this, what am I going to do? What are you going to replace it with?' ... It's the hare and tortoise approach. You're the hare and I'm trying to show you the tortoise and they ain't prepared to kinda go for the tortoise, right? They're on the fast track, which means that you know it's very, very difficult to kind of shift them from that mode.

Norma, another detached youth worker from Brixton, made a similar point about the young heroin sellers she was working with:

> When I speak with them they're like, 'Yeah we're gonna go to college and we're gonna do this.' They go on about what they're gonna do. They speak real positive, but when you lay down grounds, sort of passages and say 'Here's an application. Let me sit down and fill this out with you', the enthusiasm's gone after a while. They have to be on a low, really in a sense for them to, whether they're facing jail or whether they're facing some other issue/conflict, yeah? ... But when everything's good it's not an issue that they look at ... The temptation, the lifestyle; they get cars and the girls. They're earning what we do in half a year.

Declan, a youth justice worker, made similar claims about young people he has worked with:

> They would say, some of them, 'Oh, I'd like to fly an aeroplane': you know, some nice jobs. They would mention they have aspirations. They were also quite prepared to sell drugs at a drop of a hat ... They were as intelligent as you or I, but how they were going to own that and control that. You know, they weren't academically, they weren't literate ... They would aspire to things [but] they knew it would be easier to burgle and rob or sell drugs. They would make it that way. They wouldn't make it flying an aeroplane.

Looking at how those in my sample felt about employment in their future tells us a little more about their worldviews in relation to work in general. Most did not see conventional, legitimate occupations as something out of their reach, or something the young people were non-compliant with. Furthermore, in the main, the young people were not completely rejecting their prospects for legal work, and did not believe that supporting themselves (and their future families) with money earned from offending, or committing other criminal acts, such as joyriding and vandalism were behaviours that would extend much further into their lives. These young people were not located outside the dominant culture, but firmly rooted in it. They appeared to value legitimate work highly, much like everyone else, and perhaps like young people elsewhere. Pryce (1979: 68) in his research on the inner city suggested this when he noted that for 'the hustler' the situation was 'less a case of permanently rejecting the work ethic of the outside world and more a case of temporarily seeking to circumvent it'. Likewise, many in my sample who committed acquisitive offences for money, like Pryce's 'hustler', perhaps believed earning money this way was only 'temporary'.

While this may be the case, young people who commit serious offences in Lambeth run a risk of becoming negatively stigmatised, which, in turn, can have a serious knock-on effect. For instance, if a young person commits an offence, they may be labelled as 'deviant' or 'criminal' by those within their community. In turn, this young person may come to see themselves as criminal or deviant and act accordingly (Becker 1963). If a young person is labelled as such, a result might be their permanent exclusion from lifestyles outside those generally considered deviant. Crucially, these young people may find it difficult to fully reintegrate into society, particularly in terms of being employed, which, in turn, may lead to more delinquency (McGahey 1986; Pitts 1999). So while the young people may have viewed offending only as something temporary, by behaving this way they placed their futures in serious jeopardy, for these actions can have radical, perhaps unforeseen, consequences for the rest of their lives.

General impressions: looking beyond the sample

Obtaining first-hand data on young people who offend is problematic (Maguire 2000; Wright *et al.* 1992), particularly in-depth interview material. As such, the conglomeration of responses offered by the professionals I interviewed who worked with such young people in Lambeth hold potentially valuable insights. The professionals were knowledgeable or 'wise'[2] about young offenders in the borough. In other words, I interviewed the 'right' people in Lambeth when it came to those with accurate information about these young people. Furthermore, each of the adults interviewed offered a unique perspective on young offenders, due, in part, to the variability in their relationship with them. For instance, police and supervision or probation officers might be seen as having more 'official' relationships due to their involvement with young people who offend at the entry level of the criminal justice system. Other youth and community workers and, particularly, detached youth workers, due to the nature of their work, hold more 'unofficial' relationships with juveniles. Such relationships generally tended to be 'tighter' because these professionals talked about having more personal relationships with the young people and their families, discussed serving as 'appropriate adults' when the young people were arrested, and also held community social functions, which were attended by young people and their families. The point is that these interviews with the professionals are able to tell us much about young people who have offended in Lambeth more generally.

So what can my data tell us about young offenders in Lambeth? Throughout the book, I attempted to make it clear that my data do not claim to be representative of young people from any one area, estate or street, let alone the whole borough. However, I attempted to show that many similarities existed between how those in my sample interpreted their offences and, according to many professionals interviewed, the interpretations of other young people in Lambeth from similar backgrounds they worked with. Indeed, the phrase 'this point was confirmed in interviews with professionals' has been used throughout this book when making statements on the behaviour of those in my sample. In this respect, the interpretations of *my* young people seem somewhat typical of others in the borough. The responses from the professionals thus not only served to help support my claims, but also established a general impression of young offenders in Lambeth. In building this impression, it is important to highlight the instances when those in my sample offered interpretations of their illegal or illicit behaviours that matched those offered by the professionals interviewed, who have years of experience working with young people in Lambeth.

One of the more striking discoveries made about young people in Lambeth was the sheer ubiquity of crime in their lives. In other words crime seemed to be all around them, and the young people knew about it. Almost every single person interviewed, from the young people to the professionals, mentioned knowing at least one person or place involved in illegal behaviour. This included the numerous individuals and second-hand electronics stores that peddled in stolen goods, the garages that acted as 'chop-shops' trading in stolen car parts, or just 'someone' doing 'something' illegal. And because knowledge about 'crime' or 'criminals' in Lambeth did not seem to be exclusive amongst a small section of the community, many, no doubt, were given the opportunity to commit offences through various associations. The persistent presence of these opportunities is, no doubt, partially responsible for Lambeth's stifling and consistently high crime rates.

The image of the borough as a Mecca for criminal opportunities may suggest that in Lambeth, in terms of offending, 'anything goes'. This, however, does not seem to be the case. I laboured to explain that the data suggest the young people, even those most seriously involved in offending, made (or were still making) normative judgements regarding their offending in terms of their willingness to only commit particular offences against specific individuals or targets to certain degrees. The professionals interviewed also noted how young people they worked with, including those committing relatively serious offences, such as street robbery and burglary, have made similar judgements. As with my sample, the professionals also noted how the young people they have worked with made general distinctions, such as not robbing old ladies or little children, making excuses for their burglaries and thefts, or not fighting without an acceptable 'reason'. Furthermore, the professionals noted how offences such as graffiti, vandalism and joyriding were basically an extension of youthful play, as opposed to being motivated out of malice, politics or any other discernible reason. Additionally, the professionals continued to suggest that young people have only committed these offences to a certain degree. For instance, they noted how young people *only* did graffiti inconsistently and in small spates, vandalism primarily concerned *only* breaking car windows, bottles or smashing up bus stops, and joyriders pretty much just drove around in their immediate area, and then dumped the car or moped when finished. In other words, the impression is that young people in Lambeth who committed such offences only took them so far, and their value systems did not allow their offences to overstep self-imposed guidelines, similar to the 'codes' those in my sample followed.

My data also suggest young people in Lambeth are likely to come across someone who sells illegal drugs – specifically crack, heroin and, to a larger degree, cannabis. For many of those in my sample, their knowledge about illicit drugs ranged from those who sold drugs 'under the counter' at newsagents or off-licences to the young men who sold cannabis and crack on Coldharbour Lane, or those who sold heroin on Atlantic Road – two well-known streets in Brixton where such drugs could be purchased. In fact, professionals such as Quincy, a youth justice worker, Fred, a drugs squad officer, and Patrick, a NACRO worker, all mentioned something to the extent that some places in Lambeth, particularly the Brixton area, were *the* place in London to buy these drugs. However, they and other professionals also said that the young people they worked with did *not* treat all illicit drugs equally. Like those in my sample, the professionals noted how the use of cannabis by young people in Lambeth was practically celebrated, but the use of other drugs, particularly crack and heroin, was often viewed with distaste. This distinction was even the case with those who *sold* such drugs. For instance, Norma, a detached youth worker, Amanda, a youth justice worker, and a couple of the police officers interviewed who worked with young people who sold 'hard' drugs in the borough all noted how these distinctions were made. In this sense, it may have been the norm that young people who sold crack or heroin in Lambeth not only did not use such drugs, but also held those who did in contempt.

My data also help to establish a general impression of young people who have offended in Lambeth because those in my sample and, according to the professionals, other young people in the borough all shared similar cultural indicators. These include a similar style, group behaviour, and interactions with the police. In other words many professionals discussed that other young people in Lambeth placed a similar importance on looking 'good' by wearing sportswear and designer clothing, and they listened to the same general genre of music – some even discussed a certain 'connection' between what the lyricists were rapping about and events that had taken place in their lives. Also, the professionals offered no evidence that US-style gangs existed in Lambeth, and some went so far as to suggest the term 'gang' itself was culture bound, having no place in a discussion of young people in the borough, let alone England (Downes 1966; Foster 1990). Rather, the impression received from the professionals was one of young people 'hanging around' in small groups with others they grew up with; that these groups had no lasting names; that long-standing rivalries between two different groups of young people did not exist and that young people in general did not have any visual identifiers (such as colours, tattoos or hand signals) connecting them with an area, organisation or 'turf'. A final point where the interviews with those in my sample corroborate those of the professionals is on young people's interactions with the police. Many of the professionals said the young people they worked with talked about being 'pulled on a suss' quite often. Overall, it appeared that not only did young people who offend in Lambeth more generally seem to make distinctions about their offences similar to those in my sample, but they also looked very similar and shared many cultural traits.

Young people who have offended: a theoretical discussion

Accurately testing any theory of crime and delinquency lies outside the scope of this research. However, seeing how these theories 'fit' with my data is possible. We can explore how, why and in what ways these theories explain the young people's offending or evoke a greater understanding of it. This theoretical discussion does not review an exhaustive list of theories on crime and delinquency, but does address the major ones. After doing this, I offer my own theoretical viewpoints on *why* young people in Lambeth commit certain offences.

Theories on crime: strain, control, rational choice, subcultural, transcendent

To an extent, my research reflects the interests of postmodern criminologists (such as Henry and Milovanovic 1994; Nelken 1994). For one, my approach has been interpretative, focusing on the immediate situations bound up in young people's offending, aiming to see what offending means to them and understand the context of their illegal or illicit behaviours within the course of their everyday lives. Secondly, my analyses have not concentrated on broad theories of crime and delinquency (for example strain, control, rational choice, subcultural, transcendent), and, in hindsight, none of them seems to be able to adequately explain or capture all the various forms of offending committed by those in my sample. As I will soon argue, these theories do not entirely fit with my data. Finally, as I will also attempt to illustrate, the young people in my sample, for the most part, did not compromise the 'criminal Other' (Nelken 1994). In other words, with the exception of a few of those more seriously involved in offending who risked developing an 'outsider status', not much emerged within either their moral universes or their appearances to suggest that the rest of these young people were completely dissimilar from everyone else.

To begin with, I discuss the inapplicability of some of the major theories of crime and delinquency towards my data. Take those that look at social inequality, such as strain theories, for example. Strain theories basically assume that people, primarily those within the lower or working classes, commit offences as a result of some sort of perceived pressure or injustice they have suffered in their lives, whether this is due to social structural variables (Merton 1938, 1957), or social psychological ones (Agnew 1992). The idea that the young people committed specific offences as a way to overcome their economic strain (for example commit a burglary in order to sell the goods so they can go and buy clothing, cannabis, and so on), or as a way to lash out at others because they felt they were 'wronged' is persuasive, but as a general explanation of crime and delinquency strain theories have some major shortcomings. Among them, as my data are able to highlight, are its failure to indicate the direction crime and delinquency may take, and to explain how two people in the same financial situation will have completely different offending histories (see Downes and Rock 1988). Furthermore, Merton's explanation of drug use within society is antiquated. Drug use was too widespread amongst those in my sample, and indeed in Lambeth more generally, to consider those who used drugs as 'retreatists' – individuals giving up on everything else in life – nor did drug use appear to be the result of a 'shock' within the young people's personal lives (Agnew 1992). Far from being the marginalised activity that Merton and other researchers (Cloward and Ohlin 1960; Cohen and Short 1958) first suggested, drug use was widespread, and in some cases perhaps routine 'normalised' behaviour (Parker *et al.* 1995, 1998).

Control theories (Gottfredson and Hirschi 1990; Hirschi 1969) represent another major theoretical tradition in the explanation of crime and delinquency. These theories look beyond social inequality and instead address degrees of individual self-control. Where strain theories proposed that the 'presence of negative stimuli' is at the heart of understanding why someone would commit an offence, control theories suggest the *absence of positive relationships* foster offending. Rather than asking 'Why do people commit crime?' the theory essentially asks 'Why *don't* they commit crime?' To answer this, control theory holds that individuals have a series of social bonds that, in effect, 'control' their behaviour. When these bonds weaken or break off completely, crime or delinquency may be the result. Control theory seems somewhat applicable to my data in that those more seriously involved in offending did have a series of weakened social bonds, such as their tenuous attachment to school and the absence of one or both parents in their homes. However, as discussed in Chapter Two, crime appeared to be ubiquitous in the lives of these young people; opportunities existed everywhere in Lambeth to commit them. As such, if it was only these social bonds keeping the young people in check, then it should be expected that they would have committed *many more* offences than they actually did (Jones 1998). Likewise, as the same set of weakened social bonds were experienced by those less involved in offending in my sample, then it should also be expected that they, too, would have committed many more offences. However, this situation was not the case, and we still are left wondering why the young people *didn't* do it. Furthermore, control theory essentially holds that individuals' self-control is shaped early in their lives, and, once established, does not fluctuate. The theory contends that an individual's 'commitment', 'attachment', 'involvement' and 'belief' in society are solidified at a young age and that these conditions do not change. Several of the young people had offended in their pasts and then stopped altogether, perhaps suggesting they passed through a 'delinquent phase'. This, in turn, suggests that the self-control they exerted over their offending had oscillated. To these effects, control theories are not completely helpful in explaining crime and delinquency amongst my sample.

Social learning theories, such as rational choice theory, have also been applied in attempts to understand human behaviour, including crime and delinquency (Coleman and Fararo 1992; Cornish and Clarke 1987; Cromwell *et al.* 1991; Jacobs and Wright 1999). Rational choice theory suggests offending is the result of an individual's free will, that someone commits an offence because they 'want to'. It assumes crime is a rational decision. The theory holds that offending occurs in response to the presence of specific opportunities when expected benefits (stolen goods; peer approval) outweigh expected costs (community penalties; peer disapproval). Evidence emerged to suggest that a few young people did make decisions about their offending this way, such as Tolu and Marc's drug selling, Travis and Noel's office burglaries and Kevin's shoplifting. Nonetheless, one of the shortcomings of rational choice theory in its general applicability to my sample is that, once again, given the numerous criminal associations these young people mentioned and that crime seemed 'everywhere' in Lambeth, the expectation would be that the young people would have committed many more offences than they actually did. Also, rational choice theory seems to hold an automated view of people, that all decisions, including those about offending, are completely well thought out, and thus rational. My findings clearly indicate that not only were the young people's decisions to offend often sudden and not well thought out, they also made finely graded distinctions about their offending based, in part, on how they *felt* about a particular offence. In other words, a degree of impulsiveness and emotion was involved in this behaviour (Schell 1992), and many of their offences did not seem to be entirely rational decisions.

Subcultural theories of crime and delinquency (Cloward and Ohlin 1960; Cohen 1955; Cohen and Short 1958; Spergel 1964) also fail to accurately capture all the offending committed by all the young people. To a degree, the young people were perhaps part of a very broad youth subculture, such as one that may be labelled 'inner-city young people with histories of offending'. Many of them did share similar values, such as their attitudes towards drug use and fighting, and they all seemed to follow the same fashion. To these effects, they both looked similar and had similar views on particular aspects of their lives. Perhaps they comprised part of a large and ill-defined 'subculture of delinquency' (Matza and Sykes 1961; Matza 1964) within Lambeth where certain offences were 'allowed' to be committed under specific circumstances. However, these young people did not consist of a 'delinquent subculture' defined by its anti-middle class values and rejection of 'conventional' values (Cohen 1955). Rather, outside of offending, they seemed very much like everyone else. Furthermore, delinquency in a delinquent subculture was characterised either by its 'malicious, hedonistic, and wanton' behaviour (Cohen 1955), or its criminal, fighting, theft or drug-taking objectives (Cohen and Short 1958; Cloward and Ohlin 1960; Spergel 1964), and those within such delinquent subcultures frowned upon middle-class goals and ideals. The picture of the young people in my sample was not like this. In the main, their offences were instrumental towards a goal, and only on some occasions committed 'for the sake of it'. Also, these young people, particularly those more involved in offending, committed all sorts of different illegal acts, and did not necessarily focus on just one. Moreover, almost all of the young people said they wanted to eventually lead 'normal' lives, and did not reject conventional values. In these respects my data offer little support for the delinquent subcultures.

What might be best thought of as a 'crime as an act of transgression' approach towards explaining crime and delinquency represents another tradition (Katz 1988; O'Malley and Mugford 1994; Presdee 2000; Stanley 1997; see also Rojek 2000). Katz (1988), for instance, explores what he defines as the 'seductive' nature of crime and the 'moral and sensual attractions in doing evil'. Katz claims that crime can be stimulating, exciting and liberating, and that those who commit crime do so in order to transcend the banality that is characteristic of much of everyday life, or to diffuse some sort of moral or emotional dilemma in their lives. Presdee (1994, 2000) also discusses the differences between 'doing wrong' and 'doing crime', and the 'carnavalesque' nature of specific offences. To this extent, he suggests that young people engage in some offences simply as a matter of looking for something to do because they produce excitement. This theoretical standpoint suggests that an offence may be committed by someone so as only to change how they feel, however temporary, and that such behaviours generate 'sneaky thrills'. To this degree, such a standpoint seems to be suggesting that all offences have an expressive element to them. This view is very useful in explaining some of the offences committed by some of the young people. In particular, joyriding and vandalism seem to fit the transcendent model. Many of the young people said they joyrode or vandalised things for no other purpose than simply to commit these acts, which were interpreted by them as 'fun' or producing a 'buzz'. Outside of this, however, transcendent theory seems more limited in its applicability towards explaining the offending committed by the young people. Fundamentally, street crimes, such as robbery, burglary and theft, were mainly interpreted by the young people, particularly those more involved in offending, as being committed in order to get money or goods, which, in turn, bought them a lifestyle highly valued by young people more generally. It just does not hold that robberies, burglaries or thefts, nor the investment of hours spent selling crack or heroin, were committed in order to emotionally or morally transcend. True, the money earned from these offences may have allowed the young people to temporarily transcend the poverty around them. Nonetheless, these *actions themselves* – the act of robbery, burglary or shoplifting – produced tangible results, not just emotional ones. So while the transcendent approach is beneficial in explaining why some of the young people committed some of the offences, and contributes to a broader understanding of such behaviour, the theory cannot adequately capture all of it.

Towards an explanation

Several problems exist with all-inclusive theories of crime and delinquency. For one, they generally tend to ignore or give peripheral attention to issues of ethnicity and gender. Such a stance is unhelpful when attempting to explain the differential experiences of young men and young women within the criminal justice system and amongst young men from various ethnic backgrounds. Also, general theories tend to view the individual as a passive agent, unable to make personal decisions, but rather helplessly propelled into committing an offence due to some particular 'reason'. Furthermore, they attempt to set up one series of postulates to describe a wide variety of behaviours, suggesting, in part, a similarity amongst all offences. Surely the analytical framework for, say, comprehending the nature of vandalism needs to be completely different from when attempting to understand why someone would commit murder. Crime and delinquency are not a simple equation. Rather, several social, structural and emotional variables exist that need to be taken into consideration when attempting to comprehend why someone at a particular moment in time will commit an offence (see, for example, Henry and Milovanovic 1994). It seems a rather fruitless endeavour to attempt to draft a theory aiming to explain all crimes at all times. Crime is not a separate reality. Crime is, as Durkheim held, part of a *normal* society (Collins 1982); a society without crime is simply impossible. Without acknowledging crime as an integral part of our complex everyday lives, and thus analysing it from this viewpoint, we will come no closer to completely or accurately understanding it, nor know what can be done about it.

What I offer here is not a grandiose theory that attempts to explain crime and delinquency amongst young people in Lambeth in general. Rather, I work towards an explanation by piecing together parts of existing theories and general observations about crime. I then relate these to the young people's various experiences with offending. First and foremost, any explanation that attempts to adequately explain crime and delinquency needs to take gender issues into account. The great majority of all offences in Lambeth are committed by males, which reflects national and general trends (Flood-Page *et al.* 2000; Messerschmidt 1993, 2000; Newburn and Stanko 1994; Sutherland and Cressey 1978). Furthermore, the professional's conceptualisation of a 'young offender' in Lambeth was one of a young man. As such, issues of masculinity, of what it means to 'be a man', of 'doing masculinity' need to be addressed when attempting to construct an explanation for such behaviours (Messerschmidt 1993, 2000).

In explaining the acquisitive offences amongst those in my sample who committed many of them, strain theories (Agnew 1992; Merton 1938, 1957) are somewhat helpful. In the main these young men said they committed these offences in order to get money, which, in turn, allowed them to obtain goods and participate in activities they would otherwise have been excluded from or denied. Young people in Lambeth in general are constantly showered with images of affluence advertised on television, on billboards, and amongst the 'haves' in Lambeth; every day of their lives the young people are bombarded with images of the fruits of consumerism. The young men in my sample talked of receiving little or no money from parents or legitimate work. Being strapped for cash and wanting what everyone else does, the young people may have felt pressures to attain these coveted goods. Given the socioeconomic heterogeneity of Lambeth, the fact that rich and poor live right next to each other, the pressures these young men may feel towards attaining the 'right' clothes and participating in the 'right' activity must be considerably strong, perhaps more so than in an area where a greater consistency amongst people's socioeconomic status exists (see Downes 1998). This point is based on the premise that boys and young men who are constantly reminded on a daily basis of how little they possess may be seduced by the ubiquitous affluent images that surround them and, as a result, commit acquisitive offences in order to procure them. In order to attain these valued goods these young men, similar to Merton's (1938, 1957) 'innovators', employed unconventional means (acquisitive offences) in order to attain conventional goals (money; going out; looking 'good'). The extent to which other, conventional forms of making money were available to them is open to debate. Nonetheless, their interpretations of using acquisitive offences as a way to earn money, and the fact that no other money was coming to them, suggests the applicability of strain theories in explaining such behaviour. Marc and Tolu's involvement in selling of crack, heroin, and/or cannabis may also be explained in a similar vein. For these young people, selling these drugs, like acquisitive offences, was a means to achieve a specific goal – financial success or independence – a goal widely valued not only by them, but by conventional society more generally. To this degree, strain theories seem somewhat applicable in explaining why these young people behaved this way.

Travis, Theo, Quentin and Lenny all eventually stopped robbing, burgling and thieving. Why was this? Perhaps they 'aged out' of offending? Indeed, significant support exists for the idea that offending peaks between the ages of 16 and 18 and declines thereafter (see Sampson and Laub (1992) for a discussion). Simultaneously, evidence also exists to suggest young people do *not* 'age out' of offending (for example Audit Commission 1996; see also Gottfredson and Hirschi 1990). Nonetheless, Travis (18), Quentin (17), Lenny (23) and Theo (22) discussed how they had eventually stopped committing acquisitive offences. So what exactly made them stop in the end? This question is difficult to answer. What seemed to be the case was that an important event occurred within their lives that made them radically question the extent of their involvement in acquisitive offences and reflect profoundly on how they wanted to lead their lives (Graham and Bowling 1995; Sampson and Laub 1992). For instance, Quentin mentioned wanting to stop offending and focus on his new family, when his 17-year-old girlfriend became pregnant. Travis saw 'his man', the one who bought all of his stolen goods, get raided and arrested by the police, and, when finding out how much trouble his man was now in, decided that particular life was not for him. Lenny said that, when one of the individuals involved in his 'strong arming' practices and robberies wound up dead 'in pieces', he took this as a sign that he should stop. Theo witnessed his friends become heavily involved in offending and the repercussions of such behaviour (being arrested and sent to prison). He said, 'I made my own decision not to turn to that kind of life of crime', and discussed how his other friends, alternatively, did not. Theo elaborated:

> When you're younger, everyone like that: you don't know what's right and wrong really. Like but you learn from your mistakes. But some of the guys they don't learn from their mistakes. They carry on. Come out of jail, whatever. They do the same thing. They don't try to push themselves to do the right thing.

Evidence from interview material with the professionals supports the 'ageing out' scenario. For instance, Steven, a detached youth worker from Stockwell, mentioned how some of the young people he worked with desisted from offending when 'they just kinda grow up. It's like an awakening.' Wendy, a NACRO worker from Brixton, concurred:

> I think they tend to grow up a little bit [and stop offending] … I think that something like a girlfriend coming onto the scene has an element of appeal.

Ben, a youth and community worker from Clapham, also discussed how he had seen young people desist from offending as they aged, and related this to the opening of other opportunities to make money and their self-realisation that such behaviour was not for them.

> I would say in the main they gave some sort of indication, and that [they were saying] 'Yes, we do know that these things are harmful and that these sort of things are not for the well-being of the community.' Whether or not that was because they were saying what was necessarily was expected of them or that there was a sort of genuine concern and feelings about it, I couldn't really say. But given their overriding sort of interest involved in it, I think there might be some sort of, umm, internal conflicts. Because I've seen some of them move away they have moved into something more legitimate ways of making money, and it is due to the fact because it's too risky both for their own sort of, umm, safety and for their, uh, freedom, y'know? Or is it also because they, umm, truly understand that: 'Wait a second, y'know? I could be one of the people who is contributing to the demise of my community.'

So, in sum then, what seems to have led the young people in my sample towards desisting from committing acquisitive offences as they aged was some sort of self-realisation that such a lifestyle was not conducive to these young people's impressions of how they consider themselves living their lives. This realisation, in turn, appeared to be largely due to some event that made them profoundly question such behaviour. To a degree, similar comments could be made about young people who have offended in the borough more generally. If this 'realisation' is the case, then the idea that salient life events have a significant influence on young people's desistance from crime and delinquency as they mature receives some support (Graham and Bowling 1995; Sampson and Laub 1992). Perhaps younger 'active offenders' in my sample, such as Sonny, Marc, Tolu, and even Nathan, will experience similar events that may lead them away from acquisitive offences.

For those who only committed a couple of acquisitive offences, strain theories are less applicable. While these young people were in roughly similar socioeconomic situations as everyone else, their acquisitive offences, for the most part, did not seem to be committed to overcome any pressures they might have felt. The young people did not say they used such offences towards monetary gain. Rather, their interpretations of such offences suggested they became caught up in the offence, that such behaviour was a one-off that occurred 'a long time ago' when they were younger, or that they took something off the shelves because they 'just wanted it'. The idea that strain theories adequately capture the acquisitive offences committed by some and not all of these young men highlights a general shortcoming of these approaches: how can young people in very similar socioeconomic situations, education, and housing tenure, living in a lower- or working-class community have completely different experiences of strain, and, as a result, of their participation in offending? To this degree, as suggested by recent research, additional social psychological attributes of young people need to be addressed when looking at their socioeconomic background status in relation to their offending (for example Broidy 2001; Dunaway *et al.* 2000; Wright *et al.* 1999). These attributes may be able to tell us more about how individual young people *respond* to the 'presence of negative stimuli' – the central crux of strain theories.

While strain theories help in constructing a viable reason *why* those in my sample who committed many acquisitive offences did so, addressing other explanations of crime and delinquency is beneficial when looking at *how* the young people are able to gain from them. Perspectives that have focused on the opportunity young people have to commit certain offences (such as Cloward and Ohlin 1960; Hagan 1994) have much to offer when explaining the young people's offending. The *many* legal second-hand shops in Lambeth offer young people accessible outlets where they can easily pawn stolen goods for instant cash. These shops act as a support matrix for this type of offending (Cromwell *et al.* 1991, 1996; Foster 1990; McGahey 1986; Sullivan 1989). There exists within Lambeth a network of adults, such as those who sell stolen goods 'door-to-door' and those who sell drugs, who also advertise the idea of behaving this way, and perhaps offer the opportunity to do so. This influence of 'delinquent peers' further contributes to young people in the borough becoming involved in such offending, and differential associations to these peers could help explain varying rates of involvement in offending (Sutherland 1947; Sutherland *et al.* 1992; see also Flood-Page *et al.* 2000; Graham and Bowling 1995).

The young people's interpretations of their use of specific illegal drugs also have theoretical implications. Amongst both those in my sample and those in Lambeth more generally, the use of cannabis was incredibly widespread, and not located within a distinct drug-using subculture (Cloward and Ohlin 1960; Cohen and Short 1958; Spergel 1964). Cannabis use appeared to be so common amongst young people, if not people in general, as to be considered 'normalised' (Parker *et al.* 1995, 1998). For young people in Lambeth, using cannabis should almost come to be expected; cannabis seemed to be a 'normal' aspect of their adolescence. Certainly the 'softly-softly' approach introduced by officers in the borough towards policing the casual use of cannabis reflected this. In other words a harmony existed between the use of cannabis in the borough and the police's new attitude towards it.

Since the 1960s, the theoretical conceptualisation of a 'drug user' has evolved from someone considered one of society's 'double failures' (Cloward and Ohlin 1960) into someone engaging in 'normal', routine, and perhaps expected youthful behaviour (Parker *et al.* 1998; although see Shiner and Newburn 1997, 1999). Whereas the belief was once that very few people in society used illicit drugs, contemporary viewpoints suggest young people in general are very likely to try at least one, particularly cannabis. But while this may be the case, a very different story emerged for other drugs in Lambeth, especially 'harder' drugs, such as crack and heroin. Crack and heroin use amongst those in my sample was unheard of, and the general impression received in the borough was that these drugs were widely avoided by young people. In these respects, crack and heroin use in Lambeth may be subcultural (Cloward and Ohlin 1960; Spergel 1964). By this I refer to how, regardless of the overall stigmatisation associated with the use of such drugs in Lambeth, clearly groups of people in the borough did use them with some consistency. In turn their 'values' and 'norms' regarding crack and heroin use appeared to be significantly distinct from the majority of the people in Lambeth. Both the limited number of users of these drugs and the distinctions between their values regarding such use and those of the majority of people in the borough suggest that heroin and crack use in Lambeth may be subcultural.

The 'crime as an act of transgression' approach (Katz 1988; O'Malley and Mugford 1994; Presdee 2000; Stanley 1997) seems helpful in explaining many of the expressive offences committed by young men across offending categories. Their vandalism, joyriding and graffiti, with the exception of Kenny's 'artistic' graffiti, were interpreted by them as being committed, in the main, 'for fun' because they produced a 'buzz', or simply because it was 'something to do'. These explanations appear to suggest they committed these offences in order to break away from the routine boredom they suffered on a daily basis, something that seems to be characteristic of many contemporary urban areas (Campbell 1993; Presdee 2000; Rojek 2000). A couple of acquisitive offences mentioned by a few young people, and a violent incident by one of them, may be best explained by this approach. For instance, Karl talked about how he used to 'sniper people' with his pellet gun on the rooftop of his estate 'for fun'. Martin and Tom also discussed how they once committed a burglary in order to generate some excitement in their lives. One of the attractions of this perspective is its focus on the phenomenological aspects of the offence, rather than structural inequality. To this degree, the approach is beneficial in explaining certain types of offending – expressive offences in the main – regardless of the young person's socioeconomic status or other background issues in their lives.

Katz (1988: Chapter 3) also suggested that this perspective offered much in the way of explanation of violence amongst young men. He argued that young men's aggression towards one another had much to do with presenting themselves as 'hard', 'tough', or, as Katz puts it, as 'badasses' (see also Patrick 1973). To this degree, fighting supports a lifestyle, a desired image, and, more crucially, was an activity they enjoyed. In the main this is *not* the picture of the young people in my sample or in Lambeth more generally. A couple of examples of this did emerge, but my data suggest, for the most part, the young people presented themselves as defenders, not attackers; not individuals seeking out and relishing violence, but rather only engaging in it when 'necessary'. What my data suggest in terms of the young people's violence is that, in the main, violence was something brought about for particular reasons. The reasons discussed for fighting outline a culture of masculinity, a culture of machismo, a culture of respect. These young people, primarily young men, defended any attacks that might have damaged or compromised their self-perceptions of what it means to be 'tough', to be someone 'nobody messes with', to be a young man. Respect is a valued commodity in their world, and actions that jeopardise it were dealt with violently, usually through fighting. Only in a couple of examples, such as those offered by Nathan, were these attacks relatively extreme and vicious. Overall, the values those in my sample had regarding fighting seemed to be shared by a broad section of people within Lambeth. Indeed, much research in inner-city lower- or working-class environments has suggested that attitudes towards fighting, not unlike those offered by the young people in Lambeth, exist amongst a broad population of young people and adults alike (Anderson 1990, 1999; Hannertz 1969; Kennedy and Forde 1999; Messerschmidt 2000; Miller 1958, 1969; Patrick 1973; Shover 1996). To this degree, the young people's values regarding fighting may simply be an extension of those in the adult community.

When developing an explanation for crime and delinquency amongst the young people, taking gender issues into account is important. So is ethnicity. From the beginning of the book I suggested that, in terms of offending, the interpretations and experiences of young black, white and 'mixed race' people have been relatively the same, and that a great many cultural similarities existed between them. Nonetheless, in Lambeth, young black men, which would include those generally considered 'mixed race', are disproportionately represented as offenders of serious street crimes, such as burglary, robbery, theft, and drug sales. How do we explain these differences? Should there be an explanation for their offending that differs from that for young white men? Clearly, the histories of young white and black people within the borough are fundamentally different. Black people have only been in England en masse since the middle of the twentieth century. Since they have been here they have faced discrimination in the housing and employment markets, been policed by a force considered 'institutionally racist' and hyper-represented as 'criminals' within the mass media (see, for example, Hall *et al.* 1978; Harris and James 1993; MacPherson 1999; Pryce 1979; Surette and Otto 2001). In short then, to answer the questions raised, to include ethnicity in an explanation of crime and delinquency amongst these young people would seem imperative. The fundamental differences in history between young white and black people and the various discriminatory practices black people have endured surely need to be recognised and properly addressed when developing a theory to explain crime and delinquency in their lives (for example Sampson and Wilson 1995; Wilson 1987).

Overall then, in terms of attempting to better comprehend the young people's offences, what I find applicable is not a broad, all-inclusive theory. Rather, what best explains and evokes reasons for these behaviours are excerpts from a variety of different theories. Strain theories seem beneficial in explaining their acquisitive offences, particularly for those who committed many. The normalisation thesis appears to be persuasive in explaining the widespread use of cannabis amongst them. The 'crime as an act of transcendence' approach is somewhat useful in explaining why they committed expressive offences, such as joyriding and vandalism. And when explaining their violence, theories that address a culture of masculinity, a culture of respect and continuity in values between youth and parent lower- or working-class cultures have much to offer. These theories do not *exactly* explain all of these behaviours, but they seem to be relatively adequate in capturing them. Also and importantly, when drafting explanations for crime and delinquency amongst the young people, taking issues of gender and ethnicity into account is important. This consideration is due to the overwhelming majority of males involved in offending in general, and the disproportionate number of young black people within local offending statistics. Only from constructing an explanation that incorporates all of these perspectives will we get closer towards answering *why* young people in Lambeth commit their offences.

A final point I want to make in this section concerns how we view young people in the inner city who offend, in general. Basically, those in my sample did not comprise a criminal 'type', nor the 'criminal Other' (Nelken 1994). By this I refer to how no consistencies emerged amongst any of them to suggest a series of specific or distinct qualities existed that were the mark of someone who offends. For one, these young people dressed typically; nothing they wore, no special insignias on them suggested they belonged to a distinct clique. Moreover, their *values* seemed to be very much akin the majority of people living in Lambeth, if not in general. Stereotypical images of the inner-city street thug, yardie, rude bwoi or gangsta who cares nothing about anyone else, who completely disregards society in general, and who lives his life strictly by his wits and survives only through crime are largely unsupported by my data. The young people, in the main, were nothing like this at all. Rather, with a few exceptions, the young people were very similar to everyone else. By this I refer to how they did the same things as typical young people: went to some form of schooling, were involved in sports or some organised extracurricular activity, played on 'the computer', partied, chased the opposite sex, and just 'hung out'. Crime was a very small part of their lives, not something that dominated their thoughts and actions. This situation was, perhaps, slightly different for a few within my sample, particularly those more deeply involved in offending, who thus ran the risk of an 'outsider' status. Having said this, evidence emerged to suggest the 17- and 18-year-olds who did commit relatively serious offences were well on their way towards desisting from offending, and that the most serious offences were part of their past, at least according to their interviews. Even for them, slipping back into the mainstream should not be too difficult because they never really left it. This, perhaps, is the best way to view *all* of these young people: as youngsters who were primarily grounded within conventional, normal, everyday society and observed its general norms, laws and rules, but from time to time dipped over into the world of offending for a variety of reasons when particular opportunities arose and when their moral universes allowed it. In sum, findings indicate that these young people were hardly detached from the world around them, but in many respects were very similar to all of us.

Conclusions

What I attempted to demonstrate within this book is that all of the young people, including those who committed relatively serious offences, made (or were still making) normative judgements about their acquisitive, expressive, violent and drug-related offences. The young people imposed limits upon themselves, and were only willing to commit certain offences against particular individuals or targets to a degree. These judgements appeared to be based both on instrumental and practical grounds (Is it worth it? Will I gain what I want?) as well as moral and ethical ones (Is it right? Should I do this?). For them, offending was only allowed under specific conditions, when the right opportunities arose, and the victims or targets were deemed appropriate. And even when these opportunities presented themselves, the young people were still only willing to take these offences to a certain level of harm, a certain amount of damage. Overall, findings indicate that the young people's illegal or illicit behaviour was highly self-regulated. However, these findings are largely based on what the young people said, which may not always be exactly what the young people do.

I also attempted to show that, for these young people, not only was offending a small part of their lives currently, but also they viewed such behaviours as events that were not going to be occurring when they were older. For the most part, the young people held very conventional outlooks about their futures. They desired families, their own places to live, and their own jobs. But while practically all of them said they would like to lead these kinds of lives later on, many of those with more serious offending histories had unrealistic expectations in terms of the occupations they wanted. That these young people will ever attain the jobs they discussed is doubtful. This partially suggests that these young people's offending may drag on a bit longer, as links between desistance from offending and being legally employed have been previously considered. If this course is true, then we may come to expect that all the other young people, who were on the right paths towards the careers they mentioned, may leave offending in their pasts as they move successfully towards the futures they desire. Evidence emerged to suggest the young people were already doing this.

Next, I attempted to paint a broad picture of young people and crime and delinquency in Lambeth by suggesting that, according to interviews with professionals,
the way those in my sample interpreted, felt and made distinctions regarding their
offences, how they looked and what they got up to on a daily basis, their interactions with the police, and their overall outlook on their offending in the future
appeared to be somewhat typical of other young people in the borough with similar
backgrounds. This is not to claim my data are completely representative, but these
professionals have been working in various capacities with young people who have
offended for many years. Such individuals were Lambeth's police officers and
youth justice workers, representing 'official' criminal or youth justice agencies. The
professionals were also youth and community workers connected to youth clubs
and youth activities organisations, who discussed working with young people who
have offended, as well as detached youth workers, a very specialised and select
number in Lambeth, who discussed working with relatively serious 'young offenders' outside of any organisation or club, but rather 'on the street'. All of the youth
workers represent more informal agencies with a hands-on approach. The combination of all of the interview material from professionals representing both these
formal and informal agencies in Lambeth has allowed for a more well-rounded
view of young people who have offended in the borough. What I pointed out to
some degree in each of the chapters, and what I stressed again in this chapter, is
that many of the normative judgements those in my sample made about their
offending behaviour and many of their cultural aspects were confirmed by the
professionals as being congruent with their experiences of working with young
people who offended in Lambeth.

In the second half of the chapter I raised some points about the applicability of
general theories of crime and delinquency towards my data. Here, I argued that
the theories I discussed – strain, control, subcultural, rational choice, and transcendence – were unable to accurately explain all of the various forms of offending
committed by those in my sample. These theories were useful in explaining some
aspects about these behaviours, but none entirely captured all of them. One of the
shortcomings I highlighted within these and other general theories of crime was
that they tend to view the individual as someone who was helplessly propelled into
this behaviour through forces beyond their control, or as someone on automatic
pilot on a collision course towards some sort of offending. Furthermore, such theories seem to throw an entire catalogue of criminal and illicit acts into one giant pot
called 'crime and delinquency' and then attempt to explain all of this behaviour
within the same analytical framework.

Using bits and pieces of existing theories, I offered my own theoretical viewpoints on the young people's offences. I suggested that the essence of strain theories
seems to best capture the reasons *why* those who committed many acquisitive
offences did so. Profiting from these offences was largely facilitated by the network
of second-hand shops that purchase goods with no questions asked, which also
stresses the importance of perspectives that address the opportunities to offend. I
then discussed how applicable the normalisation thesis was to the use of cannabis
amongst young people in Lambeth, and that since the 1960s sociologists have

come a long way in their conceptualisation of illicit drug use amongst young people. Also, theories that suggest the criminal act is actually an act of transcendence, whereby the individual commits an offence solely for the purpose of changing how they feel, seem somewhat applicable in explaining their expressive offences, such as joyriding, vandalism, and some violent episodes. Finally, I forwarded that the perspectives addressing issues of machismo, respect and the continuity of values between adult and youth populations in lower- and working-class environments better contextualise the young people's violence, specifically their fighting. Based on my data, fighting amongst the young people may be viewed as them defending attacks on their masculinity or 'respect' under conditions that have been acceptable within their community for many years. Concomitantly, when looking at *why* the young people committed various offences, addressing issues of gender and ethnicity is important due to the fact that most crimes are committed by males, and that young black men are arrested for a disproportionate number of offences in Lambeth. Lastly, I suggested that these young people were not 'the criminal Other', if such a character ever existed in society. For one, I pointed out that the young people looked like everyone else, and had no specific 'uniform' that could easily demarcate them from the rest of their community. Furthermore, their values were primarily grounded within the dominant culture, and not located outside of it. In the main, offending was a relatively small part of their lives. Most of the time these young people were doing what may be considered routine youthful activities.

9   What is to be done about crime and delinquency in Lambeth?

I studied various forms of crime and delinquency in Lambeth for several years. I also experienced what it is like to live around certain forms of crime in ways perhaps not too dissimilar from your 'average' Lambeth citizen. What follows are my own reflections on these experiences, as well as some ideas that might be beneficial towards doing something about them. Specifically, I offer a couple of ideas regarding what can be done about acquisitive and some drug-related offences in the borough.

Pressed for cash: being young, earning money, and Stop and Swap Inc.

That young people who committed acquisitive offences did so primarily in order to get money, which enabled them to participate in activities and present themselves in a certain way, is clear from my data (Jacobs and Wright 1999; Shover 1996). If this situation is the case more generally then perhaps as a society we should make it easier for young people to get money legitimately (Graef 1993).

In the last chapter I suggested young people, young men in particular, in their early teenage years, who desire all of the fancy clothes and youthful activities they see all around them yet are pressed for cash, may turn to acquisitive offences (or other profitable offences) as a means to an end. And while these young people are probably told, from many different angles and in many different ways, that crime is wrong and not to behave this way, what alternatives are they offered? What other options are they allowed to choose from that will enable them to earn money legitimately, so as to experience these activities and purchase these fashions they covet so highly?

My purpose is not to review the policies and practices within Lambeth that may or may not have been implemented since the early1990s attempting to tackle acquisitive offences amongst young men. What I call attention to are the options available to boys and young men who want to earn money. What I suggest, rather simply, is this: let us make it easier for young people to earn money legitimately; let us offer young people more job opportunities or vocational training in fields they find gratification in. Considering the significant relationship between a young person's involvement in the legitimate labour market and their desistance from offending (McGahey 1989;

Pitts 1999; Sullivan 1989), perhaps their participation within such a market at earlier stages of their lives might contribute to them desisting sooner rather than later. This idea was brought up by many of the professionals I interviewed, particularly the youth and community workers and the detached youth workers. Mick, a detached youth worker in Brixton, mentioned 'education' as a way for young people in Lambeth to 'break the circle', the offending pattern:

> The way you gotta break it is with education. There's no two ways about it: education is priority number one. You've got to educate those young people so that they can make choices. You have to give those young people the word we call 'opportunity'. What is opportunity? What is opportunity? The most fundamental point ... one of the most vital parts in a young person's life is ... they need to have a positive setting around them to change the kinds of influences that's going to affect their lives when they are older ... I would say a positive environment, and definitely a support structure.

In order to make these opportunities happen and to advertise their existence amongst young people greater public-sector funding is needed. It seems that the majority of the money in the UK set aside for crime and disorder is spent on more prisons and police (Audit Commission 1996; Graef 1993), rather than on what might be thought of as the 'intermediaries' between the young people and the initial stages of the criminal justice system, such as youth and community workers and detached youth workers. Mick acknowledged this, saying 'One of the things that's missing, Bill, is people *like me* that can talk with those young people'. Indeed, *all* of the professionals interviewed who worked in these capacities, even those in more nationally recognised agencies such as NACRO, said their hands were tied in terms of what to offer the young people, and how these limitations generally stemmed from operating on shoestring budgets. For instance, Tanya and Russell, two NACRO workers from Brixton, mentioned how their funding was limited, and how, rather than hiring people with some sort of training or experience with young people, an obligation was to use volunteers, with an emphasis on unemployed local people. While nothing is wrong in using volunteers for such important social work, there seemed to be an over-reliance on their participation. Mick mentioned his frustrations of running a youth centre on £4,000 a year and how he is not a 'voluntary organisation'.

> Give me some cash! ... What it is, though, I'm not a charity organisation. I'm not a voluntary organisation. I'm a statutory organisation led by the local authority on £4,000 a year. So what can you do? ... So where does the common sense come of it? Four weeks the police [in Lambeth] can come up with twenty grand, yeah, for four weeks, to do a programme because they are funded by the big corporate boys. Yeah, with a committee and trustees that are from the Brixton Summer Projects. But we can't get shit together for the other 48 weeks of the year through the local authority that *should* inject outside money, yeah, to come in on a bigger scale.

Fortunately, he, and a couple of the other detached youth workers in the borough, had other, mature, altruistic young adults from the community helping out voluntarily. Interestingly, in a couple of instances these young adults had offended themselves once, and were now 'giving something back' to the organisations that helped them in their troubled teen years. Steven and Ayo are two prime examples of this. Without these volunteers, the difficulties of detached youth work would become compounded. Surely, those who work in such organisations in Lambeth not only deserve more money, but require it in order to do their job effectively.

Aside from greater public-sector funding, additional aspects of Lambeth need to be addressed in order to curb its high rates of acquisitive offences. In particular, it may be useful to focus on the trading and selling of stolen merchandise, primarily electrical, and the many shops within the borough where these transactions go down. I observed *numerous* such shops in the borough; such 'businesses' are an intrinsic part of Lambeth. These economic practices flourish, in part, due to the cracks, the deficiencies in Lambeth's overall structure (Coleman 1988; Cromwell *et al.* 1996; Hagan 1994; McGahey 1986; Sullivan 1989). As such, these practices are firmly rooted within the community, and are not simply going to go away. No doubt, many 'average' citizens benefit directly from them.

The proliferation of these shops in Lambeth contributes to the large number of burglaries, shopliftings, thefts and robberies in the borough. The harm these shops cause is related to the loss of personal property by individuals who live within their vicinity. As mentioned, my data suggest young people were stealing things from their own communities, from their more 'affluent neighbours' (Pitts 1999; Sutherland and Cressey 1978). To this degree, these second-hand shops are feeding off their own communities, paying one neighbour for the property of another.

These second-hand shops are not necessarily illegal per se, and surely not all the merchandise that circulates within them was initially stolen, but they act as a support network for certain acquisitive offences, such as burglary, theft and even some robberies. These stores make it easy for those who commit such offences to make money from their stolen goods, their 'swag'. No doubt the buying and selling of stolen merchandise goes on in other private settings behind closed doors. These shops, nonetheless, facilitate acquisitive offending, perhaps to a larger degree than expected. These shops are everywhere, easy to find and may have an influence on young people. If, for example, 'Joe', who lived, 'near Brixton' wanted to sell his stolen television, Joe would not have to look far to do this. Many second-hand shops exist around that area and will buy it from him. Such shops are a convenience. Joe does not have to ask around, hoping someone will take interest in this television; all Joe has to do is bring it down to one of the many second-hand shops near to his home, and the likelihood of him walking out with cash in his pocket is high. Selling stolen goods in Lambeth is that simple.

Also, the sheer number of these shops may suggest to people that selling stolen goods is acceptable – 'everyone's doing it' (Matza 1964; Sykes and Matza 1961) – another way these shops may exert a degree of influence over the young people's decision to commit acquisitive offences. Surely, the simple knowledge that stolen goods will be purchased somewhat influences people to commit these offences in the first place. In a sense, these shops advertise: 'sell your stolen goods here; we'll give you some cash; it's not a big deal.' Certainly this knowledge is not privileged; many people knew about these shops. A recent television game show called *Swag* has previously set up contestants to see if they purchase stolen goods from one of the show's ersatz 'vendors'. This show seems to contribute to the idea that buying stolen goods is acceptable; they make a joke of it. I observed *many* of these second-hand electronics shops in Lambeth, much more than in some of the 'nicer' boroughs of London, areas with lower rates of burglary and robbery. In other words, there seemed to be a large number of shops that buy and sell stolen goods in an area where high rates of acquisitive crimes have existed for years. Is there any connection? Perhaps future research will inform us.

The legality of these shops is fuzzy. They apparently follow some sort of 'point' system, whereby certain pieces of personal identification – such as passports, driver's licences, utility bills or birth certificates – will establish the identity of those wanting to sell goods, and thus entitle them to do so. These identifications do not necessarily have pictures attached to them, leaving it more difficult to confirm authenticity. According to my informal conversation with Bobby who worked at Stop and Swap – a chain of second-hand stores in Lambeth, and London more generally – as long as the person had enough identity 'points', Bobby's boss would buy the items regardless of how many times the individual came in with goods to sell, and whether they believed the items truly belonged to them or not. Thus, while 'the bosses' at such shops may adhere to some sort of policy that attempts to regulate the amount of goods anyone comes in to sell, cases were reported where it seemed very clear the people behind the counters at these stores knowingly purchased goods that were probably stolen. This points system seems to be put in place so that those who work in such shops can cover their tracks, so to speak. As Will, a detective constable from Streatham, said about the employees of such second-hand shops, 'It's like they know it's stolen, they just don't care.'

Regulating such practices so as to monitor the amounts of potentially stolen items that are filtered through them is, perhaps, not a bad place to start. To control what comes into these businesses, tighter regulations are needed on identification, proof of purchase, and the amount of merchandise individuals are allowed to bring in over a certain period of time. This regulation should proceed both internally through legislation (in other words rewriting the 'rules' of purchasing goods), and externally through the development of independent 'watchdog' organisations responsible for monitoring these shops in all their forms, including Stop and Swap and the various independent second-hand electronics and mobile-phone shops. In short, let us not make it so easy for people to make money through acquisitive offences in the area. In the late eighteenth century, magistrate Patrick Colquhoun commented on the critical link between 'thieves' and 'receivers' in London:

> Nothing … can be more just than the old observation, 'that if there were no receivers there would be no thieves' … Deprive a thief of a safe and ready market for his goods and he is undone.
>
> (Colquhoun 1795, quoted in Cromwell *et al.* 1991: 71)

Crack and heroin users and sellers on the street

In the heart of Brixton between an imaginary 'red triangle' connecting the high street (Brixton Road), Coldharbour Lane and Atlantic Road I encountered many crack and heroin users and sellers. Experiences include being offered these drugs, seeing discarded drug paraphernalia, and various encounters with people who use these drugs. During the course of this research many times in mixed circles I brought up the evidence of the proliferation of crack and heroin use and sales in Brixton to the response of 'Oh, that happens *everywhere*'. Statements such as these are misleading, and not founded in empirical research. Not all of Brixton is like this and certainly not all of Lambeth. Furthermore, I walked through many communities in London and failed to find evidence of heroin and crack users and sellers. Such individuals were, however, very evident in Brixton's 'red triangle'.

Coming into Brixton via public transport and *not* noticing the signs of crack and/ or heroin use is difficult. For one, it seemed common knowledge, at least according to my interviews and many informal conversations, that individuals 'hanging about' the Brixton underground station frequently used these drugs. On a couple of occasions, I actually *saw* them purchasing either crack or heroin. The Brixton train station is another area congested with evidence of crack and heroin use, and I observed many discarded needles and makeshift pipes made from aluminium foil and empty soda cans littering the stairwell leading up to the platform and the platform itself. During the evenings the top of the stairwell at the station has served as a 'hang out' for crack and/or heroin users. I observed them there on several occasions. Just outside of the Brixton train station, on the corner of Atlantic Road and Electric Avenue, you can find people selling heroin and/or crack. Even on the television I watched an undercover reporter for *Sky News* film people buying these drugs here.

Not only is there heavy human traffic at both the train and tube stations, but Brixton's 'red triangle' is right in the middle of an extensive commercial zone, with grocers, butchers, shops of all kinds, and an intricate open-air market and covered bazaar. Probably *thousands* of people work or interact within the parameters of this triangle, if only to pass through, on a daily basis. Probably thousands more lie in its shadow. That crack and heroin use and sales occur within these areas is no secret. Many people, including police officers interviewed, seemed to know exactly what was going on down the streets of Atlantic Road and Coldharbour Lane. Apparently, the sales and use of crack and, to a lesser degree, heroin have been happening in this area for *many years* before I arrived in Brixton. Informal conversations with people in Lambeth suggest this 'red triangle' has existed within the area since the mid-1980s, just slightly shifting its location.

What about the people who live and work in these areas? Do the drug users and drug sellers affect them in any way? No doubt, to some degree for the 'average' citizens who live and/or work within this 'red triangle', crack and heroin users and sellers have become a part of their lives; they interact with and negotiate their presence frequently, if only by attempting to avoid them altogether. This effort alone compounds their daily lives. More importantly this effort is on top of a mountain of other social ills people within this inner city may face. This drugs' atmosphere in central Lambeth affects some of the most disadvantaged people in London; it adds to the struggle, the pressures and the challenges that low-income or benefit-dependent people living in crowded public-sector housing within Lambeth must endure.

Surely those who sell and use crack and heroin must exert a degree of influence upon the people who live near them, particularly young people. Many young people must walk past the crack and heroin sellers on Atlantic Road and Coldharbour Lane, and the users elsewhere in central Brixton, on a daily basis as part of their routine. Some may come to find that selling crack and heroin presents them with an opportunity to make 'big, easy money', an opportunity perhaps only available to them due to their consistent contact with such individuals, even only to frequently walk past them. They then become part of the cycle of crack and heroin sales which, according to interviews and observations, have been occurring in this area – Brixton's 'red triangle' – for many years. If nothing is done to break this cycle, to intervene in the perpetuation of crack and heroin sales in this area, these harms in their many forms will continue to be present in these areas, perhaps for many more years to come.

Obviously, no easy answers, no quick-fix solutions, exist to curb the proliferation of crack and heroin use and sales in Lambeth. This drugs 'problem' is not a simple matter of using or selling crack or heroin, but also encompasses living around those who do. So what is being done about this? For all the efforts of the police in Lambeth, crack and heroin use and sales in Brixton's 'red triangle' were rife.

My proposed solution is rather simplistic. Rather than over-relying on closed-circuit television (CCTV) to catch people either selling or using crack or heroin, thus having a potential deterrent effect, perhaps a stronger police presence is required. If police officers were strategically placed both outside the train and tube station, or even patrolled a small stretch of space surrounding those areas, then the blatant use and sales of crack and heroin might slowly subside, and, eventually, become non-existent. I observed police officers do this occasionally with seemingly positive results. When I noticed officers either at the underground or train stations, I saw less of the individuals who use or sell crack or heroin. Of course, if police officers are stationed at the underground and train stations, the crack and heroin users and sellers might simply abandon these areas and set up camp in others. To this degree, the crack and heroin problem is only pushed away, and not necessarily solved. However, due to the strong history of the use and sales of these drugs in the central Brixton area, the thousands of 'everyday' people who must interact within them, and the potential influence that individuals who sell or use crack or heroin might have on young people, it is perhaps not such a bad idea to push these practices out of such a populated area with a high flow of human traffic through a stronger and continued police presence.

Living next door to crack and heroin

My experiences with crack and heroin users and sellers were not only limited to those within Brixton's 'red triangle'. Remarkably, between the years 1996 and 2002, three houses on my street, located directly behind the Brixton high street, reportedly sold heroin and/or crack. In addition, a couple of crack and heroin 'dens' – pockets in the street where the use of these drugs occurred – appeared. By all other means the street seemed fairly 'normal' by Lambeth standards, with a mixture of rich and poor, young and old, families with children and those without.

These crack and/or heroin houses and dens were a great concern amongst neighbours. Some expressed being tired of finding needles and other paraphernalia strewn across their property, as well as of the users lurking around. Little, however, seemed to be done about these houses by the police. Rather, people on my block took matters into their own hands to tackle this issue. For instance, in 1997 one neighbour firebombed a reported crack house located directly opposite from me. About a year later another house that sold heroin located at the other end of the street was set ablaze, apparently by another disgruntled neighbour.

The traffic and commotion of the first two heroin/crack houses on my street paled in comparison to that of the third one, which was located right next door to me. This neighbour had visitors all hours of the night, some whom I recognised buying crack and/or heroin on Atlantic Road, and I constantly found discarded needles outside his door and sometimes mine. I figured he sold heroin. To confirm this, I asked him once to please try and be quieter at night, and brought up selling and using heroin. He admitted selling heroin and said would attempt to keep the noise down.

Unfortunately, nothing changed. As the noise and commotion, not to mention the potential dangers of living next to such a house, became overbearing, I decided to do something about it. I called several people – the police, Lambeth Council and Lambeth Housing Association, and each of them told me to call the other. The police said the situation was something for the Council to take care of, the Council said the property was under the jurisdiction of the Housing Association, and the Housing Association said it belonged to the Council. Both the Council and the Housing Association also told me to call the police.

Eventually it turned out to be a house belonging to Lambeth Council, but they told me it would take several months to get the 'squatters' out, as much legal paperwork needed to be sorted out. I informed them of all the drug paraphernalia and the flow of late-night visitors, and that I believed this to be a house used only by heroin sellers and users, with the hopes that the Council might expedite the situation. They, again, told me to call the police. The police said the situation was not their problem, but 'made a note' of the probable drug-selling going on, and mentioned the quickest way to expel them was to call the Council. This circle of finger-pointing was very frustrating; all I wanted to do was get these people out. I eventually was given the name of the legal representative for that area of Brixton by someone at the Council, who suggested this representative could act immediately on this house, particularly if other people in the neighbourhood were making the same complaint, and if this house was used by people selling heroin, not by a family or permanent resident.

Unfortunately nothing happened. Several more months passed and no one did anything, not the police, Lambeth Council, the Housing Association nor the legal representative. In a bizarre twist, the legal representative refused to do anything until he knew *my* name. I suggested he simply visit the residence to see for himself if action was necessary. He did nothing. Overall, I found it curious that no one in the borough with supposed 'power' could do anything about squatters with a some-what tenuous hold on a relatively expensive house who, crucially, were using and selling heroin. This residence was a 'smack' house, one where the blatant use of heroin was occurring. What was going on here? How much evidence was needed to remove such an obvious illegal and dangerous nuisance? Surely someone could have put the house to better use?

While a general feeling of disgust at crack and heroin users existed in Lambeth, as suggested by my interviews and other informal conversations 'on the street', there also seemed to be great feelings of apathy about what could be done about crack and heroin in the area. The general impression received about this drugs problem was: just get on with it; what can you do? I talked to neighbours and some of the owners of businesses on my street who all disapprovingly shook their heads at the crack and heroin houses down the street, but did not take any action against them. Perhaps they, like myself, have talked to the people supposedly 'in charge' of these things in the borough and failed to get any results. In a couple of instances, people have taken matters into their own hands and done something about these residences: firebomb them. This final solution, however, can easily lead to much more immediate and serious damage to both property and persons. Also, these people should not *have* to do these things. There *must* be an easier way to tackle the problem of blatant and obvious drugs sales occurring in all housing, particularly that belonging to the public sector. If more direct action is taken against these prop-erties and people who use and sell these drugs, and everyday citizens in Brixton are shown results, then perhaps the apathy regarding such behaviours, the perceived feeling of 'we can't do anything about these crimes, so don't try' will eventually lift, and citizens may begin to feel they actually can make a difference by speaking out about heroin and crack use and sales occurring in their backyard. This process could lead to a great sense of empowerment and autonomy, a sense of control people in these areas have over their environment, a sense such individuals can do something about some problems in their 'manor'.

Again, my proposed solution to better tackling the seeming proliferation of crack and smack houses in Brixton, and Lambeth more generally, is rather simple: listen more closely to those who live around them. Foster (2002) discussed the impor-tance that everyday people can and should have in tackling crime and disorder in high-crime communities. She argues that these 'people pieces' are extremely valu-able, but often neglected in community crime-prevention strategies. My experi-ences in attempting to tackle the problem of crack and heroin houses on my street confirmed this. It might be beneficial to allow the police greater resources in order to enable them to handle such complaints with greater efficiency, rather than simply 'making a note' of the presence of such houses. Furthermore, greater communication between the police and Lambeth's public-sector housing may also further expedite the legal recourse needed to evict those using such property to sell crack and heroin. Home Secretary David Blunkett recently (2004) enacted measures, as laid out in the Anti-Social Behaviour Act, giving police greater power and resources to close 'drug' houses within 48 hours. Perhaps such measures will make a difference.

Conclusions

In this chapter I discussed some of my experiences with crime and delinquency in Lambeth. In doing so, I offered some very general, perhaps relatively obvious, ideas of what might be done to reduce the high rates of acquisitive and some drug-related offences.

From looking at the young people's responses, and of those of some of the professionals, I offered a three-pronged approach towards tackling acquisitive offences in the borough. I suggested we make it easier for young people to get money, either through employment or direct vocational training, and allocate more money to the public sector, in particular youth and community centres and detached youth workers – those closest to the young people 'on the street' – so that these people can bring the youngsters into these training programmes. Concomitantly, better regulation of the hive of second-hand shops throughout the borough, shops where the trading of stolen merchandise seems so common, is important.

The problem of crack and heroin in Lambeth, and of living within the atmosphere these drugs create, was also discussed. I suggested, perhaps simply, that more officers be put on the streets within Brixton's 'red triangle' in attempts to perhaps push the highly visible network of crack or heroin users and sellers somewhere else with a lighter flow of human traffic, and thus reduce the potential danger from interaction or influence from such characters. These drugs have a really strong presence in the central Brixton area, which has reportedly been there for many years. This problem will not go away by itself. Neither, did it seem, will houses in residential areas that blatantly sell crack or heroin. In fact, such houses did not even seem to go away when people in the community rang all the bells and blew all the whistles they believed proper in order to rid themselves of these nuisances. Certainly my experiences suggested this. The police, public-sector housing and those knowledgeable about squatter's rights need greater correspondence to come up with quick, safe and efficient means to evict those who so obviously use any property, particularly valuable public-sector property, to peddle crack and heroin, drugs which appeared to be considered the most dangerous by those in Lambeth.

In this book I attempted to demonstrate that young people who offended in Lambeth did not appear to be mindless thugs who committed random, purposeless offences against anyone or anything. My data countered the stereotype of the young villain completely immersed within a criminal or delinquent culture, cut off from the outside world, or the idea that a sense of lawlessness is associated with young people in the inner city. I hope the evidence presented within has served to offer a clearer idea of the complexities within the moral universes of young people who offend in Lambeth, and how this behaviour appeared to be governed by an unwritten code many of them seemed to have followed. What their normative judgements about their offending suggest is that certain rules are to be adhered to when behaving this way in their neighbourhood. What they also suggest, theoretically, is that to young people 'crime' refers to several different behaviours, which they commit for a variety of different reasons, against many different people, and to different degrees. If this research has questioned the way we think about young people who commit crime in the inner city and, consequently, what we might be able to do in order to steer them away from such behaviour, then my intentions have been realised.

Notes

1 Research in the inner city

1 I have renamed all the people, businesses and organisations in this research.
2 Becker (1970), for instance, discussed approaching individuals whose occupational position possibly placed them in contact with relevant information concerning the subject matter. He (1970: 42) suggested, 'We can learn about the contingencies of deviant lives and organizations by studying the operations of the professionals who come into contact with them … specialists accumulate a great deal of practical experience and lore. They know what kinds of things go on, who is who in the deviant community and where he maybe found, relevant local history, and a host of other things a researcher can use.'
3 Many interpretations and definitions of the terms 'race' and 'ethnicity' exist (see, for example, Gilroy 1993; Goldberg 1993). For purposes here, the terms 'ethnic' and 'ethnicity' are employed as social constructs aiming to distinguish minority populations whose heritage originally stems from that outside of 'white' Europe.
4 Throughout the book citations from the interviews are employed that contain argot and idioms. Some variations emerged in the way respondents spelt some slang words and idiosyncrasies. In those cases the argot is spelt phonetically.
5 Hobbs (1988: 10) said that during his research 'My family, friends, and neighbours were all potential sources of data. There was no social situation I encountered during the three years of this research that did not warrant some inductive analysis.'
6 Slang for somebody.
7 Warren (1988: 19) concluded from her personal research experience that 'role taking in fieldwork is subsumed by a more interactive process in which respondents assign the field worker to what they see as his or her proper place in the social order.' In this sense, my role while employed at the shop held more of a 'co-worker' status as opposed to a researcher status (see also Adler and Adler 1991).
8 *Lambeth Education Statistics* 1997–98.
9 Data on Lambeth's ethnic demography presented in this section are derived from *National Statistics Online, Census 2001, Profiles, Lambeth*. Available online at www.statistics.gov.uk/census2001/profiles/00AY-A/asp. Downloaded 09/05/2003.
10 Data on police statistics in this section are from the Metropolitan Police Service, Performance Information Bureau (PIB) data for Recorded Persons Accused FY 2000–2002.
11 Information on The Movement for Justice was provided by informal conversations with volunteers who work for them. According to one of the volunteers, these quotes are within the manifesto of the Movement for Justice.
12 Cockney rhyming slang is where words are replaced with others that rhyme with them. In this case 'skunk', a type of cannabis, rhymes with 'punk'. For more on the history of British and Cockney rhyming slang see Kray's *Slang* (date not provided).

2 Lambeth

1 Data from the 2001 Census. Available online at www.statistics.gov.uk/census2001/ profiles/00ay.asp. Downloaded 27 March 2003.
2 DETR Index of Deprivation 1998.
3 Census 2001 data.
4 LRC *Focus on London 2000.*
5 LRC *Contrasting London Incomes* (1997).
6 PIB Crime Unit data for Recorded Offences FY 1996–2002.
7 PIB Crime Unit data for Recorded Persons Accused FY 1996–2002.
8 LRC *Focus on London 2000.* 'Economic activity' is measured by the percentage of the household population of working age who were in the labour force.
9 LRC *London at Work* (1999).
10 Census 2001 data.
11 LRC *Focus on London 2000.*
12 LRC *Focus on London 99.*
14 Generally speaking, the prices of food are significantly higher at Tesco and Sainsburys when compared to Lidl and Kwik Save.
15 These were businesses I came across numerous times during the course of the research. Several young people and professionals also mentioned such practices at all three establishments. I have been propositioned for crack and smelled crack in the air outside of the take-away restaurant in Brixton on a couple of occasions. This restaurant is located opposite the shop I worked at.

3 Robbery, burglary, theft

1 PIB Crime Unit data for Recorded Offences FY 1996–2002. Street robberies may contain an element of violence and are often thought of as 'violent offences'. I have included my analysis and discussion of the young people's street robberies alongside that of their burglaries and thefts because of the similarities in the reasons, as expressed by the young people, as to why such acts were carried out. Within this book, I consider 'violent offences' as individual or group fighting and the use of weapons. These violent offences are discussed in Chapter Six.
2 Slang for burglary.
3 Interestingly enough, a couple of individuals quoted in Matthews (2002) said that the television programme *Crimewatch* had given them the idea to commit robberies.
4 Slang for car stereo. 'Sets' may also refer to home stereos.
5 I have paraphrased Travis' account of breaking into this vehicle for brevity. His full account verbatim of this incident is lengthy, and detailing it here in full runs the risk of redundancy.

4 Drug use and drug selling

1 PIB Crime Unit data for Recorded Offences FY 1996–2002.
2 The names 'skunk' and 'bush' were two general classifications of cannabis I came across in the borough. The prices are rough estimates of numbers offered by several of the young people in my sample, as well as others within the borough.
3 PIB Crime Unit data for Recorded Persons Accused FY 1999–2002.
4 This was an internal, private policy that was specific to Lambeth only, which, at the time of writing, was to be extended to other London boroughs (and perhaps the UK more generally).
5 After a reprimand, which, according to CID officers in Brixton and Kennington, takes about 10 minutes, the individual caught with cannabis is allowed to go free. Furthermore, a reprimand stays *only* on Lambeth's police record, whereas a caution remains on an individual's criminal record for three years.

6 I briefly spoke with CID officers at the Brixton and Kennington stations, who said that the general feeling amongst police officers was that they were in favour of the new policy. What other police officers and the public in Lambeth had to say about this cannabis pilot scheme in Lambeth was reported in *The Guardian* (9 February 2002).
7 For more on how cannabis is a theme within hip-hop music see Fernando (1994).
8 PIB Crime Unit data for Recorded Persons Accused FY 2000–2002 for the 10–25 age range.
9 Misuse of Drugs Act 1971.

5 Graffiti, joyriding, vandalism

1 Nathan purposely spelt 'Assassin' this way.
2 Cisco is a mass-produced, relatively inexpensive wine that has a high percentage of alcohol and comes in several 'exotic' flavours. It is similar to other wines such as MD 20/20 and Thunderbird.
3 For more on such youth subcultures see Brake (1985), S. Cohen (1972), Fyvel (1963), Hall and Jefferson (1976), Redhead (1993) and Thornton (1995).

6 Violence

1 PIB Crime Unit data FY 1996–2002 rates for 'violence against the person', which refers to crimes such as murder, grievous bodily harm (GBH), actual bodily harm (ABH), assault, harassment and 'other' violence.
2 Kenny's account is paraphrased by me for brevity; his version runs long.
3 To 'screw' someone means to look at them in a menacing way. This word comes from the Jamaican vernacular, where to have a 'screw face' means to squint your eyes and have a scowling, foreboding expression.
4 Goffman (1967: 5) described 'face' as 'the positive social value a person effectively claims for himself by the line others assume he has taken during a particular contact'.
5 Spergel (1995) also noted how some gang research has shown that gang members fought more in late adolescence and early adulthood.
6 PIB Crime Unit data show that for the FY 1999–2002, in Lambeth there were more recorded offences involving a firearm than any other borough. Roughly 10 percent of all London's firearms offences occurred in Lambeth.
7 Officers showed me a picture of about fifteen firearms of various makes and models that were collected during Lambeth's 'Gun Amnesty', all of which appeared to be older makes and models, many of which looked to be in poor shape. In this sense, this 'word on the street' seems somewhat credible.
8 Both the Twenty-Eight Posse and the Untouchables, apparently, spawned younger generations of these groups named, respectively, the 'Younger Twenty-Eights' and the 'Younger Untouchables'. However, information on these groups was vague and sometimes conflicting. Nonetheless, nearly all of the interviews suggested that by 1994/95 these groups ceased to exist.

7 Style, group behaviour, interactions with the police

1 I am not suggesting that those wearing designer clothing and living on estates are committing offences in order to get the money to pay for such clothing. Maybe they set aside a large chunk of their wages/dole cheque for designer clothing. However, it is more probable that Heidi, Theresa and others in similar economic situations who highly valued sportswear and other designer clothing knew someone who was selling the designer clothing at lower prices that would be expected at a shop on the high street. As discussed in Chapter Two, observations and interviews suggest that trading in stolen designer clothing was not uncommon in Lambeth.

2 The descriptions of the music discussed in this section are my own, and are based on a personal interest and a history of listening to these types of music.
3 Themes of deadly violence, violence against women, misogynist attitudes, profanity and alcohol abuse – those which spurned this 'moral panic' – are not exclusive to 'hard-core' hip-hop. Rather, these themes can be found in country, blues and bluegrass, even though such music is considered, at least in the general perception, more 'wholesome' (see Tunnell 1995).
4 Although it is not always a requisite for a group to be a gang, some gang researchers in the US have argued that territorial violence is a central characteristic of gangs (see Sanders 1994).
5 For instance, Spencer and Hough (2000: v) concluded that '1) Public confidence in the police in Lambeth was significantly below the average of the Metropolitan Police in the late 1990s; 2) This largely reflects the poor image of the police given by black people.'
6 Newitz (1997) noticed a similar point in her analysis of the television show *Cops*, which shows footage of police officers on patrol and arresting people in various US cities. Newitz (1997: 138) pointed out how in one show 'a white biker is beaten and thrown to the ground by white police who suspect that the biker is dealing drugs. He turns out to be carrying only a small packet of speed, but the police continue to believe that he must be part of a "ring." We assume they believe this because he is a white biker, and fits the Hell's Angels stereotype of low-class white males who wear leather and ride Harley's. This kind of logic – informed by racial and class prejudice – drives police officers in other shows to behave violently with inner city blacks wearing high-priced sporting gear.'

8 The moral universes of young people who have offended

1 See N.W.A.'s *Dopeman* and Notorious B.I.G.'s *The 10 Crack Commandments*. These songs discuss both using and selling crack, and one point they say 'Don't get high on your own supply'.
2 This is Goffman's (1963: 41) meaning of the word. Goffman defined 'wise' as applying to 'persons who are normal but whose special situation has made them intimately privy to the secret life of the stigmatised individual and sympathetic with it, and who find themselves accorded a measure of acceptance, a measure of courtesy membership in the clan. Wise persons are the marginal men before whom the individual with a fault need feel no shame nor exert self control, knowing that in spite of his failing he will be seen as an ordinary other.' Goffman (1963: 42) continues by differentiating between types of persons who are 'wise'. 'One type of wise person is he whose wiseness comes from working in an establishment which caters either to the wants of those with a particular stigma or to actions that society takes in regard to these persons.' Later Goffman (1963: 43) continued, 'A second type of wise person is the individual who is related through the social structure to a stigmatised individual – a relationship that leads the wider society to treat both individuals in some respects as one' (see also Armstrong 1993; Becker 1970).

Appendix

Interview schedules

These questions were asked in this order and generally phrased as they appear here. At times, the respondents answered or brought up questions earlier than anticipated.

Questions asked to the professionals

- What do you do and how long have you been doing it? (general discussion)
- What do you know about groups of young people who have a history of offending (or individual offenders that commit crime within the context of a group)?
- How long have you known them?
- How did you get to meet them?
- Where do they live?
- How old are they? How many?
- What is their racial origin? (Is the group mixed or is it all one race?)
- Do you know about their school performance? If so, how well they did, if they're still enrolled, and potential further education: GNVQs, GCSEs? Above?
- Do you know if they have jobs? If so what? Are they contributing to the household?
- Do you know if they want to have career-type jobs? If so what? If not, do you know how they feel about future employment prospects? What do they want or see themselves doing when they get older?
- What type of family histories do the members have? Who raised them? How were they earning income? What types of housing do they live in? Condition? Persons per household?
- What are they wearing? How would you describe their overall appearance/presentation?
- Do you know what types of music they listen to? Why do they like that?
- Do you know if they use drugs? (Prompt: smoke cannabis? any others?)
- What's an average day like for this group?
- How cohesive is this group? How long have they known each other?
- Why do you think that they hang out in a group/together?
- Do they have a group name? Do they have individual tags or street names? What are they?

- Are there any leaders in the group? If so, why are they the leaders? Any specific roles? (Prompt: Are some of their friends particularly good at certain things within their group?)
- Do any of the groups claim or protect a certain territory or area? If so, what and why?
- What types of crimes are they committing? Have all of the young people that hang out in this group committed offences? If so, which members and what types?
- Have they been arrested? If so, for what? Alone or with others? Where?
- (If they have burgled or robbed, then what was stolen and how are the goods dispersed? How much do they get for the goods?)
- Why are they committing those types of crimes? (Prompt: Is it out of necessity? If not, then what is your opinion on the matter?)
- Do you know how they feel about committing those crimes? (Prompt: do they seem to care and/or feel any remorse about committing the crimes?)
- Do any of them carry weapons? If so, what?
- Have you heard of the TEP/UT/YB/ PYB/PRG/GB/JCT.BS/FK? (These are abbreviations for names of other groups of young people.) What can you tell me about them? – Re-ask same questions regarding the groups.

Final section

- What does the term 'street wise' mean to you?
- How would you define the term 'gang'?
- Do you think that any of the groups we talked about are gangs? Which ones? Why?
- What do you know about adult organised crime in Lambeth? Does it exist?
- What can you tell me about legitimate businesses that might also conduct illegal business: for instance, off-licences or newsagents selling drugs, garages that are also chop shops, electronics stores that buy and sell stolen merchandise?
- Is there anything you want to ask me?

Questions asked to young people

Personal

- How old are you?
- How many years have you lived in Lambeth? Where?
- How would you describe your ethnic origin?

School

- Have you completed school?
- If no, why not?
- If you dropped out, why?

- If you were kicked out, what was it for?
- How did you feel afterwards? (Prompt: good, bad, didn't care.)
- Have you earned any GCSEs or GNVQs or A-levels or any other additional education? If so, what?
- If not, then why not?
- What are you going to do afterwards?

Employment

- Do you have a job? If so, what?
- If not, how do you earn money?
- Have you ever had a job? If so, what?
- Do your friends have jobs? If so, what are they doing?
- If not, how do they earn money?
- Can you see yourself having a career-type job? If so, what?
- If not, why not?
- Do you think you'll get that job?

Family

- Who were you raised by?
- Do they have a job? If so, what?
- If not, how do they earn money?
- Do you have any brothers and sisters? If so, how many?
- Do you contribute to your family's expenses? (Prompt: do you buy food or clothes for other members in your family or do you help pay bills or any other way in which you financially help those who live in the same house as you?)
- What type of place do you live in (flat, house, estate)?

Culture / style

- What type of music do you listen to?
- What do you like about the music?
- What does the term 'street wise' mean to you?
- Do you smoke gear?
- Have you used any other drugs? If so, what?

About the group

- Do you usually hang out with a group of guys? How many?
- What's the age range?
- How tight are you guys? How long have you known them?
- Why do you hang out with these guys?

- How much of your time would you say that you spend with them?
- What do you guys do on a typical day? How many do you typically hang out with?
- Why do you hang out together in a group? (Prompt: how did this group form? attraction.)
- How do you decide if someone is part of your group?
- What do you feel distinguishes your group of friends from other groups of youths? (Prompt: do you feel that there are things that are specific to your group only?)
- Does your group have a name?
- Are there any leaders in your group? Who? Why?
- Do the guys in your group have street names or tags?
- Is there any territory or area that you guys protect or consider your turf? If so, what area is it and why do you feel that way?
- Do you or anyone in your group ever carry any weapons? If so, what kinds?

Police encounters / crime

- Have you ever been stopped by the police? If so, how many times?
- What have they stopped you for?
- Have you ever been arrested? If so, for what?
- How did you feel after being arrested? (Prompt: good, bad, didn't care.)
- Were you arrested alone or with others for the same act?
- How well did you know the others you were arrested with?
- Are they members of your group?
- Why did you commit the act?
- If you burgled or robbed, what did you steal?
- What happened to the goods? If sold, how much money did you get?
- How did you feel about it afterwards? (Prompt: good, bad, didn't care.)
- How did you learn to commit the act?
- What other illegal acts have you committed that you haven't been caught for?
- Do you ever get into fights? If so, why?
- How did you feel about it afterwards? (Prompt: good, bad, didn't care.)
- Have all the people that you hang around/used to hang around with committed crime?

Other groups

- Have you heard of the TEP/UT/YB/ PYB/PRG/GB/JCT.BS/FK? (These are abbreviations for names of groups of young people in the borough that I came across.)
- Do you know members from them? If so, how well?
- How old were you when you first heard of them?
- Where were you living at the time?

- Do you know how they got that name?
- Do you know how many members there were?
- What distinguished the group of guys from another?
- Could you explain how this group of guys became known as the group?
- Were there any hangouts that they had?
- Did they have any leaders? Who? Why? How much control? (Prompt: did everyone always do as they asked? What would happen if someone didn't like their choices?) Any roles?
- How did the guys from the group spend most of their time? (Prompt: what was an average day?)
- Was there any territory or areas or estates that the group protected or considered their turf?
- Did they have any rivals or arch-enemies? If so, how did this rivalry emerge?
- What happened to the guys in the group? (Prompt: how come they don't exist any more?)
- Do/did they carry any weapons?

Final section

- What do you know about organised crime in the area? Does it exist? Do you know anyone involved?
- Do you know any adults who have committed any offences?
- What do you know about legitimate business as fronts for illegal activity? (Prompt: off-licences selling drugs, garages as chop shops, electronics stores buying and selling stolen property.)
- How would you define the term 'gang'?
- Do you think that the members of the group were a gang? Why/not?
- Is there anything you want to ask me?

References

Ackroyd, S. and Hughes, J.A. (1992) *Data Collection in Context*. London, Longman.

Adler, P.A. and Adler, P. (1991) *Membership Roles in Field Research*. London, Sage.

Agnew, R. (1992) 'Foundation for a general theory of crime', *Criminology* 30(1) February: 47–88.

Aldridge, J., Parker, H. and Measham, F. (1999) *Drug Trying and Drug Use Across Adolescence*. Drugs Prevention Advisory Service, paper 1, London, Home Office.

Alexander, C. (1996) *The Art of Being Black: The Creation of Black British Youth Identities*. Oxford, Clarendon Press.

Anderson, E. (1990) *Streetwise: Race, Class, and Change in an Urban Community*. Chicago IL, Chicago University Press.

—— (1999) *Code of the Streets: Decency, Violence, and the Moral Life of the Inner City*. New York NY, W.W. Norton and Co.

Anderson, H. (1997) *Contrasting London Incomes*. London, London Research Centre.

Arksey, H. and Knight, P. (1999) *Interviewing for Social Scientists: An Introductory Resource with Examples*. London, Sage.

Armstrong, G. (1993) 'Like that Desmond Morris?', in D. Hobbs and T. May (eds), *Interpreting the Field: Accounts of Ethnography*, Oxford, Clarendon Press, p. 3.

—— (1998) *Football Hooligans: Knowing the Score*. Oxford, Berg.

Audit Commission (1996) *Misspent Youth: Young People and Crime*. London, Audit Commission.

Back, L. (1996) *New Ethnicities and Urban Culture: Racism and Multiculturalism in Young Lives*. London, University College London Press.

Barker, M. and Bridgeman, C. (1994) *Preventing Vandalism: What Works?* Police Research Group, Crime Detection and Prevention Series, paper 56, London, Home Office.

Becker, H. (1963) *Outsiders: Studies in the Sociology of Deviance*. London, Macmillan.

—— (1970) 'Practitioner of vice and crime', in R.W. Habenstein (ed.), *Pathways to Data*, Chicago IL, Aldine, p. 30.

Benyon, J. and Solomos, J. (eds) (1987) *The Roots of Urban Unrest*. Oxford, Pergamon.

Berger, P. and Luckman, T. (1967) *The Social Construction of Reality: A Treatise in the Sociology of Knowledge*. New York NY, Anchor.

Bourgois, P. (1995) *In Search of Respect: Selling Crack in El Barrio*. Cambridge, Cambridge University Press.

Braithwaite, J. and Daly, K. (1994) 'Masculinities, violence and communitarian control', in T. Newburn and E. Stanko (eds), *Just Boys doing Business?*, New York, Routledge, p. 189.

Brake, M. (1985) *Comparative Youth Culture: The Sociology of Youth Cultures and Youth Subcultures in America, Britain and Canada*. London, Routledge.

Britton, N.J. (2000) 'Race and policing: a study of police custody', *British Journal of Criminology* 40: 639–58.

Broidy, L. (2001) 'A test of general strain theory', *Criminology* 39(1) February: 9–36.

Burney, E. (1990) *Putting Street Crime in its Place*. A report to the Community/Police Consultative Group for Lambeth, London, Goldsmiths College.

Campbell, A. (1991) *The Girls in the Gang*. Oxford, Blackwell.

Campbell, B. (1993) *Goliath: Britain's Dangerous Places*. London, Methuen.

Cashmore, E.E. (1984) *No Future: Youth and Society*. London, Heinemann.

Chamberlain, M. (1989) *Growing Up in Lambeth*. London, Virago.

Clarke, J. (1976) 'Style', in S. Hall and T. Jefferson (eds), *Resistance Through Rituals*, London, Hutchinson, p. 175.

Cloward, R. and Ohlin, L. (1960) *Delinquency and Opportunity: A Theory of Delinquent Gangs*. London, Collier-Macmillan.

Coffield, F. (1991) *Vandalism and Graffiti: The State of the Art*. London, Calouste Gulbenkian Foundation.

Cohen, A. (1955) *Delinquent Boys: The Culture of the Gang*. New York NY, Free Press.

—— and Short, J. (1958) 'Research in delinquent subcultures', *The Journal of Social Issues* 14: 20–37.

Cohen, P. (1972) 'Sub-cultural conflict and working class culture', *Working Papers in Cultural Studies* 2, Birmingham, University of Birmingham, pp. 5–51.

Cohen, S. (1972) *Folk Devils and Moral Panics: The Creation of the Mods and Rockers*. London, MacGibbon and Kee.

—— (1973) 'Property destruction: motives and meanings', in C. Ward (ed.), *Vandalism*, London, Architectural Press, p. 23.

Coleman, J.S. (1988) 'Social capital in the creation of human capital', *American Journal of Sociology* 94: S95–S120.

—— and Fararo, T.J. (eds) (1992) *Rational Choice Theory: Advocacy and Critique*. London, Sage.

Collins, R. (1982) *Sociological Insight: An Introduction to Non-obvious Sociology*. Oxford, Oxford University Press.

Connell, R.W. (1987) *Gender and Power: Society, the Person, and Sexual Politics*. Stanford CA, Stanford University Press.

Cooley, C.H. (1964) *Human Nature and Social Order*. New York NY, Schocken Books.

Cornish, R. and Clarke, R. (1987) 'Understanding crime displacement: the applicability of Rational Choice Theory', *Criminology* 25(4) November: 933–48.

Corrigan, P. (1979) *Schooling the Smash Street Kids*. London, Macmillan Press.

Cromwell, P.F., Olson, J.N. and Avary, D.W. (1991) *Breaking and Entering: An Ethnographic Analysis of Burglary*. London, Sage.

——, —— and —— (1996) 'Who buys stolen property?: a new look at criminal receiving', in P. Cromwell (ed.), *In Their Own Words: Criminals on Crime: An Anthology*. Los Angeles CA, Roxbury, p. 47.

Davidson, J. (1997) *Gangsta*. London, Vision.

Davies, N. (1997) *Dark Heart: The Shocking Truth about Hidden Britain*. London, Chatto and Windus.

Decker, S. and Van Winkle, B. (1996) *Life in the Gang: Family, Friends and Violence*. Cambridge, Cambridge University Press.

Denzin, N.K. (1970) *The Research Act in Sociology*. London, Butterworth.

Downes, D. (1966) *The Delinquent Solution: A Study of Subcultural Theory*. London, Routledge and Kegan Paul.

—— (1998) 'Back to the future: the predictive value of social theories of delinquency', in P. Rock and S. Holdaway (eds), *Thinking about Criminology*, London, University College London Press, p. 99.

—— and Rock, P. (1988) *Understanding Deviance: A Guide to the Sociology of Crime and Rule Breaking*. Oxford, Clarendon Press.

Dunaway, G.R., Cullen, F.T., Burton Jr, V.S. and Evans, T.D. (2000) 'The myth of social class and crime revisited: an examination of class and adult criminality', *Criminology* 28(2) May: 589–632.

Fagan, J. (1996) 'Gangs, drugs, and neighborhood change', in C.R. Huff (ed.), *Gangs in America*, Thousand Oaks CA, Sage Publications, p. 39.

Fernando Jr, S.H. (1994) *The New Beats*. New York NY, Payback Press.

Ferrell, J. (1993) *Crimes of Style: Urban Graffiti and the Politics of Criminality*. Boston MA, Northeastern University Press.

—— (1995) 'Style matters: criminal identity and social control', in J. Ferrell and C. Sanders (eds), *Cultural Criminology*, Boston MA, Northeastern University Press, p. 169.

—— and Sanders C. (1995) 'Culture, crime, and criminology', in J. Ferrell and C. Sanders (eds), *Cultural Criminology*, Boston MA, Northeastern University Press, p. 3.

Finestone, H. (1957) 'Cats, kicks and color', *Social Problems* 5: 3–13.

Fitzgerald, M. (1998) 'Race and the criminal justice system', in T. Blackstone, B. Parekh and P. Sanders (eds), *Race Relations in Britain*, London, Routledge, p. 158.

Flood-Page, C., Campbell, S., Harrington, V. and Miller, J. (2000) *Youth Crime: Findings from the 1998/99 Youth Lifestyles Survey*. Home Office Research Study 209, London, Home Office.

Foster, J. (1990) *Villains: Crime and Community in the Inner City*. London, Routledge.

—— (2002) '"People pieces": the neglected but essential elements of community crime prevention', in G. Hughes and A. Edwards (eds), *Crime Control and Community: The New Politics of Public Safety*, Cullompton, Devon, Willan Publications, p. 167.

Fraser, S. (ed.) (1995) *The Bell Curve Wars: Race, Intelligence and the Future of America*. New York NY, Basic Books.

Fyvel, T.R. (1963) *The Insecure Offenders*. Harmondsworth, Penguin.

Geason, S. and Wilson, P.R. (1990) *Preventing Graffiti and Vandalism*. Canberra, Australian Institute of Criminology.

Geis, G. (2002) 'On cross-disciplinary qualitative research: some homilies', *The Criminologist* 27(3) May/June: 1–5.

Gibbons, D. (1971) 'Observations on the study of crime causation', *American Journal of Sociology* 77: 262–78.

Gilroy, P. (1987) *Ain't no Black in the Union Jack: The Cultural Politics of Race and Nation*. London, Hutchinson.

—— (1993) *The Black Atlantic: Modernity and Double Consciousness*. London, Verso.

Glass, R. (1960) *Newcomers: The West Indians in London*. London, George Allen and Unwin.

Glassner, B. and Loughlin, J. (1990) *Drugs in Adolescent Worlds: Burnouts to Straights*. London, Macmillan.

Goffman, E. (1959) *Presentation of Self in Everyday Life*. Harmondsworth, Penguin.

—— (1963) *Stigma: Notes on the Management of Spoiled Identity*. Englewood Cliffs NJ, Prentice-Hall.

—— (1967) *Interaction Ritual: Essays on Face-to-face Behaviour*. Garden City NY, Doubleday.

Goldberg, D.T. (1993) *Racist Culture: Philosophy and the Politics of Meaning*. Oxford, Blackwell.

Gottfredson, M. and Hirschi, T. (1990) *A General Theory of Crime*. Stanford CA, Stanford University Press.

Graef, R. (1993) *Living Dangerously: Young Offenders in their Own Words*. London, Harper Collins.

Graham, J. and Bowling, B. (1995) *Young People and Crime*. Home Office Research Study 145, London, Home Office.

Groves, B.W. and Lynch, M.J. (1990) 'Reconciling structural and subjective approaches to the study of crime', *Journal of Research in Crime and Delinquency* 27: 348–75.

Hagan, J. (1994) *Crime and Disrepute*. Thousand Oaks CA, Pine Forge Press.

—— and McCarthy, B. (1992) 'Mean streets: the theoretical significance of situational delinquency among homeless youths', *American Journal of Sociology* 98: 597–627.

Hagedorn, J. (1988) *People and Folks: Gangs, Crime and the Underclass in a Rust-belt City*. Chicago, Lake View Press.

Hagell, A. and Newburn, T. (1994) *Persistent Young Offenders*. London, Policy Studies Institute.

Hakim, C. (1987) *Research Design: Strategies and Choices in the Design of Social Research*. London, Allen and Unwin.

Hall, S. and Jefferson, T. (eds) (1976) *Resistance Through Rituals: Subcultures in Post-war Britain*. London, Hutchinson.

——, Critcher, C., Jefferson, T., Clarke, J. and Roberts, B. (1978) *Policing the Crisis: Mugging, the State, and Law and Order*. London, Macmillan.

Hannertz, U. (1969) *Soulside: Inquiries into Ghetto Culture and Community*. New York NY, Columbia University Press.

Harris, C. and James, W. (1993) 'Introduction', in W. James and C. Harris (eds), *Inside Babylon: Caribbean Diaspora in Britain*, London, Verso.

Hebdige, D. (1979) *Subculture: The Meaning of Style*. London, Methuen.

Henry, S. and Milovanovic, D. (1994) 'The constitution of Constitutive Criminology: a postmodern approach to criminological theory', in D. Nelken (ed.), *The Futures of Criminology*, London, Sage, p. 110.

Herrnstein, R.J. and Murray, C. (1994) *The Bell Curve: Intelligence and Class Structure in American Life*. New York NY: Free Press.

Hirschi, T. (1969) *Causes of Delinquency*. London, University of California Press.

Hobbs, D. (1988) *Doing the Business: Entrepreneurship, the Working-class and Detectives in the East End of London*. Oxford, Oxford University Press.

—— (1993) 'Peers, careers, and academic fears: writing as field work', in D. Hobbs and T. May (eds), *Interpreting the Field: Accounts of Ethnography*, Oxford, Clarendon Press, p. 45.

Huff, C.R. (1989) 'Youth gangs and public policy', *Crime and Delinquency* 35: 524–39.

Jacobs, B.A. (1999) 'Crack to heroin?: drug markets and transition', *British Journal of Criminology* 39: 555–74.

—— and Wright, R. (1999) 'Stick-up, street culture, and offender motivation', *Criminology* 37(1) February: 149–73.

Jefferson, T. (1993) 'The racism of criminalisation: police and the reproduction of the criminal other', in L. Gelsthorpe (ed.), *Minority Ethnic Groups in the Criminal Justice System*, Cropwood conference series, No. 21, Cambridge, University of Cambridge Institute of Criminology, p. 26.

Jones, C. (1993) *A London Atlas*. London, London Research Centre.

Jones, S. (1998) *Criminology*. London, Butterworths.

Katz, J. (1988) *Seductions of Crime: Moral and Sensual Attractions in Doing Evil*. New York NY, Basic Books.

Keiser, L. (1969) *The Vice Lords: Warriors of the Street*. New York NY, Holt, Rinehart, and Winston.

Keith, M. (1993) *Race, Riots and Policing: Lore and Disorder in a Multi-racist Society*. London, University College London Press.

Kennedy, L.W. and Forde, D.R. (1999) *When Push Comes to Shove: A Routine Conflict Approach to Violence*. New York NY, State University of New York Press.

Kershaw, C., Budd, T., Kinshott, G., Mattinson, J., Mayhew, P. and Myhill, A. (2000) *The 2000 British Crime Survey*. Home Office Statistical Bulletin 18/00, London, Home Office.

Kirk, B. (1996) *Negative Images: A Simple Matter of Black and White?* Aldershot, Avebury.

Klein, M. (1971) *Street Gangs and Street Workers*. Englewood Cliffs NJ, Prentice-Hall.

—— (1995) *The American Street Gang: Its Nature, Prevalence and Control*. New York NY, Oxford University Press.

Kray, R. (n.d.) *Slang*. Birmingham, Wheel and Deal Publications.

Lee, R. (1993) *Doing Research on Sensitive Topics*. London, Sage.

Liebow, E. (1967) *Tally's Corner*. Boston MA, Little, Brown.

Linder, R. (1996) *The Reportage of Urban Culture*, translated by Adrian Morris. Cambridge, Cambridge University Press.

Lofland, J. and Lofland, L.H. (1984) *Analyzing Social Settings*. Belmont CA, Wadsworth.

MacDonald, N. (2001) *The Graffiti Subculture: Youth, Masculinity and Identity in London and New York*. New York NY, Palgrave.

Macpherson, W. (1999) *The Lawrence Inquiry: Report of an Inquiry by Sir William Macpherson of Clung*. London, The Stationery Office.

Maguire, M. (2000) 'Researching "street criminals": a neglected art', in R. King and E. Wincap (eds), *Doing Research on Crime and Justice*, Oxford, Oxford University Press, p. 121.

Marlow, A. (1999) 'Youth, minorities, drugs and policing: a study of stop and search', in A. Marlow and G. Pearson (eds), *Young People, Drugs and Community Safety*, Dorset, Russell House Publishing, p. 81.

Matheson, J. and Edwards, G. (eds) (2000) *Focus on London 2000*. London, London Research Centre.

—— and Holding, A. (eds) (1999) *Focus on London 99*. London, London Research Centre.

Matthews, R. (2002) *Armed Robbery*. York, Willan Publishing.

—— and Pitts, J. (2001) *Crime, Disorder and Community Safety*. London, Routledge.

Matza, D. (1964) *Delinquency and Drift*. London, John Wiley & Sons.

—— and Sykes, G. (1961) 'Juvenile delinquency and subterranean values', *American Sociological Review* 26: 712–19.

Maxwell, J.A. (1996) *Qualitative Research Design: An Interactive Approach*. Thousands Oaks CA, Sage.

Mays, J.B. (1954) *Growing Up in the City: A Study of Juvenile Delinquency in an Urban Neighbourhood*. Liverpool, Liverpool University Press.

McGahey, R. (1986) 'Economic conditions, neighborhood organization, and urban crime', in A.J. Reiss Jr and M. Tonry (eds), *Communities and Crime*, Chicago, University of Chicago Press, p. 231.

Melly, G. (1970) *Revolt into Style: The Pop Arts in Britain*. London, Allen Lane.

Merton, R.K. (1938) 'Social structure and anomie', *American Sociological Review* 3: 672–82.

—— (1957) *Social Theory and Social Structure*. London, Glencoe Free Press.

—— (1972) 'Insiders and outsiders: a chapter in the sociology of knowledge', *American Journal of Sociology* 78: 9–47.

Messerschmidt, J.W. (1993) *Masculinities and Crime: Critique and Reconceptualization of Theory*, Lanham MD, Rowman and Littlefield.

—— (2000) *Nine Lives: Adolescent Masculinities, the Body, and Violence*. Oxford, Westview.

Miller, W.B. (1958) 'Lower class culture as generating a milieu of gang delinquency', *Journal of Social Issues* 14: 5–19.

—— (1969) 'White gangs', *Trans-action* 6: 11–26.

Mirrlees-Black, C., Mayhew, P. and Percy, A. (1996) *The 1996 British Crime Survey*. Home Office Statistical Bulletin 19/96, London, Home Office.

——, Budd, T., Partridge, S. and Mayhew, P. (1998) *The 1998 British Crime Survey*. Home Office Statistical Bulletin 21/98, London, Home Office.

Moore, J. (1991) *Going Down to the Barrio: Homeboys and Homegirls in Change*. Philadelphia PA, Temple University Press.

Muncie, J. (1984) *The Trouble with Kids Today: Youth and Crime in Post-war Britain*. London, Hutchinson.

NACRO (1989) *Vandalism*. London, National Association for the Care and Resettlement of Offenders briefing.

Nelken, D. (1994) 'Reflexive criminology?', in D. Nelken (ed.), *The Futures of Criminology*, London, Sage, p. 7.

Newburn, T. (1998) 'Young offenders, drugs and prevention', *Drugs: Education, Prevention and Policy* 5: 233–43.

—— and Stanko, E. (1994) 'Introduction', in T. Newburn and E. Stanko (eds), *Just Boys Doing Business?* New York NY, Routledge.

Newitz, A. (1997) 'White savagery and humiliation, or a new racial consciousness in the media', in M. Wray and A. Newitz (eds), *White Trash: Race and Class in America*, New York NY, Routledge, p. 131.

O'Malley, P. and Mugford, S. (1994) 'Crime, excitement, and modernity', in G. Barak (ed.), *Varieties of Criminology: Readings from a Dynamic Discipline*. London, Praeger, p. 189.

Padilla, F. (1992) *The Gang as an American Enterprise*. New Brunswick NJ, Rutgers University Press.

Park, R. (1950) *The Collected Papers of Robert Ezra Park: Race and Culture, Volume One*, edited by E. Hughes, C. Johnson, J. Masuoka, R. Redfield and L. Wirth. Glencoe IL, Free Press.

Parker, H. (1974) *A View from the Boys*. London, David and Charles.

——, Bakx, K. and Newcombe, R. (1988) *Living with Heroin: The Impact of a Drugs Epidemic on an English Community*. Milton Keynes, Open University Press.

——, Measham, F. and Aldridge, J. (1995) *Drugs Futures: Changing Patterns of Drug Use amongst English Youth*. London, Institute for the Study of Drug Dependence.

——, Aldridge, J. and Measham, F. (1998) *Illegal Leisure: The Normalisation of Adolescent Recreational Drug Use*. London, Routledge.

Patrick, J. (1973) *A Glasgow Gang Observed*. London, Eyre Methuen.

Patterson, S. (1965) *Dark Strangers: A Sociological Study of the Absorption of a Recent West Indian Immigrant Group in Brixton, South London*. Harmondsworth, Penguin.

Pearson, G. (1983) *Hooligan: A History of Respectable Fears*. London, Macmillan.

Phillips, S.A. (1999) *Wallbangin': Graffiti and Gangs in LA*. Chicago IL, University of Chicago Press.

Pitts, J. (1999) *Working with Young Offenders*. London, Macmillan.

Polsky, N. (1969) *Hustlers, Beats and Others*. New York, Doubleday.

Presdee, M. (1994) 'Young people, culture and the construction of crime', in G. Barak (ed.), *Varieties of Criminology: Readings from a Dynamic Discipline*, London, Praeger, p. 179.

—— (2000) *Cultural Criminology and the Carnival of Crime*. London, Routledge.

Pryce, K. (1979) *Endless Pressure: A Study of West Indian Lifestyles in Bristol*. Harmondsworth, Penguin.

Ray, O. and Ksir, C. (1999) *Drugs, Society and Human Behavior*. Boston MA, McGraw-Hill.

Redhead, S. (ed.) (1993) *Rave Off: Politics and Deviance in Contemporary Youth Culture*. Aldershot, Avebury.

Reiss, A.J. (1986) 'Why are communities important in understanding crime?', in A.J. Reiss and M. Tonry (eds), *Communities and Crime*, Chicago, Chicago University Press, p. 1.

Reynolds, S. (1997) *Wargasm: Military Images in Pop*. Available online at http://members.aol.com/blissart/militpop.htm (downloaded November 1997).

Robins, D. (1992) *Tarnished Vision: Crime and Conflict in the Inner City*. Oxford, Oxford University Press.

Rojek, C. (2000) *Leisure and Culture*. London, Macmillan.

Rubin, H.J. and Rubin, I.S. (1995) *Qualitative Interviewing: The Art of Hearing Data*. London, Sage.

Ruggiero, V. and South, N. (1995) *Eurodrugs: Drug Use, Markets, and Trafficking in Europe*. London, University College London Press.

Runnymede Trust (1996) *This is Where I Live: Stories and Pressures in Brixton*. London, The Runnymede Trust.

Russell, K.K. (2001) 'Racing crime: definitions and dilemmas', in S. Henry and M.M. Lanier (eds), *What is Crime?: Controversies over the Nature of Crime and What to Do About It*. Oxford, Rowman and Littlefield, p. 155.

Sampson, R. and Groves, W.B. (1989) 'Community structure and crime: testing social disorganization theory', *American Journal of Sociology* 94: 774–802.

—— and Laub, J. (1992) 'Crime and deviance in the life course', *Annual Review of Sociology* 18: 63–84.

—— and Wilson, W.J. (1995) 'Toward a theory of race, crime, and urban inequality', in J. Hagan and R. Peterson (eds), *Crime and Inequality*, Stanford CA, Stanford University Press, p. 37.

Sanders, W.B. (1981) *Juvenile Delinquency: Causes, Patterns, and Reactions*. New York NY, Holt, Rinehart and Winston.

—— (1994) *Gangbangs and Drive-bys: Grounded Culture and Juvenile Gang Violence*. New York NY, Aldine De Gruyter.

Scarman, Lord (1981) *The Scarman Report: The Brixton Disorders 10–12 April 1981: Report of an Inquiry by Lord Scarman*. Harmondsworth, Penguin.

Schell, T.J. (1992) 'Rationality and emotion: homage to Norbert Elias', in J.S. Coleman and T.J. Fararo (eds), *Rational Choice Theory: Advocacy and Critique*, London, Sage, p. 101.

Schneider, E. (1999) *Vampires, Dragons and Egyptian Kings*. Princeton NJ, Princeton University Press.

Schrag, C. (1962) 'Delinquency and opportunity: analysis of a theory', *Sociology and Social Research* 46(2) January: 167–75.

Schuman, H. and Converse, J. (1971) 'The effects of Black and White interviewers on Black responses in 1968', *Public Opinion Quarterly* 35: 44–68.

Scott, P. (1956) 'Gangs and delinquent groups in London', *The British Journal of Delinquency* 7: 4–26.

Shaffir, W.B. (1991) 'Managing a convincing self-presentation: some personal reflections on entering the field', in W.B. Shaffir and R. Stebbing (eds), *Experiencing Fieldwork*, London, Sage, p. 72.

Shaw, C. and McKay, H. (1942) *Juvenile Delinquency and Urban Areas*. Chicago IL, University of Chicago Press.

Shiner, M. and Newburn, T. (1997) 'Definitely, maybe not? The normalisation of recreational drug use amongst young people', *Sociology* 31(3): 511–29.

—— and —— (1999) 'Taking tea with Noel: the place and meaning of drug use in everyday life', in N. South (ed.), *Drugs: Culture, Controls and Everyday Life*, London, Sage.

Shover, N. (1996) *Great Pretenders: Pursuits and Careers of Persistent Thieves*. Boulder CO, Westview Press.

Silverman, D. (1985) *Qualitative Methodology and Sociology: Describing the Social World*. Aldershot, Gower.

Simmons, J. and colleagues (2002) *Crime in England and Wales 2001/2002*. Home Office Statistical Bulletin No. 07/02, London, Home Office.

Solomos, J. (1988) *Black Youth, Racism and the State: The Politics of Ideology and Policy*. Cambridge, Cambridge University Press.

South, N. (1999) 'Debating drugs and everyday life: normalisation, prohibition and "otherness"', in N. South (ed.), *Drugs: Cultures, Controls and Everyday Life*, London, Sage, pp. 1–15.

—— and Teeman, D. (1999) 'Young people, drugs and community life', in A. Marlow and G. Pearson (eds), *Young People, Drugs and Community Safety*, Dorset, Russell House Publishing, p. 69.

Sparks, R. (1992) *Television and the Drama of Crime: Moral Tales and the Place of Crime in Public Life*. Birmingham, Open University Press.

Spencer, B.A. and Hough, M. (2000) *Policing Diversity: Lessons From Lambeth*. Police Research Series Paper 121, London, Policing and Reducing Crime Unit.

Spergel, I. (1964) *Racketville, Slumtown, Haulberg*. Chicago IL, University of Chicago Press.

—— (1995) *The Youth Gang Problem: A Community Approach*. Oxford, Oxford University Press.

Stanko, E.A. (1994) 'Challenging the problem of men's individual violence', in T. Newburn and E. Stanko (eds), *Just Boys Doing Business?* New York NY, Routledge, p. 32.

Stanley, C. (1997) 'Not drowning but waving: urban narratives of dissent in the wild zone', in S. Redhead, D. Wynne and J. O'Connor (eds), *The Clubcultures Reader: Readings in Popular Cultural Studies*. Oxford, Blackwell.

Sullivan, M. (1989) *Getting Paid: Youth Crime and Work in the Inner City*. Ithaca NY, Cornell University Press.

Surette, R. and Otto, C. (2001) 'The media's role in the definition of crime', in S. Henry and M.M. Lanier (eds), *What is Crime?: Controversies over the Nature of Crime and What to Do About It*. Oxford, Rowman and Littlefield, p. 139.

Sutherland, E. (1947) *Principles of Criminology*. Philadelphia PA, J.P. Lippincott.

—— and Cressey, D. (1978) *Criminology*. New York NY, Lippincott.

——, —— and Luckenbill, D. (1992) *Principles of Criminology*. Dix Hills NY, General Hall.

Sykes, G. and Matza, D. (1961) 'Techniques of neutralization: a theory of delinquency', *American Sociological Review* 22: 664–70.

Taylor, C. (1989) *Dangerous Society*. East Lansing MI, Michigan State University Press.

Thompson, T. (1995) *Gangland Britain*. London, Hodder and Stoughton.

Thornton, S. (1995) *Club Cultures: Music, Media and Subcultural Capital*. Cambridge, Polity Press.

Thrasher, F. (1927) *The Gang*. Chicago IL, Phoenix Press.

Toby, H. and Farrington, D.P. (2001) 'Disentangling the link between disrupted families and delinquency', *British Journal of Criminology* 41: 22–40.

Tunnell, K.D. (1995) 'A cultural approach to crime and punishment, Bluegrass style', in J. Ferrell and C. Sanders (eds), *Cultural Criminology*, Boston MA, Northeastern University Press, p. 80.

Vaid, L. (1998) *Alternative Measures of Unemployment*. London, London Research Centre.

—— (1999) *London at Work*. London, London Research Centre.

Vigil, D. (1988) *Barrio Gangs: Street Life and Identity in Southern California*. Austin TX, University of Texas Press.

Walsh, D. (1986) *Heavy Business: Commercial Burglary and Robbery*. London, Routledge and Kegan Paul.

Warren, C. (1988) *Gender Issues in Field Research*. London, Sage Publications.

Webb, E., Campbell, D., Schwartz, R. and Sechrest, L. (1966) *Unobtrusive Measures: Non-reactive Research in the Social Sciences*. Chicago IL, Rand McNally and Co.

Weber, M. (1947) *The Theory of Social and Economic Organisation*. New York NY, Free Press.

Wengraf, T. (2001) *Qualitative Research Interviewing: Biographic Narrative and Semi-structured Methods*. London, Sage.

Whyte, W.F. (1955) *Street Corner Society*. Chicago IL, University of Chicago Press.

Williams, T. (1989) *The Cocaine Kids*. Reading MA, Addison-Wesley.

Willis, P. (1977) *Learning to Labour: How Working Class Kids Get Working Class Jobs*. London, Saxon House.

—— (1978) *Profane Culture*. London, Routledge and Kegan Paul.

Willmott, P. (1966) *Adolescent Boys of East London*. London, Routledge and Kegan Paul.

Wilson, W.J. (1987) *The Truly Disadvantaged: The Inner City, the Underclass, and Public Policy*. Chicago IL, University of Chicago Press.

Wolfgang, M. and Ferracuti, F. (1967) *The Subculture of Violence*. London, Tavistock.

Wright, R.T. and Decker, S. (1994) *Burglars on the Job*. Boston MA, Northeastern University Press.

——, ——, Redfern, A. and Smith, D. (1992) 'A snowball's chance in Hell: doing fieldwork with active residential burglars', *Journal of Research in Crime and Delinquency* 29: 148–61.

Wright, B.R.E., Caspit, A., Moffitt, T.E., Miech, R.A. and Silva, P.A. (1999) 'Reconsidering the relationship between SES and delinquency: causation but not correlation', *Criminology* 37(1) February: 175–94.

Yablonsky, L. (1962) *The Violent Gang*. New York NY, Macmillan.

Zimring, F. and Hawkins, G. (1997) *Crime is not the Problem: Lethal Violence in America*. New York NY, Oxford University Press.

Index

Page numbers in *italics* indicate tables; page numbers in **bold** indicate illustrations